Jonathan Lethem and the Galaxy of Writing

New Horizons in Contemporary Writing

In the wake of unprecedented technological and social change, contemporary literature has evolved a dazzling array of new forms that traditional modes and terms of literary criticism have struggled to keep up with. *New Horizons in Contemporary Writing* presents cutting-edge research scholarship that provides new insights into this unique period of creative and critical transformation.

Series Editors:

Martin Eve and Bryan Cheyette

Editorial Board: Siân Adiseshiah (University of Lincoln, UK), Sara Blair (University of Michigan, USA), Peter Boxall (University of Sussex, UK), Robert Eaglestone (Royal Holloway, University of London, UK), Rita Felski (University of Virginia, USA), Rachael Gilmour (Queen Mary, University of London, UK), Caroline Levine (University of Wisconsin–Madison, USA), Roger Luckhurst (Birkbeck, University of London, UK), Adam Kelly (York University, UK), Antony Rowland (Manchester Metropolitan University, UK), John Schad (Lancester University, UK), Pamela Thurschwell (University of Sussex, UK), Ted Underwood (University of Illinois at Urbana-Champaign, USA).

Volumes in the series:

David Mitchell's Post-Secular World, Rose Harris-Birtill
Life Lines: Writing Transcultural Adoption, John McLeod
New Media and the Transformation of Postmodern American Literature, Casey Michael Henry
The Politics of Jewishness in Contemporary World Literature, Isabelle Hesse
South African Literature's Russian Soul, Jeanne-Marie Jackson
Transatlantic Fictions of 9/11 and the War on Terror, Susana Araújo
Wanderwords: Language Migration in American Literature, Maria Lauret
Writing after Postcolonialism: Francophone North African Literature in Transition, Jane Hiddleston
Postcolonialism after World Literature, Lorna Burns
The Contemporary Post-Apocalyptic Novel, Diletta De Cristofaro

Forthcoming volumes:

Contemporary Posthumanism, Grace Halden
Northern Irish Writing after the Troubles, Caroline Magennis
David Foster Wallace's Toxic Sexuality, Edward Jackson

Jonathan Lethem and the Galaxy of Writing

Joseph Brooker

BLOOMSBURY ACADEMIC
LONDON · NEW YORK · OXFORD · NEW DELHI · SYDNEY

BLOOMSBURY ACADEMIC
Bloomsbury Publishing Plc
50 Bedford Square, London, WC1B 3DP, UK
1385 Broadway, New York, NY 10018, USA
29 Earlsfort Terrace, Dublin 2, Ireland

BLOOMSBURY, BLOOMSBURY ACADEMIC and the Diana logo are trademarks
of Bloomsbury Publishing Plc

First published in Great Britain 2020
This paperback edition published in 2021

Copyright © Joseph Brooker, 2020

Joseph Brooker has asserted his right under the Copyright, Designs and
Patents Act, 1988, to be identified as Author of this work.

For legal purposes the Acknowledgements on p. viii constitute an extension
of this copyright page.

Cover design: Eleanor Rose
Cover illustration © Alice Marwick

All rights reserved. No part of this publication may be reproduced
or transmitted in any form or by any means, electronic or mechanical, including
photocopying, recording, or any information storage or retrieval system,
without prior permission in writing from the publishers.

Bloomsbury Publishing Plc does not have any control over, or responsibility for,
any third-party websites referred to or in this book. All internet addresses given in this
book were correct at the time of going to press. The author and publisher regret any
inconvenience caused if addresses have changed or sites have ceased to exist,
but can accept no responsibility for any such changes.

A catalogue record for this book is available from the British Library.

A catalog record for this book is available from the Library of Congress.

ISBN: HB: 978-1-3500-0376-7
PB: 978-1-3502-3592-2
ePDF: 978-1-3500-0378-1
eBook: 978-1-3500-0377-4

Series: New Horizons in Contemporary Writing

Typeset by Integra Software Services Pvt. Ltd.

To find out more about our authors and books visit www.bloomsbury.com
and sign up for our newsletters.

For Nigel Parke
Books, with occasional music

Contents

Acknowledgements	viii
Note	x
Introduction	1
1 Sources	11
2 Genres	45
3 Worlds	83
4 Heroes	119
5 Streets	155
Conclusion	196
Works Cited	203
Index	209

Acknowledgements

I am glad to have worked with Bloomsbury Academic on this book. I am grateful to the staff who have assisted its progress, including Clara Herberg, Lucy Brown and most especially David Avital, whose efficiency and encouragement have been greatly helpful. The book joins the series *New Horizons in Contemporary Writing*, and I am grateful to the series editors Bryan Cheyette and Martin Paul Eve, as well as Peter Boxall and Stephen J. Burn who were involved with the series at an earlier stage.

The Department of English & Humanities at Birkbeck, University of London, has provided a supportive environment in which to produce this work. I am grateful to all those colleagues who have contributed to this environment, but must especially name those who work in areas related to the present book. Roger Luckhurst has crucially advanced the study of science fiction and other genres, along with colleagues including Mark Blacklock, Caroline Edwards and Grace Halden, and the London Science Fiction Research Community based at Birkbeck. Other colleagues including Anna Hartnell, Esther Leslie and Mpalive Msiska have also contributed to varied discussions of contemporary culture. I have benefited from working with postgraduate students in these areas, many of whom have since gone on to greater things in their own careers. This includes those who contributed to a symposium on Lethem at Birkbeck, *Occasional Music*: Zara Dinnen, Dennis Duncan, Bianca Leggett and Tony Venezia. I also thank the other contributors to that event, including Samuel Cohen, Adam Gearey, Richard Greenwald, James Peacock and Benjamin Widiss.

My parents, Liz and Pete Brooker, have given me invaluable support. My grandfather, Peter Stray, who met Olaf Stapledon in the 1940s, has frequently asked if I was writing something related to science fiction: I hope that this book may satisfy him. My brother Will has shared particular expertise on the Western film and on comic book superheroes. During the composition of this book, his wife Fiona gave birth to my nephew Ethan, a name to make a reader of Lethem think: '*That'll* be the day'. I am grateful to Helen Saunders for her support and encouragement during 'Project Lethem'. While the resources of London's academic libraries are indispensable, the writing of the book was also facilitated by the hospitality of Manor House Library and Halcyon Books, SE13.

Writing about an author from the United States, I have been fortunate to have friends and acquaintances from that country. In particular I thank those, of diverse origins, who over several years have shown me their New York and helped me to know the city better: Nitsuh Abebe, LD Beghtol, Carrick Blair, Lisa Borodkin, Amrita Brard, Zoe Dolce, Robyn Fadden, Laurel Girvan, Peter Goodrich, Michael Grace Jr, Ara Hacopian, Mary Jacobi, Lindsay Kay, Dudley Klute, Laura Kunkel, Stephin Merritt, Linda Mills, Peter Nicholls, Gail O'Hara, Anna Persson, Carey Price, Roque Ruiz, Kathryn Schubert, Elisha Sessions and Hong-An Tran. The first person who ever told me about Lethem was Stephen Troussé, characteristically ahead of the game. I also enjoyed sharing an appreciation of Lethem's writing with our friend Carey Lander (1982–2015), whose passion for contemporary American literature was inspiring.

Thanks, finally, to everyone who has ever given me any of Lethem's works. That includes Nigel Parke of Undercover Books, who let me pluck a copy of *You Don't Love Me Yet* from his voluminous backroom stock. Over the years, Nigel's warmth, wit and enthusiasm have enhanced my own love of literature. I dedicate this book to him in friendship and gratitude.

Note

References are given as (author, date: page number), corresponding to the Bibliography at the end of the book. Where the author is clearly mentioned nearby, their name is omitted from the reference. Where an author is not specifically indicated, the author is Jonathan Lethem.

In sections that discuss one text extensively, page numbers for that text are given in parentheses without further details.

Book titles are occasionally abbreviated in the text, thus: *Gun* for *Gun, with Occasional Music*; *Table* for *As She Climbed across the Table*; *Fortress* for *The Fortress of Solitude*.

Introduction

The American novelist Jonathan Lethem has expressed scepticism about literary canons. His writing has sometimes shunned elevated status, effacing his own creative role amid a chorus of other voices. Yet the present book contends that Lethem himself is among the most compelling literary voices to emerge in the past three decades. Within contemporary American letters, in the pages of the *New York Times* or *Los Angeles Review of Books*, Lethem is a recurring character: essayist, reviewer, interviewee. In other contexts, for instance among readers in the UK, Lethem remains a more esoteric taste, though his fiction has remained consistently in print. Either side of the Atlantic, notwithstanding his constant productivity, to the casual bookshop browser he remains less familiar than several of his direct contemporaries and sometime associates: Bret Easton Ellis, Jonathan Franzen, Donna Tartt. Perhaps more surprisingly, academic writing about his work has remained limited in quantity. The surprise is in part because Lethem's writing, as the present book will show, speaks directly to numerous concerns in contemporary literary studies. *Jonathan Lethem and the Galaxy of Writing* argues for Lethem's importance in relation to five main themes that will be explicated below. The facts of Lethem's life and career, the arc of his development, his own statements (and others') on these: all will be relevant. Describing and interpreting Lethem's writing, the book posits it as a rich and complex contribution to contemporary literature.

Lethem's work is peculiarly enmeshed in the work of others. This is a crucial theme of Chapter One, below, which sets significant terms for the rest of the book by elucidating how Lethem has developed an aesthetic that embraces connection, citation and borrowing as a model for creativity. In discussing his work, therefore, the present book will often venture outwards, building contexts and making juxtapositions. In providing detailed treatments of Lethem's own works, we will also consider crucial sources, such as Raymond Chandler, Franz Kafka or superhero comics. The 'galaxy' in this book's title connotes such a plethora of writings, connected and overlapping. Such breadth and multifariousness are evident both in Lethem's constantly proliferating work and in the reams of other material on to which, with conscious intertextuality, his writing opens. In this sense the titular term is not far from the sense invoked by Roland Barthes at the start of *S/Z*: 'this text is a galaxy of signifiers, not a structure of signifieds; it has no beginning; it is reversible; we gain access to it by several entrances, none of which can be authoritatively declared to be the main one; the codes it mobilizes extend *as far as the eye can reach*' (Barthes 1974: 5–6). Lethem himself deploys the word in a relevant context early in his novel *Chronic City*, when the narrator marvels at the conversation of the critic Perkus Tooth, who 'catalogued speculative connections among the galaxy of cultural things that interested him' (2010: 19). At the same time, 'galaxy' can be taken more literally, to indicate Lethem's roots in science fiction, and to carry a fond sense of pulp novels or magazines. Edited by the New Yorker Horace Gold, *Galaxy* was among the most distinguished science fiction magazines of the 1950s, publishing Philip K. Dick, Robert Sheckley, Frederik Pohl and many more. The present book's title might thus be heard as a cousin of *Jonathan Lethem's Amazing Stories*. This is true to some of the most important tones and sources of his work, which have also become increasingly important within contemporary literary studies more generally.

Following Chapter One's exploration of influence and intertextuality, the book's chapters will read Lethem in the light of four more themes. Chapter Two explains the importance of genre, which Lethem's writing has extensively put to use. This theme is intimately connected to those of the first chapter, as to write in a genre is inherently to work intertextually. The next two chapters then focus on particular genres. Chapter Three discusses world-making as fictional practice, notably in Lethem's science-fictional work of the 1990s. Lethem's worlds are shown to range from the creation of an alien planet through fictions in which the fabric of the known universe is rent and multiplied. Chapter Four looks more closely at Lethem's use of the superhero genre. His essays about superheroes as a formative aesthetic experience are read alongside a range of works that both use the superhero to renew the content of contemporary fiction and recontextualize the superhero mode itself. Chapter Five, lastly, presents Lethem as a writer of place and space, arguing for his status as a crucial writer of New York City.

Life Stories

Before we proceed to these detailed analyses, a chronological synopsis of Lethem's career can situate us. He was born in 1964 and raised in Brooklyn, New

York City, the child of bohemian radicals. His father Richard Brown Lethem is a painter. Jonathan Lethem's own aspirations to visual art were displaced by the parallel course that he developed on the typewriter that his mother Judith gave him at fourteen. A social worker and activist, she was of German Jewish background; Lethem can thus define himself as a Jewish writer, though this aspect has not thus far been prominent in discussion of his work. It does begin to emerge, though, in a 2013 essay on Philip Roth, where Lethem records that he had 'been raised so as not to take being Jewish, or in my case half-Jewish, in any way personally', and that the Jewish-American writing of Roth, Bernard Malamud, Norman Mailer and others showed him 'That something aggravated and torrential in my voice, or perhaps I should call it my attempt at having a voice, was cultural in origin, even if aggravated and torrential frequently in the cause of disputing or even denying that point of origin' (2017: 43). A more immediate and evident influence than this, though, was Judith Lethem's death from cancer in 1978, a loss that would leave extensive traces on his fiction.

From his upbringing Lethem drew an easy openness to art and creativity: 'a lot of my parents' friends were [my father's] students or colleagues, and so this activity – specifically, going into the studio every day and trying to make paintings – seemed normal to me' (Clarke 2011: xiv). This sense of the openness of art to life, and vice versa, has been an enabling condition of Lethem's later output: continuous, garrulously expansive, and often making light of boundaries between fact and fiction, between pictures and writing, or between intellectual property and common inheritance. Lethem also inherited his parents' political sympathies. Even when not ostensibly political, his fiction has consistently tended to a sceptical view of the world and those in power. In a 2003 interview he is explicit about the inescapably political character of his upbringing, as a crucial root for this attitude: 'The first third of my life was spent at political demonstrations, shouting my lungs hoarse. […] I was a protester by birthright. […] My life *was* a demonstration'. All this, Lethem concludes, is 'there in my work'; 'My politics are everywhere' (Clarke 2011: 48–9).

This sceptical view derived also from his reading. When still a teen, Lethem read much literature that would be formative for his work; but most distinctively and significantly, he discovered science fiction, consuming the genre 'like a machine' (Clarke 2011: 35). The California-based novelist Philip K. Dick (1928–1982) quickly became the master author of Lethem's life, offering political 'solidarity' (Clarke 2011: 49) as well as imaginative resources. Lethem read his voluminous body of work multiple times, becoming not only an expert but, in the mid-1980s, an early member of the Philip K. Dick Society. He would eventually introduce editions of Dick's work for the Library of America (making Dick the first science fiction author to be granted entry to this notably official canon), and in 2011 he co-produced, with Pamela Jackson, a vast edition of Dick's late journals known as his *Exegesis*. Meanwhile, Lethem also consumed much of the rest of the science fiction canon, from Olaf Stapledon to Samuel R. Delany, and that of hard-boiled crime fiction (Dashiell Hammett, Raymond Chandler, Stanley Ellin) (Clarke 2011: 35). The overall effect – of many of these writers, but especially Dick – was to install paranoia and dystopia as default settings for Lethem's imagination. He recalls: 'So when I found that Rod Serling [creator of the television series *The Twilight Zone*] and Philip K. Dick and Thomas Pynchon also agreed with me that the president was probably an evil robot programmed by a computer, it was merely a matter of pleasurable recognition that someone was naming the world' (Clarke 2011: 48). Much later, Lethem's 2010 short book on John Carpenter's 1988 film *They Live* would confirm his fascination with how a 'pulp' narrative could productively articulate political paranoia.

From 1982 Lethem spent a year at Bennington College in Vermont, a setting that he would later fictionalize. In hindsight, Lethem's college year (also featuring the novelists Jill Eisenstadt, Donna Tartt and Bret Easton Ellis) looks a distinguished literary generation. But Lethem himself soon dropped out and relocated to San Francisco, drawn in part by the spell of Philip K. Dick, who had died shortly before. Settling a few streets from Dick's old home, Lethem worked for years in bookshops, honing his knowledge of literary obscurities and the backroads of the canon. He also wrote short stories, publishing (from 1989) mainly in genre-based magazines such as *Isaac Asimov's Science Fiction Magazine* and *Interzone*. His career as a novelist began with *Gun, with Occasional Music* (1994). The novel is a hard-boiled detective story after Raymond Chandler, but set in a near-future dystopian California akin to Dick's, in which animals have been genetically modified to act like humans.

Lethem's second novel *Amnesia Moon* (1995) draws on numerous attempts at fiction that he had written since his teens (Lethem 2011: xix). They add up to another near-future dystopia, this time particularly preoccupied with a multiplicity of worlds or distinct zones of reality. As a slim campus novel, *As She Climbed across the Table* (1997) seems closer to life as we know it. But it centres on a physics laboratory which has discovered a portal in reality that comes to be called Lack. Lack mysteriously captures the affection of Alice, partner of the protagonist Philip. The novel thus recounts his romantic quest to regain her love, while staging larger questions about reality, perception and the production of worlds. Set on a campus in California, it also completes an opening trilogy of

Californian novels; *Amnesia Moon*, like *Gun*, had spent much of its narrative time in San Francisco.

Lethem had moved back to Brooklyn in 1996, and his next three novels would treat of the borough in some way. *Girl in Landscape* (1998) is Lethem's last indisputable science fiction novel to date, set on a distant planet while drawing on the resources of the Western genre. Through the 1990s Lethem had continued to publish short stories located between science fiction, contemporary realism and conceptual allegory. A significant selection of these appeared in the volume *The Wall of the Sky, The Wall of the Eye* (1996). But at the decade's end he issued a novel that withdrew from science fiction, while enriching his engagement with genre. *Motherless Brooklyn* (1999) was Lethem's most commercially and critically successful novel thus far, bringing him into higher visibility in American letters. The novel's narrator Lionel Essrog has Tourette's syndrome – a neurolinguistic condition which Lethem creatively adapts for literary effect. Lionel narrates the action to us without complication, but his speech to others is punctuated by outbursts of word salad and extraneous verbal content. This feature and Lionel's compulsion to tic or repeatedly touch things play their part in the story, in which Lionel investigates the murder of his mentor Frank Minna.

Reviewing the first few years of Lethem's published career, it bears remark that the chronology of composition may not correspond simply with that of publication. Most simply, his volumes of short stories have often appeared several years after individual pieces within them, while the US and UK editions of *The Wall of the Sky, The Wall of the Eye* (1996 and 2002, respectively) differ in two stories. Several other stories from the 1990s – 'Using It and Losing It', 'The One about the Green Detective' and more – have not yet been collected in any volume dedicated to Lethem, but currently form an obscure area of the corpus which could receive more prominent republication in future.

Lethem's accounts of composition indicate that multiple early novels were written and redrafted simultaneously. In a 2006 piece about debut novels, he records starting three first novels which never saw the light of day, followed by 'a series of short stories': some becoming the first four chapters of his second-published novel *Amnesia Moon*. The hidden complexity of literary chronology now becomes apparent:

> Next, at twenty-four, I began *Gun, with Occasional Music*, which, six years later, would be my first published novel. Before completing the as-published version of *Gun*, however, I wrote two more novels: *Amnesia Moon* and *As She Climbed across the Table*. All three (*Moon, Table, Gun*) were, in early versions, circulated simultaneously by a literary agent; *As She Climbed across the Table* came within

a hair's breadth of being published in its nascent form by Bantam Books, and would therefore have become my first-published book. No dice, so a much-rewritten *Gun* had the privilege instead. (Lethem 2006b)

This account is corroborated by another essay which records revelling in the writing of *As She Climbed across the Table*, 'in 1990 or '91' (Lethem 2011: 313). To this first trio of novels we can add the fourth: *Girl in Landscape*, which Lethem in another essay mentions drafting as early as 1989; by 1991 'I was two years into the first draft of my quasi-Western' (2005: 10), even though the book would not appear until 1998. All this means that the first four novels, and the stories of their period, do not belong to a straightforward chronological sequence, but rather emerged from an intense period of simultaneous and overlapping recomposition. *Motherless Brooklyn* (1999) was the first novel to belong definitively to a later period subsequent to the publication of Lethem's debut. Even then, *The Fortress of Solitude* (2003) had a root in one of his earliest attempts at fiction in the early 1980s (Clarke 2011: 62).

Though preceded by the fantastical novella *This Shape We're In* (2001), *The Fortress of Solitude* was Lethem's first major statement of the new century. By far his longest book to that date, it turned to his own life and upbringing as raw material, yet processed them through additional narratives of the music business and, most strikingly, the superhero genre. That concern was also picked up in the story collection *Men and Cartoons* (2004), and in a new commission as a writer of the revived Marvel comic *Omega the Unknown* in 2007, which followed Lethem's prose reminiscences about the character. As a novelist, though, he deliberately changed tack with the breezier 'romantic comedy' *You Don't Love Me Yet* (2007). His critical writing was now also finding book publication, with essays collected in *The Disappointment Artist* (2005) and in the much larger *The Ecstasy of Influence: Nonfictions, etc.* (2011). This last, bolstered by much new writing to make it cohere as a volume, serves not only as a set of key critical interventions but as a surrogate autobiography. Meanwhile Lethem published *They Live* (2010) and another succinct, energetic critical volume on Talking Heads' LP *Fear of Music* (2012). By 2017 he had written more than enough occasional essays, reviews and prefaces for yet another collection of non-fiction to be issued, the items' dates ranging back to the late 1990s. *More Alive and Less Lonely* is specifically about books and writers; and in demonstrating the depth and breadth of Lethem's immersion in literature, it dispels any remaining notion that this was a writer who would rather take a shortcut to culture through Spider-Man or the Ramones. Plainly, he has never agreed to choose between any of these options.

In a 2007 interview, Lethem remarks that for Dick's generation, to place a story with John W. Campbell's *Astounding Science Fiction* 'was seen in science fiction circles as being analogous to placing a story with *The New Yorker*' (Kelley 2007). As it happens, from around the same point, Lethem's own stories began more often to appear in the *New Yorker*, a destination that could suggest a new degree of respectability; the fruits of this period would appear in the collection *Lucky Alan* (2015). His rate of production has hardly slowed. The substantial novel *Chronic City* (2009), a 'reality-shifted' view of Manhattan with a trace of post-9/11 melancholy, was followed by *Dissident Gardens* (2013), a multi-decade saga of the American political left centred around Queens and Greenwich Village, and in turn by the mysterious tale of a globetrotting backgammon player, *A Gambler's Anatomy* (2016), whose UK title *The Blot* refers to a tumour on its protagonist's vision. Lethem compounded the title's ambiguity by collaborating with the academic Laurence A. Rickels on *The Blot: A Supplement* (2016), a textual dialogue circling the novel and other shared themes. Meanwhile, from 2010 Lethem relocated to California once more, this time to take a Chair in Creative Writing at Pomona College, in Claremont on the outskirts of Los Angeles. This area would suggest a setting for his eleventh novel, *The Feral Detective*, published in late 2018.

Analytical Relevance

The work listed above comprises a prolific record. At the time of writing – Autumn 2018 – Lethem has published eleven novels, one novella, three full short story collections and two more slim volumes containing short stories; three substantial collections of essays and memoirs and two critical books on film and music. To this one can add his role as writer for a superhero comic; extensive labour as co-editor of Dick's writings; editing of multiple anthologies of others' essays (from the *Vintage Book of Amnesia* in 2000 to a collection of writing about rock music, *Shake It Up*, co-edited with the academic Kevin Dettmar, in 2017); and numerous other uncollected short works. Auxiliary spin-offs have included a 2007 film of the short story 'Light and the Sufferer', a 2014 Off-Broadway musical of *The Fortress of Solitude*, and a documentary film, *Lethem* (2017), while *Motherless Brooklyn*'s film adaptation is due in 2019. With many contemporary writers, one is necessarily dealing with a nascent oeuvre of uncertain weight and longevity. With Lethem, the mass of work has reached a point where it is difficult for any one reader to be sure that they have read everything.

One corollary of this is that the present book cannot be exhaustive. It reads numerous key works in the light of the five themes indicated above, but cannot do justice to the whole of Lethem's output. Two novels, *Motherless Brooklyn* and *The Fortress of Solitude*, prove richly relevant enough to demand substantial treatment in different chapters below. Other works typically either receive a single sustained passage of consideration, or are cited more briefly across multiple contexts, but not all are given the lengthy treatment they might merit. This is true of most of Lethem's short stories, which merit a critical volume on their own; his most recent fiction, whose new aesthetic strategies will generate critical conversation in the years ahead; and much of his critical writing. The relations between Lethem and music or film, for instance, merit substantial studies in their own right. So too do themes raised in the pages below, yet not developed at full length, such as race or politics. All this can be considered work for the future, which the present book aims to encourage and assist.

At present, though, the amount of academic discussion dedicated to Lethem's work is smaller than could be expected. Prior to this volume, such published criticism primarily includes two insightful books, by James Peacock and Matthew Luter, and several critical essays. An evident comparison would be with Lethem's close contemporary David Foster Wallace (1962–2008), whose work has amassed a critical industry of its own along the lines of canonical forebears like James Joyce or Thomas Pynchon. Lethem is alert enough to know that such extensive critical attention is often conditioned by factors of social identity – in short, that the work of white male authors has most often benefited from such attention – and that as a figure of relative 'privilege', he is not in a position to demand more of it. At the start of *The Ecstasy of Influence* he acknowledges that the role of the novelist he currently occupies, as a figure whose opinions are valued, has its 'aristocratic' dimension: 'akin to being borne aloft in a chair like a conquistador over mountain terrain everyone else is made to traverse barefoot and with supplies on their backs' (2011: xviii). Accordingly, he has had the opportunity to shape his own reception, not only in his extensive non-fictional writing but in numerous interviews. Several of the most significant of these are collected in *Conversations with Jonathan Lethem* (2011), a volume that stands among the most indispensable critical resources on this writer. It is not merely that Lethem, in interview, provides facts and background otherwise unavailable, but also that he frequently provides exegeses of his own work, which can reach a level of interpretation that it would normally be the job of the professional critic to produce. An example is Lethem's insistence to the *Paris Review* that the second half of *The Fortress of Solitude* is in fact closely analogous to the whole of

Motherless Brooklyn, a case he spontaneously explains in detail (Clarke 2011: 62). The case makes sense, yet would hardly be taken as proven if made by anyone other than the author himself. That is equally true of Lethem's explanation, immediately before this, of 'a strict alternation in my books' between those 'Organized by the setting' and those 'Organized by a compulsive voice', which find a unity in *The Fortress of Solitude*. His interviewer Lorin Stein responds: 'If you see it that way you'd be completely insane. No one would believe that you actually sat down to write alternating books'. Lethem's reply despatches any notion that the author should not be too conscious of what he is doing: 'But I did' (Clarke 2011: 62).

Stein is thus persuasive in averring that this writer is 'his own best, most curious biographical critic' (Clarke 2011: 48). 'Biographical' even undersells Lethem, given his readiness to talk formally and conceptually about the fiction. This capacity for self-analysis is so unusually extensive that the critic might feel redundant in the face of it, as Lethem playfully says he does amid the 'flood of analytical relevance' in Shelley Jackson's commentary on *Motherless Brooklyn* (Clarke 2011: 42). Yet there remains more to say, in dialogue with the novelist's own understanding of his work. If he is peculiarly able to explain it, he also accepts that his own understanding remains partial – and that, over the years, he has contradicted himself on every significant subject, such that a reader can construct the Lethem they prefer (2011: 244). The pages ahead will frequently cite Lethem's own account of what he is doing, but as part of a critical narrative necessarily beyond his control.

1

Sources

What are the sources of creative work? One answer is the individual artist's personal experience. In *The Fortress of Solitude*, Jonathan Lethem drew deeply on memories of the Brooklyn of his childhood decades earlier. Real experiences are rendered, such that the reader of Lethem's autobiographical essays may find them closely prefigured by his novel. They are also disguised or transmuted. Richard Lethem became a partial model for Abraham Ebdus: a figure related to the real painter yet also more withdrawn from society than the original. The real Judith Lethem died in 1978; the fictional Rachel Ebdus absconds, leaving her son orphaned in a different way. So too, an artist might seek out distinctive experiences, such as travel to unfamiliar places, to gather material for artistic creation. That *A Gambler's Anatomy* sets early scenes around Berlin is plainly related to the fact that Lethem had spent time in the city while preparing the novel. Phoebe Siegler, protagonist of *The Feral Detective* (2018), matches Lethem's own career in travelling from Brooklyn to Claremont, California, where her impressions of a town 'fitted around a college campus as empty and perfect as a stage set' may be taken as something of an in-joke on her author's adopted residence (Lethem 2018b: 25).

That art draws from life is clear. Yet it is also true that art is often made from other art. For one thing, to recognize something as art at all may rely on its adoption of pre-existing conventions. As Graham Allen avers: 'Works of literature, after all, are built from systems, codes and traditions established by previous works of literature' (2000: 1). A longer historical perspective can also emphasize the relative nature of creativity. For much literature and art prior to the Romantics, the success of artistic creation centred less on novelty than on the skilful imitation of extant models. The most celebrated author of Anglophone literature, William Shakespeare, was an innovator, introducing hundreds of new words to the English language; yet he is well known to have derived the majority of his stories from pre-existing sources such as other plays or chronicle histories.

Entire aesthetics like Classicism in art and architecture have been founded on the adherence to styles of the past. It can be argued that an emphasis on original creativity as a key criterion in artistic value is a relatively recent development, which would itself be challenged by the openness to borrowing and replication in work since the early twentieth century: say, from T.S. Eliot's 'Gerontion' and 'The Waste Land' to the possibilities of digital copying and pasting made commonplace by the early twenty-first century.

Such issues are important to Lethem. He has talked and written extensively about how art, notably his own, appropriates materials from other works. This chapter thus investigates this issue, which Lethem has raised more consistently than any other comparable author. The chapter will start by looking closely at Lethem's treatment of these themes in his non-fictional statements. Attention will be given first to his essay 'The Ecstasy of Influence', then to essays that describe the importance of particular artists. Next we turn to Lethem's interviews, comparing them to those of other contemporary writers to highlight the distinctiveness of his approach. Finally, we shall consider how these themes are dramatized in Lethem's fiction.

Public Knowledge

In transferring the title 'The Ecstasy of Influence' from his 2007 essay to his substantial 2011 collection of essays, Lethem made 'influence' his chosen banner. Before Lethem, its most prominent critical association was with the American critic Harold Bloom, whose book *The Anxiety of Influence* (1973) provides his best-known catchphrase and idea. Bloom sees artistic history as agonistic: a given writer battles his precursors for supremacy. The highly masculinist model is based on Sigmund Freud's notion of an Oedipus complex in which sons are driven to overcome their fathers. Literary creation thus needs to be understood as thoroughly intertextual; in Terry Eagleton's formulation of Bloom's doctrine, 'All literary works were a kind of plagiarism, a creative misreading of earlier efforts' (2003: 168). The struggle with one's 'strong' precursor in literary history produces a 'swerving' away from it. Lethem acknowledges that his title comes from an academic, Richard Dienst, making a 'rebuking play' on Bloom's phrase (Lethem 2011: 112). His project is in large part to rethink and invert the aggression and competitiveness embedded in ideas of artistic influence, and replace them with a more positive approach which also better corresponds to his sense of how creativity works.

'The Ecstasy of Influence' itself was first published in *Harper's* magazine in February 2007. Its subtitle 'A plagiarism' (2011: 93) is the main hint to the reader of its unusual means of composition. This is spelled out more fully at the essay's end, as Lethem offers a new section headed: 'KEY: I IS ANOTHER': 'This key to the preceding essay names the source of every line I stole, warped, and cobbled together as I "wrote" (except, alas, those sources I forgot along the way)' (112). This might be the first time that the reader is aware that the whole text has been written this way: patched together from pre-existing sentences, which Lethem has also then tweaked. His 'Key' moves through the ten titled sections of his essay (each title announced with block capitals), naming the dozens of authors who have been quoted – without quotation marks – to form it, before he provides a final 'KEY TO THE KEY'. Here he offers precursors for his own method. His statement that 'The notion of a collage text is, of course, not original to me' (120) echoes the views advanced in the essay itself. The essay is about not being original; the method of composition uses materials not original to Lethem; and this method, he now notes, is itself not original. Precursors include Walter Benjamin's *Arcades Project* and a collage novel by Eduardo Paolozzi, and certain writers more contemporary with Lethem including David Shields, whose *Reality Hunger* (2010) would appear three years after the *Harper's* essay. In interview years later with the magazine *Right to Copy*, Lethem would state that his 'big idea' was to 'do it by stealing. To practice intertextuality. And of course, even that was not a new idea. The great thing is, I knew there were plenty of people who'd done things like this too, and so I couldn't claim originality in my disclaiming of originality' (2016b: 38).

The most celebrated writers of Lethem's generation – perhaps especially male ones – have periodically produced essays announcing aesthetics and world views. David Foster Wallace's lengthy essay 'E Unibus Pluram: Television and U.S. Fiction' (1993) is perhaps the most cited such proclamation of its era, for its exploration of what Wallace presents as the corrosive effect of irony on American writing. A rival in the genre is Jonathan Franzen's 'Why Bother?' (1996), a rumination on the fate of the novel in a contemporary American society decreasingly interested in the form. 'The Ecstasy of Influence' might be considered Lethem's bid to occupy a similar sphere of literary-critical authority. But no comparable writer of Lethem's generation has composed a major essay in the way that he does here. It is a *coup de théâtre* to hang together an argument from the sentences of others in this way. The essay is a performance of its theme, an exercise in imitative form: a collage of pre-existing pieces which is about the idea that art is made from pre-existing pieces. Given its importance in Lethem's thought, we shall now outline its claims, while seeking to discern the overall pattern they form and how they relate to wider intellectual contexts.

The first section, 'LOVE AND THEFT', introduces ideas of art echoing other art. Vladimir Nabokov's repetition, in *Lolita*, of the plot outline of an earlier story of the same name demonstrates how art can echo and repeat earlier art, whether coincidentally, deliberately or unconsciously. Likewise Bob Dylan's apparent derivation of a 1966 line from a 1958 Don Siegel film highlights how far his work has been characterized by 'appropriation', including the 2001 LP title *'Love and Theft'* itself – taken from the title of a 1993 book by Eric Lott, which Lethem suggests was itself a 'riff' on Leslie Fiedler's *Love and Death in the American Novel* (1960). (Lott was in turn commissioned to write an essay on the LP *'Love and Theft'* for the *Cambridge Companion to Bob Dylan*, a book that also includes an essay by Lethem: these streams of connection can be playfully diverted.) 'Dylan's originality and his appropriations are as one', Lethem summarizes, before adding: 'The same might be said of *all* art' (2011: 94). A related case has since been made by Lewis Hyde, one of Lethem's intellectual inspirations, who observes the casual range of Dylan's sources in traditional song and proposes that the emergence of Dylan's individual talent was made possible by the 'creative ecology' (2011: 206) of the early 1960s, in which copyright was less exclusive than it would later become. Hyde's use of Dylan as an example demonstrates how Lethem's own intervention would in turn influence the terms of the debate that had shaped it.

Section two, 'CONTAMINATION ANXIETY', describes the multiple modes of creativity and influence forming a blues song, illustrating the 'open source' culture of the musical genres blues and jazz, 'in which preexisting melodic fragments and larger musical frameworks are freely reworked' (96). 'Technology', Lethem explains, 'has only multiplied the possibilities', as copying and allusion are replaced by technologies of sampling. These tendencies echo twentieth-century movements in the visual arts – 'futurism, cubism, Dada, musique concrète, situationism, pop art' – to the point where 'collage, the common denominator in that list, might be called *the* art form of the twentieth century, never mind the twenty-first'. The idea of originality implied by 'finding one's own voice' as an artist is problematic and needs rethinking: 'Finding one's voice isn't just an emptying and purifying of oneself of the words of others but an adopting and embracing of filiations, communities, and discourses' (97). The artist finds his or her voice through other voices, rather than in silence.

'The theory of intertextuality', write Judith Still and Michael Worton, 'insists that a text […] cannot exist as a hermetic or self-sufficient whole, and so does not function as a closed system'. Both writer and reader contribute to this. The former is most pertinent here: 'the writer is a reader of texts (in the broadest sense) before s/he is a creator of texts, and therefore the work of art is inevitably shot through with references, quotations and influences of every kind' (1990: 1). That baseline is consistent with Lethem's views. Those views are inflected by the development of technology for copying cultural work, an earlier stage of which had been prominently highlighted by Walter Benjamin's essay 'The Work of Art in the Age of Mechanical Reproduction' (1936). Benjamin asserted that while 'Objects made by humans could always be copied by humans' (2008: 20), such a process had greatly intensified with the advent of such technologies as printing, photography and film. Lethem's 2007 polemic belongs to a later stage of this story, in which digital means of reproduction were coming to augment and displace earlier 'analogue' technologies, and thus further intensify the speed and prevalence of copying. As Hyde observes: 'In the 1990s, digital copying and the global Internet appeared almost simultaneously, and all of a sudden many of the useful old fences simply disintegrated. [...] in less than a decade, the heavy, slow, and local became light, swift, and global' (Hyde 2011: 11). Zara Dinnen (2012) thus suggests that Lethem's verbal collage, though prominently disseminated in the analogue form of print, is profoundly attuned to the possibilities of remix afforded by the digital era. At the same time, Lethem's views are also congruent with the model of intertextuality that became consensual among Parisian thinkers some decades earlier. Roland Barthes, writing in 1973, concurs: 'Every text is an intertext; other texts are present within it to different degrees and in more or less recognisable forms. [...] Every text is a new tissue of recycled citations. [...] The intertext is a field of anonymous formulae whose origin is rarely recoverable, of unconscious or automatic citations without speech marks' (cited in Orr 2003: 33). Barthes's contemporary Michel Foucault, writing in 1968, makes the case in a way very close to Lethem's understanding in 2007: '[N]o book can exist by itself; it is always in a relationship of support and dependence in regard to others; it is a spot in a network; it contains a system of landmarks which refer [...] explicitly or not [...] to other books, other texts, or other sentences' (Cancalon and Spacagna 1994: 2).

Lethem draws a paragraph from Wallace's 'E Unibus Pluram' to suggest the place of the fiction writer in this scenario. Wallace had recalled a seminar in which 'a certain gray eminence' had advised writers to avoid contemporary reference in their work, on peril of making it go swiftly out of date. Pressed on the point, the authority figure resisted the 'frivolous Now' and 'trendy mass-popular media' reference (99). Lethem aligns himself with Wallace and with the musical collagist Mark Hosler, as members of a generation for which such 'frivolity' is the appropriate stuff of art, being 'the stuff of the world' (99) in which they have grown up. On this view, brand names like 'Band-Aid' and 'Xerox' are normal elements of discourse, available also to literary art, and not to be shunned. In a very characteristic statement that seems not to be a plagiarism, Lethem avers that he 'came of age swamped by parodies that stood for originals yet mysterious to me', and into a 'commercial and cultural environment with which we've both supplemented and blotted out our natural world': 'I can no more claim it as "mine" than the sidewalks and forests of the world, yet I do dwell in it, and for me to stand a chance as either artist or citizen, I'd probably better be permitted to name it' (100). Lethem's recollection of experiencing parodies of artistic items before the originals themselves has become characteristic; thus, in a retrospect on this essay, he refers to 'how it felt to surmise the existence of Edward G. Robinson from a Bugs Bunny aside' (2011: 123). (He does not advertise an unexpected, subtle parallel between his thought here and that of Harold Bloom, for whom an 'influenced' poet's 'best misinterpretations may well be of poems he has never read' [Bloom 1973: 70].) In Lethem's reference to 'the sidewalks and forests of the world', which he does not own yet dwells in, we see the beginnings of the essay's imagining of 'the Commons'.

In the first sections Lethem has made an aesthetic case for appropriation. In the fourth section, 'USEMONOPOLY', he turns more closely to law. Lethem questions the way that copyright goes as unquestioned as the law of gravity, in an increasingly 'bloated' way that contradicts, for instance, Thomas Jefferson's proposal of a pragmatic and limited model of copyright to promote the exclusive development of ideas 'for limited Times' (101). Lethem's treatment of copyright as an unquestioned norm that merits fresh scrutiny derives from the legal theorist Lawrence Lessig, as does his citation of Jefferson's defence of 'non-rivalrous' goods that can be reproduced without detriment to their owner: 'he who lights his taper at mine, receives light without darkening me' (Lessig 2002: 5, 94). Continuing to criticize the abuse of copyright, Lethem's short sixth section 'SOURCE HYPOCRISY, OR DISNIAL' notes that Disney has drawn source material from the work of others, from fairy tale tradition to stories by particular authors, but refuses to share its own creations. Lethem labels this 'source hypocrisy', stating that if one makes art by drawing on others' work, one should be prepared to share in turn. The borrower must be willing to lend. The fifth section, 'THE BEAUTY OF SECOND USE', offers a more benign view of art's afterlife: from a newspaper used to wrap fish to making a Halloween costume or visual artwork inspired by a book. The work's audience, 'poaching' inspiration from the artwork, thus enters the picture as an agent of second use. Art can give unintended extras to its audience, not planned for by the creator, who should not seek to guard jealously such second or further uses. The concept of second use will be a recurrent one in this book.

The seventh section, 'YOU CAN'T STEAL A GIFT', mobilizes Lewis Hyde's notion of the gift to describe the generous possibilities of art just suggested. Works of art, Lethem proposes, 'exist simultaneously in two economies: a market economy and a *gift economy*'. He draws on Hyde's book and on David Bollier's *Silent Theft: The Private Plunder of Our Common Wealth* (2002) to argue that impersonal commercial exchanges coexist happily with kinds of activity that must not be subject to financial valuation. Some things, like votes, are in principle not for sale. Art seems different – 'it can be sold in the market and still emerge a work of art' – yet 'it may be possible to destroy a work of art by converting it into a pure commodity' (107). The relation between gift and commercial transaction is delicate. Lethem here carefully downgrades the role of the market or cash nexus as the only norm governing social relations. His emphasis is moderate, yet remains challenging amid what has been called the era of neoliberalism – in Paul Mason's words, an era of 'marketisation of public sector decision making', 'financialisation' exercising increased influence over everyday life, and the 'colonisation of non-market spaces inside industrialised societies' (Mason 2018), as much in the United States as anywhere.

It is in and against this context that the eighth section, 'THE COMMONS', enshrines another key term. The commons can be envisaged as a physical reality: 'the streets over which we drive, the skies through which we pilot airplanes, or the public parks or beaches on which we dally'. It is also broader and more figurative, the name for that which 'belongs to everyone and no one', its use 'controlled only by common consent' (108). The Commons is a concept with a long history. Lewis Hyde's account considers its role in land use by the medieval English peasantry, demonstrating that at this stage it was already a sophisticated social institution: 'not simply the land but the land plus the rights, customs, and institutions that organize and preserve its communal uses' (2011: 31). As such, the Commons was historically not an unbounded free-for-all but involved a carefully managed, 'stinted' set of mutual rights of access and use: a fact that diminishes the force of critiques of the Commons as unsustainable (Hyde 2011: 32–5). From the 1970s, such ideas were given detailed practical form in the political economist Elinor Ostrom's work on sustainable collective uses of diverse ecosystems, which she showed could be effectively managed by emergent structures at the local level (Ostrom 1990). The prominence of the Commons as an explanatory concept has been further boosted in the internet era, in which, as Ostrom and Charlotte Hess recount, multiple scholars simultaneously 'started to notice behaviors and conditions on the web [...] that had long been identified with other types of commons' (2011: 4).

Addressing a wide public, both Hyde and Lessig have sought to revive the concept as a model for intellectual property regimes in the twenty-first century, in relation both to the internet and to the new 'enclosures' undertaken by recent tightenings of copyright law. Lethem's borrowed examples of a modern Commons typically overlap with theirs: folk music tradition, writing in the public domain, Einstein's theory of relativity, even 'The silence in a movie theater [...] constructed as a mutual gift by those who compose it' (Lethem 2011: 108). Hyde's reminder of the need for management of the Commons – viewing it not as a given but as a set of practices – is heeded by recent scholars of the 'Knowledge Commons' who have sought to promote legal and technological norms to protect the common status of intellectual property and scholarly communication (Hess and Ostrom 2011; Eve 2014). While legal and technical, the issue also has political resonance, as Lethem indicates in shifting ground from law to society as a whole. Thus the 'American commons' includes the likes of 'public forests and minerals' or 'the broadcast airwaves and public spaces' (108). Lethem proposes that culture and art are equivalent realms, 'a vast commons', albeit 'salted through with zones of utter commerce'; 'The notion of a *commons of cultural materials* goes more or less unnamed' (108–9). To name it as such is one of the essay's goals.

Lethem's ninth section, 'UNDISCOVERED PUBLIC KNOWLEDGE', notes that a problem – as in science or medicine – may be most efficiently solved by studying extant research. The analogy with art suggests that good art might be best made by drawing on what has come before: rather than 'the violence and exasperation of another avant-garde', we can ratify 'the *ecstasy of influence*', implying an art drawing on earlier 'methods and motifs' (109–10). In the tenth section, 'GIVE ALL', Lethem offers '[a] few assertions', bringing his essay closer to the manifesto form. The (often plagiarized) assertions include: that texts that have 'infiltrated the common mind' should be treated as common property, as should notions and brands (such as Mickey Mouse) introduced by corporations; that perpetual copyright is wrong and 'un-American' (a nod to a leftist version of 'Americanism' that Lethem would revisit in *Dissident Gardens*); that 'the future will be much like the past', technology not making a decisive difference; that rates of remuneration will always vary, with discrepancies between what an author can make in one venue and the imperative to give away insight as a 'gift' in another.

'The Ecstasy of Influence' comprises three overlapping polemical movements. The first is aesthetic: describing how art is made, emphasizing the role of appropriation and collage, and asserting the right of artists to make use of the welter of signs and names amid which they live. The second is legal: querying the extent of copyright, criticizing those corporate interests guilty of 'source hypocrisy' and proposing that art can be simultaneously commodity and gift. The third is political, avowing the value of the Commons against a society entirely carved up as private property. Insofar as each of these strands of argument supports the other, Lethem's own tendency to make art from other art takes on an implicitly political significance.

In a 2011 retrospect, Lethem already places himself at a distance from the 2007 essay. He now emphasizes that he had tried to occupy a space between 'copyright-abolitionist anarchy' and 'corporate interest' (122). As he puts it in a later interview:

> I started to see these things in terms of a continuity. I was excited by this new conversation; but [...] It seemed to be all about saying these ideas were brand new. Something's in the air, the times they are a-changin', look out you old fuddy-duddies. And I thought, you know, Shakespeare wouldn't be all that knocked out by your appropriative techniques. (2016b: 37)

Lethem's claim to be taking a moderate stance as a 'middling type' (122) recalls the rhetorical position of Lawrence Lessig, who scrupulously detaches himself from political Left and Right and goes out of his way to emphasize the limited extent of his defence of the Commons, for good measure describing himself as 'fanatically pro-market, in the market's proper sphere' (2002: 6). Yet Lethem's retrospective claims to moderation are not particularly consistent with his essay itself. Almost none of its emphasis is on the good sense of copyright, let alone the reality of 'originality' outside appropriation. It is very heavily weighted on the side of certain themes and values: intertextuality; appropriation; the Commons; giving and the gift economy. Lethem's eventual rhetorical framing of the essay occurred in response to critical responses to it – like the one that Lethem refers to here, Marco Roth's review in *n+1* of David Shields' *Reality Hunger* (2010). Roth names Lethem as the founder of a contemporary trend involving 'hipness by analogy' or 'the fantasy of the writer as hip-hop DJ'. He accuses both Lethem and Shields of trying to 'make the reader believe they are witnessing a transgressive, transformative act', and of being on one, extreme side of the argument: 'When Shields and Lethem replace the history of literary influence with a term like "plagiarism", they reveal themselves to be secret "originalists", yin to the copyright absolutists' yang [...] Each side needs the other to validate the caricature' (Roth 2010). In this context, Lethem's later framing of his own position shows a determination to emphasize those elements of his case that Roth's own overstatement (in what had become a heavily rhetorical and polemical conversation all round) had neglected. It is convenient that Lethem in 2011 is able to disavow his words as rendered internally contradictory by their roots in others' writing. He is thus able to present the work as something he does not need to stand by: 'The essay was now an artifact whose weird repercussions I could try to fathom as innocently as anyone else' (2011: 123). Yet its underlying emphases remain the best guide to the ethics and aesthetics of his work.

Personal Testimonies

In the retrospective fragment 'Somatics of Influence', Lethem suggests that what the essay actually lacked was a celebration of the bodily ecstasy of influence, rather than an intellectual defence of it. Hearing influences within pop music is one example. Lethem notes that visceral terms are used negatively *against* influence: 'Plagiarized writing smelled wrong, originality gleamed' (123). He inverts this and makes a visceral affirmation of appropriation. Characteristically, he also seeks personal affirmation. The 'collective "I" of "Ecstasy"' is part of the problem, Lethem suggests (123): 'I'd shied from personal testimonies' (124). This is ironic, coming from a writer whose non-fiction has often been drenched in personal testimony. As Lethem wryly admits elsewhere about his penchant for youthful autobiography: 'That kid in his room: I've dragged him into the light of so many contexts he ought to be pictured by now as if blackened from head to toe with font' (2012: x). Closing 'Somatics of Influence', he unites this personal emphasis with his theme of intertextuality: 'canons not by authoritarian fiat but out of urgent personal voyaging. Construct your own and wear it, an exoskeleton of many colors' (2011: 124). The declaration of 'influence' ends as a celebration of the individual. The two elements might seem opposed. Yet in Lethem, crucially, they are profoundly and intuitively united. We can trace this point by looking at his other essays on culture, presented in *The Disappointment Artist*.

Published two years before the 'Ecstasy' essay, this book gathers essays from other sources, yet coheres in its focus on cultural works from Lethem's childhood and youth. Lethem's discussions of these works are closely tied to periods of his life. Thus, an essay on Marvel comics centres on the mid-1970s; one on *Star Wars* describes viewing the film twenty-one times in summer 1977, when Lethem was thirteen. The time-frame of 'Speak, Hoyt-Schermerhorn' again emphasizes the 1970s as the formative decade for Lethem, while his report of discovering Philip K. Dick aged fifteen records a reading experience starting in 1979. 'Defending *The Searchers*', though it concerns a film from 1956, takes place at a series of distinct temporal and spatial zones: 1982 in Bennington College, 1989 in San Francisco, 1991 in Berkeley. Lastly, 'The Beards', the one essay written especially for this volume, is divided into sections specifically dated as well as named for records, and with the state of his mother's health noted.

The Disappointment Artist is tied profoundly to time. Sometimes, as with *Star Wars*, the relevant time is simply the moment of the work's release. In other cases, like *The Searchers*, Lethem encounters the work as a latecomer. Either way, all these acts of reading are intensely personal. Be a work new or old, Lethem encounters it as part of the story of himself. To write about a cultural work is also to write about his feelings (which typically shift over time) about the work, at least as much as writing about the work as a thing apart from himself. It also typically involves writing about a time and place in Lethem's own life: home, family, friends. Critical essay becomes memoir. By the same token, 'life' becomes a recognized source of what Lethem would soon codify as 'influence'. The essays destabilize the status of the primary text, making it an occasion for reflection but not necessarily the object ultimately in need of explication. As criticism becomes memoir, we cannot be sure that we will return to criticism. Memoir – which is to say, life – may ultimately be what is more important to Lethem.

Yet it is not as though, with Lethem, 'life' exists securely beyond 'art': the ground on which art is experienced, and the mundane sphere to which one returns when one has finished with it. Rather, the sense is that life is enmeshed with art, or soaked in it, so that it cannot be located safely beyond it. This returns us to the plea for somatic 'personal testimonies' over abstract arguments for 'influence', and the construction of canons from 'urgent personal voyaging' (2011: 124). *The Disappointment Artist* recalls several such voyages, and outlines the 'canon' that results – though Lethem's writings elsewhere make clear that the body of reading described here is only a partial account of his personal canon. Disavowing, in 2011, a supposed attachment to 'pop culture', he furnishes yet another set of names barely mentioned in the earlier book, many of them British and relatively unfashionable (2011: 136). In this case, it is as though he finds that his identity has been too fixed, at least in his critics' eyes, by his own past declarations about cultural consumption, and thus wants to appear in a new guise. It is deeply characteristic that Lethem should do this by offering another list of books from his shelves. His primary way to tell us who he is is to tell us what he has read and seen. He is explicit about this tactic in the same essay: 'Writers' memoirs are supposed to wear you out with: *And Then I Wrote*. I wanted to wear you down with: *And Then I Read*' (2011: 136).

The role of the personal and the relation of original 'influence' to derivative work intertwine in the episodic essay 'Identifying with Your Parents, or The Return of the King' (2004), which we can take as exemplary of Lethem's critical method. The essay is rooted in autobiography, commencing with a recollection of his two Brooklyn schoolfriends Karl and Luke (59), enthusiasts respectively for new 1970s comics and for Jack Kirby, who had drawn *The Fantastic Four* in the 1960s. The titular 'Return of the King', a phrase borrowed from Tolkien, is Kirby's return to Marvel in 1976. We can observe a habitual critical move in Lethem's statement that Kirby's career is 'boggling in the sense that the accomplishments of a Picasso or a Dylan or a Shakespeare are boggling' (63). Characteristically, Lethem turns to a list of artists from different media to make a comparison. Characteristically again, one of the canonical greats against whom Lethem pitches his primary object is Bob Dylan: himself a figure from popular culture, though one who was elected to canons and judged to transcend genre conventions earlier than most in his field. That this instinct for analogy is native to Lethem's way of thinking about art is shown when his essay on Dick declares 'I can't keep from comparisons to other artists' of similar 'sprawling fecundity', and compares Dick in turn to Alfred Hitchcock, Robert Altman, Graham Greene, Picasso and Dylan again (2005: 83). Of his own father's painting he says, 'If he's a surrealist it's not the drawing-room gamesmanship of Magritte, but of Julio Cortázar and Bob Dylan and early Cormac McCarthy' (105) – here comparing a practitioner of one art first with another of the same art, then with workers in two other fields. As for John Cassavetes, he is more simply 'film's Bob Dylan' (114), though other artists (Charlie Parker, Miles Davis, Jackson Pollock, Donald Barthelme) are also drawn in. Back in the world of Marvel, Jack Kirby and Stan Lee are likened to John Lennon and Paul McCartney (65–6).

These analogies describe the artist in question by situating them in a field of co-ordinates. If the reader knows Dylan or Barthelme, that provides a clue to what Cassavetes is like. The analogies also encourage a sense of connection between the arts. Cassavetes and Kirby are not only to be understood in relation to film or comics respectively, but to music, literature and painting. The implication is that different arts are commensurable. Paintings are to be viewed in terms of sounds, music heard in terms of words. Lethem's tendency to leap from one art to another is something of an instinctive tic, yet also proposes a stereophonic sense of the arts as happening simultaneously and being somewhat translatable into one another. He is at it again at the close of the same paragraph on Jack Kirby: 'It's as though Picasso had, after 1950, become Adolf Wolfli, or John Ford had ended up as John Cassavetes. Or if Robert Crumb turned into his obsessive mad-genius brother, Charles Crumb. Or if Chuck Berry evolved into Sun Ra' (63). Lethem is harsher on this own tendency in himself, though, in the page elaborately dedicated to 'THE FATUOUS ZONE' (74), where a swirl of words describes 'an endlessly distended/Sequence of less and less credible or even charming analogies and equations' which would end up in the zone, where every key name in the essay 'Equals' every other. As well as playing on comics' own idiom here (the zone corresponds to the Fantastic Four's Negative Zone, and sounds like Superman's Phantom Zone), Lethem is parodying and criticizing his own mania for analogy.

Analogy is not the same as influence. The former is a critical tactic, to help describe an object by naming other objects, from cognate fields, that in their own terms resemble it. The latter is rather a causal claim, that one object is the way it is because of the preceding example of another. Despite this distinction, Lethem's habitual resort to analogy is in keeping with his general instinct for connection: for celebrating the resemblance of one artist to another, rather than highlighting an artist's uniqueness. Even if a given artist is not 'influenced' by, say, Bob Dylan, the critic who compares everything else to him clearly is.

Lethem's reflection on Chuck Berry returns us more directly to the question of 'influence' traced in this chapter. He describes having always wanted to trace the influences on a given work when encountering it: 'The notion of "influence" compelled me, at irrational depths of my being'. Yet the logic he describes has a different emphasis from 'The Ecstasy of Influence'. Learning that David Bowie was imitating Anthony Newley, Lethem 'immediately lost interest in David Bowie and went looking for the source' (63). His cultural interests, he now says, were typically earlier than those of the time or of his own generation: thus while other teens were exploring new wave records, he was pursuing Chuck Berry and Bo Diddley. It is here that the sense of the essay's title emerges: 'I tended to identify with my parents' taste in things, and with the taste of my parents' friends, more than the supposed cultural tokens of my own generation' (64).

This is like and unlike his more familiar stance. It is of a piece with his typical position simply in emphasizing influence, as something 'compelling' and 'irrational': this squares with the later emphasis on 'personal somatics' (2011: 124). But in its emphasis on origins and on rejecting that which comes later, it differs from the later position, which precisely valorizes the artist or artwork that has *been* influenced, rather than only the one that exercises influence. A large part of 'Ecstasy''s force is to argue against the dismissal of works as secondary, imitative, plagiaristic, derivative. Yet the 2004 essay suggests another outlook in which Lethem cleaves to what he might call myths of origin: equivalent to the view he later criticizes, that 'Plagiarized writing smelled wrong', and that 'You'd never listen to Led Zeppelin in the same way after you'd heard the Willie Dixon songs they'd stolen' (2011: 123).

Yet in another way 'Identifying with Your Parents' is significantly consistent with Lethem's larger case. It is, unlike Harold Bloom, anti-Oedipal. The notion that a child should 'identify with his parents' and follow their tastes is a contrary one, by the standards of the counter-cultural, generation-gap epoch that is precisely the one inhabited by Lethem's parents themselves, and which formed him. (A version of this impulse, and its frustration, is depicted in the relationship of Rose and Miriam Zimmer in *Dissident Gardens*.) Lethem's theme breaks a largely unspoken norm – that the child should struggle against the parent – just as 'Ecstasy' breaks with a standard intuition that imitation is bad and originality is good. 'Originality' would be the Oedipal position, while the embrace of 'influence' would be the one that cheerfully honours the example of one's mother and father. This is made explicit near the end of 'Ecstasy' when Lethem values an art made from the past specifically over 'another avant-garde, with its wearisome killing-the-father imperatives' (2011: 110). This reprises almost the same phrase, later in the Marvel essay, when Lethem confirms that Jack Kirby 'represented our parents' values […] which I'd sworn to uphold, against the shallow killing-the-father imperatives of youth' (2005: 70). Matthew Luter perceptively sees the point in 'Ecstasy' also applying to Lethem's relation to his own artistic successors: the author 'opens his arms wide to artists who will come after him, positioning himself as the father who does not need killing in order for successors to thrive' (2015: 15). Therefore, though 2004's report of a childhood purist take on 'origins' seems different in emphasis, a significant continuity is also discernable here. We could say that Lethem values influence and appropriation in part *because* of his comfort with 'identifying with his parents'. His relation to them – conflictual at times, but also reverential – offers a model for a relation to the cultural past. Both positions, aesthetic and familial, are taken with a certain wilful knowledge that he is happily inverting a norm.

The discussion thus far has firstly established Lethem's aesthetic stance on influence and the use of sources, and its political correlatives. Secondly, it has observed the way that Lethem's critical essays – as represented in *The Disappointment Artist* but typical of a large swathe of his non-fiction – make life and art indissoluble, while also meditating on the same conceptual questions of influence and originality, and relying on the related mode of explication by analogy. Next we shall consider how Lethem's attitude to influence emerges in another form of non-fictional discourse: the interview.

The Avowal of Influence

'Before I began publishing', Lethem remarked in 2003, 'I'd imagined that pointing out my thefts would be the occupation of my enemies. I had no idea I'd be so routinely called to take up that work myself!' (Clarke 2011: 54). As this remark indicates, he had spent much time in interviews discussing and outlining the source materials of his own fiction. The degree to which Lethem has relied on 'influence' can be seen just as clearly in such relatively spontaneous remarks as in his more extended, programmatic declarations. A sample of these will demonstrate how deeply this thread runs through his attitude to creativity.

A 1997 interview with Fiona Kelleghan, published in *Science Fiction Studies* in 1998, provides numerous noteworthy instances. Thus Lethem explains that a number of early stories, such as 'Forever, Said the Duck' and 'How We Got In Town and Out Again', 'come out of the *Galaxy*–Frederik Pohl–C.M. Kornbluth–*New Maps of Hell* tradition where the sceptical 1950s-style science fiction writer takes a debunking position on his society's infatuation with technological development, usually in light of some instinctively Marxist sense of how capitalism corrupts the reception of radical technology' (Clarke 2011: 7). The extensiveness of this explanation is almost unwittingly comic, as the writer furnishes the outline of a full-fledged critical reading of his own work in relation to its literary-historical precedents. The description of his antecedents is detached and synoptic (grouping things in a 'tradition' rather than naming individual inspirations), while also nuanced ('instinctively', rather than doctrinaire, Marxist). Put simply, a noticeable feature of Lethem's account is that it looks as much like the work of a critic – even a modern academic critic – as a creative writer.

Discussing *Amnesia Moon*, Lethem readily admits that the book is 'powerfully influenced by Dick, and also by Cornell Woolrich'. But he also adds: 'Both of those writers are characterized by their disappointing endings. It seemed to me that to write a perfect Cornell Woolrich novel, you had to find a way not to write a bad last Cornell Woolrich chapter' (Clarke 2011: 13). In this case, Lethem not only openly names two 'powerful' influences; he also focuses on the specific craft needed to make them work best as models. Turning to *As She Climbed across the Table* (1997), Lethem not only immediately agrees that Don DeLillo is a relevant influence, but declares that he read the whole of his *oeuvre* 'as well as some criticism, some secondary sources', during 'the year and a half of the first composition' of his own novel. Yet he does not stop here, but spontaneously goes on:

> Having said that, there are other really strong influences, on that book. Lem, and Lewis Carroll, and John Barth, and Malcolm Bradbury, and Terry Carr [laughs], and even Philip K. Dick are all influences. The voice is an amalgam of the voice Barth used in *End of the Road*, and *White Noise*. No one ever spots the Barth, partly because he's out of fashion, and even when he's read, it doesn't tend to be that book but the later, bigger books.

Having brought Barth's name into it, Lethem goes on to specify the way that his own novel rewrites the scenario of Barth's *End of the Road*: 'I wrote from another leg of that [love] triangle' (20). As if this were not information enough, he further specifies: 'The science comes out of *Ratner's Star*, and the campus comes out of *White Noise* and other campus novels. Malcolm Bradbury's *The History Man* was a very strong influence on the party scenes and the social atmosphere of the campus' (2011: 20).

Artists sometimes wish to deflect attention away from the precursors that have most strongly shaped their work. Certainly this would be the logic of Harold Bloom's theory of influence as that which is resented and disavowed. Here, Lethem does the opposite: first endorsing the interviewer's primary intuition of influence, then amplifying it by declaring his readership of secondary critical sources (self-evidently, again, aligning his practice with that of an academic critic as much as a creative writer). His next move is to list a plurality of other influences, yet these do not obscure the first one (DeLillo), who remains openly part of the account. The unprompted reference to John Barth is literally an assertion of influence in the face of a readership that has apparently not noticed it: as though for Lethem, in a reversal of a typical creative logic, his own creativity will gain more value and interest the more derivative it can be shown to be. The anxiety of influence here is concern that an influence will go unnoticed. Nor does Lethem merely name influences and leave readers to wonder about their relevance. He explicitly states the aspect of his own work in which he used the model. 'Voice' is often treated by creative writers as that which is most individual and in need of nurture in a writer, but here the opposite applies: the 'voice' of *As She Climbed across the Table* is an 'amalgam' of Barth and DeLillo. To extend the connection with academic life, it is as though Lethem is priming a putative future editor of a scholarly edition of his work.

This is a relatively early interview, which occurs within the ambit of science fiction, and Lethem's approach might be less unusual by the norms of this milieu than by those of literary fiction. As Gary K. Wolfe (2011: 189-90) reminds us, readers of science fiction have often needed to be scholars of their own field, alive to its range of generic conventions and what has been called its 'megatext' of extant possibilities. In Lethem's case, there is occasional evidence to support the idea of a later shift in emphasis: thus in a 2003 *Paris Review* interview upon the publication of *The Fortress of Solitude*, he suggests that the early novels were written from 'cognition and concept', rather than 'grow[ing] organically from character and voice'; the early Lethem 'wanted to be so many different writers all at once' (Clarke 2011: 68). But plenty of other statements indicate otherwise, and that being influenced by sources remains crucial to Lethem's art. In a 2001 interview during the writing of *Fortress*, he describes work on his new novel by describing what he has been reading. He names titles by half a dozen other writers, describing them as 'very long books' not primarily driven by plot, and explains: 'And I'm adamantly writing one like that myself', before further adding: 'I've become more more interested in mimetic textures like David Gates's, and Ann Beattie's, and Richard Yates's, and Philip Roth's' (Clarke 2011: 44). Lethem at once suggests a dissociation from his earlier working methods – the new novel 'will be adamantly unlike any of the previous novels' (44) – and continues them, in frankly indicating that the way to write a certain kind of novel is to read examples of it.

The pattern recurs. In the *Paris Review* interview itself, Lethem can still be seen not only reprising the same lists of influences he had given years earlier for *Table* (Clarke 2011: 54), but also offering a map of influence for *Girl in Landscape* – supposedly the book on which he had moved from 'concept' to 'character'. Thus 'I was reading Carson McCullers and Shirley Jackson and I was thinking about the teenage girl as an archetype'; 'Also Charles Portis's *True Grit*', and the non-literary source of 'John Ford Westerns, *The Searchers* especially'. More than this, though, Lethem also describes himself as replicating 'a generic postmodern move' (as in a work like Jean Rhys's *Wide Sargasso Sea*) in rewriting *The Searchers* from the point of view of a particular character – once again effectively providing his own theoretical gloss on the work. Finally, he also cites two 'large, unconscious thefts' from Philip K. Dick's Martian fiction and E.M. Forster's *A Passage to India*. For Lethem to present an influence as unconscious is a change, as so many of these statements emphasize how far he consciously knows what he is doing as an artist. Yet his account of the debt to Forster takes up two whole paragraphs and goes into detailed plot points of comparison. One might have thought that an 'unconscious' choice was uncertain enough to be left unmentioned, but Lethem drags it into the light with all the explicitness that he affords his 'conscious' borrowings.

As for *The Fortress of Solitude* marking a break with literary influence, Lethem in 2005 programmatically disavows the idea:

> [T]here's another thing that's overlooked when a book seems autobiographical: how strongly it may be influenced by other fictions. *Great Expectations* is in *Fortress*. *Portrait of a Romantic* by Steven Millhauser, too. The character of Arthur comes right out of Millhauser. Henry Roth's *Call It Sleep* was crucial too – Roth's depiction of the child's experience of life inside his house and life in the street as two opposite worlds. My earlier books are very transparent in terms of literary influence. But in *Fortress*, because of the passion of the autobiographical feeling, this fact tends to be disguised. (Clarke 201: 91)

These last lines at once signal a shift (the recent work is less 'transparent') and a continuity ('influence' goes on); and the statement as a whole removes the 'disguise' and makes the novel's relation to other texts unabashedly explicit.

Given that Lethem was still making 'influence' the keynote of his largest book of non-fiction in 2011, it is logical that he can in fact still be found naming precursors throughout his career. In a 2010 radio interview with Michael Silverblatt which refers to 'the transparency of influence, something I've always been very eager to describe' (Clarke 2011: 179–80), he explains how in *Chronic City* (2009) he used Dick as a model in a new way, having revisited him as an editor: 'I found a new usefulness, a new relevance to my own work in Dick. And I thought I can do something with this. I can make a little more of what I know from reading him now and there were things that in fact had escaped me because I wasn't already a novelist when I read them' (175). Thus: 'Dick gave me the methods, reminded me of the methods that might be useful' (176). The tone is slightly different from the earliest interview cited, yet the role of influence is undiminished: it has combined, here, with an idea of literary craft, in which a past writer furnishes a model or techniques that are usable in the present.

The suggestion here has been that Lethem, while not unusual in being subject to literary influence, has been distinctive in his open embrace of the condition. Other writers can offer telling comparison here. One example can be found in the 1993 *Paris Review* interview with Richard Price (b.1949):

> INTERVIEWER: When you're writing a book do you tend to avoid reading other books?

PRICE: I'm very protective of myself. I once made the mistake of reading *Sophie's Choice* while I was trying to write *The Breaks*. It was like trying to sing while somebody else is singing another song in the background. [...] So, when I'm writing a book all I read is genre stuff; I'm very careful not to read anything too good, that's going to make me anxious. (Gourevitch 2006: 393)

Price's answer contrasts strikingly with what we have seen from Lethem. As we have seen, for him it was normal to read fiction as part of the process of writing fiction – witness his avowal of reading the whole of DeLillo while drafting *Table*. Price's musical metaphor is cogent in itself, yet Lethem's practice shows that it need not apply universally: his accounts of his own practice imply rather a process of composition by singing along and harmonizing with the music that one has already deliberately set playing. (It is suggestive, in this context, that several of Lethem's interviews actually talk of writing while listening to music.) Price's need to be 'protective of himself' and to avoid influences that might make him 'anxious' stands in a curiously stark contrast with Lethem's approach to the same question: influences are not to be guarded against but encouraged and cultivated; Bloomian 'anxiety' is displaced by the pleasure of homage and reuse.

A close contemporary of Lethem, Jennifer Egan (b.1962) has been asked a similar question in relation to her acclaimed novel *A Visit from the Goon Squad* (2010): 'You have cited both Marcel Proust and the TV show *The Sopranos* as sources of inspiration for *A Visit from the Goon Squad*. Can you explain this unique combination of influences?' (Alford 2012). Here, evidently, Egan has previously volunteered these sources herself. Her response has two contrasting aspects. She gives a precise account of the way that she used Proust and *The Sopranos* in her work: with regard to Proust, 'the most conscious influence', 'I found myself wondering, over the years that it took me to read the whole book, what a contemporary book about time might look like'. Like Lethem in some of his answers, Egan presents influence as a matter of craft: 'how to capture the sweep and scope of those transformations and reversals without taking thousands of pages to do it. It's a technical question – how do you do that?' By the same token, Egan 'decided that using some of the techniques of a series like *The Sopranos* might be one way to try to do that'. Yet Egan begins her response to the question in a different register:

First of all, influence is always a difficult thing to pinpoint when you write as instinctively as I do because I don't really know exactly what I'm going to end up doing when I sit down to do it. I'm waiting to be surprised myself, because I find that the surprises are always the best ideas [...] the stuff that feels fun and fresh to me tends to happen fairly unthinkingly. So, sometimes it's only later that I can really parse out what actually influenced me. (Alford 2012)

Egan and Lethem have been colleagues on the Brooklyn scene, respectful about each other's work. But in this particular instance, her instinct is to think of influence in a way different from Lethem's habitual approach. Influence is 'difficult [...] to pinpoint'; writing is 'instinctive'; the writer starts writing unsure of what she will end up with; the best of the work is what comes unexpectedly, even 'unthinkingly'. Despite her insightful comments about her sources, Egan here typifies an approach to the question that Lethem's aesthetic avowals have wilfully steered away from. Her use of Proust and *The Sopranos* might have justified her offering a more ambitiously Lethemesque formulation about the creative process; but instead she speaks with a certain modesty and allows the creative act to retain some mystique. She finally offers a middle ground between deliberate craft and the mystery of creativity that can only be understood in retrospect: 'I think in some way, when I sat down to work on *A Visit from the Goon Squad*, the idea of merging some of those techniques with my conscious goal of writing a book about time must have happened' (Alford 2012).

A final and more extended comparison can be made with another contemporary of Lethem, his sometime friend Jonathan Franzen (b.1959). In his 2009 essay 'On Autobiographical Fiction', Franzen records that audiences at author events typically ask a limited range of questions, including: '*Who are your influences?*' (Franzen 2012: 121). Franzen's immediate comment on the question indicates impatient scorn: 'Sometimes the person asking this question merely wants some book recommendations, but all too often the question seems to be intended seriously'. It is difficult to imagine the author of *The Ecstasy of Influence* implying disbelief that a question about influence could be 'intended seriously'. Yet Franzen's full response is more complex. One problem he has with the question 'is that it's always asked in the present tense: Who *are* my influences? The fact is, at this point in my life, I'm mostly influenced by my own past writing. If I were still laboring in the shadow of, say, E.M. Forster, I would certainly be at pains to pretend that I wasn't' (2012: 121). (Franzen's chosen illustration of an influence to disavow is one that Lethem has openly announced as an influence on *Girl in Landscape*.) Franzen explicitly places this in terms of Harold Bloom's version of influence; but his implication is that if he ever suffered from this Bloomian version, it has passed with maturity, to the point where the writer is 'mostly' self-sufficient. On the face of it, this places Franzen in contrast with Lethem. The latter has a strong consciousness of his own body of work, and his writing can be self-referential (as in, say, the kangaroo in *You Don't Love Me Yet* acting as an enigmatic reminder of its counterpart in *Gun, with Occasional Music*). Yet it would nonetheless be uncharacteristically solipsistic of him to state that his own work was now the largest influence on itself.

Franzen goes on to assert that 'Direct influence makes sense only with very young writers, who, in the course of figuring out how to write, first try copying the styles and attitudes and methods of their favorite authors' (121). To illustrate this, he lists several writers who were important to him at age twenty-one. The list in principle looks comparable with those offered by Lethem: it even includes a precise parallel, as Franzen 'put a lot of effort into copying the sentence rhythms and comic dialogue of Don DeLillo' (122). Yet Franzen undercuts all this with the abrupt declaration: 'But to me these various "influences" seem not much more meaningful than the fact that, when I was fifteen, my favourite music group was the Moody Blues. A writer has to begin somewhere, but where exactly he or she begins is almost random' (122). The statement appears a non-sequitur, and does little for the coherence of Franzen's case. For one thing the two ages (fifteen and twenty-one) are different: by definition, one is slightly closer to the writerly maturity that Franzen values. For another, he is not a professional musician, so the importance of the two arts is not the same in a discussion of the influences that have made him the writer he is. (There is again a curiously pointed contrast here with Lethem, for whom the music he loved at fifteen *is* relevant to his identity as an adult artist: what for Franzen is self-evidently to be dismissed would for Lethem be a crucial resource that could not be easily left behind, as his book on Talking Heads demonstrates.)

Still more curious is Franzen's suggestion that his early literary influences are 'almost random', not worth further consideration, when several of them leave their mark on his published work. Indeed two of them are films from which he admits to drawing the plots of his first two novels, while his other non-fiction has made very plain the particular struggles that he has gone through with Pynchon, DeLillo and other complex American writers (notably William Gaddis), which have shaped his own aesthetic outlook (Franzen 2002: 238–69). Even the work of Horkheimer and Adorno, which he also cites here, has been seen as an influence on his mature work (Wood 2004: 190). Franzen has a right to outgrow influences, but this disavowal of them as 'random' seems symptomatic almost in Bloom's sense. Once again the contrast with Lethem is apparent, as the latter, even in middle age, is apt to describe early enthusiasms as formative in the development of an aesthetic outlook: it would be unthinkable for him to describe Philip K. Dick or David Byrne as arbitrary teenage trinkets with no bearing on his extended body of work.

Franzen is at last somewhat closer to Lethem in his remodelling of influence as a matter of contemporaneity rather than tradition: as a writer, 'I feel like a member of a single, large virtual community in which I have dynamic relationships with other members of the community, most of whom are no longer living' (123). Franzen describes other writers as 'friends' and 'enemies', and in rather characteristically combative fashion – yet another remake of Harold Bloom's narrative of aggression – declares that in writing 'I fight for my friends and I fight against my enemies' (124). Still, his coy profession that he 'befriended' (that is, read) other writers in the course of writing particular works of his own (Paula Fox for *The Corrections*, Alice Munro for *Freedom*) finally gives him some common ground with Lethem's model of creativity, in which 'You prepare [to write] by rereading books with architecture you sense will be relevant to the attempt' (Clarke 2011: 61).

The examples of Price, Egan and Franzen have shown a range of views on the idea of literary influence from US writers contemporary with Lethem. The points of overlap that Egan and Franzen have with him demonstrate that this question need not be a binary one, in which precursors are either admitted or denied. Franzen offers his own vocabulary for talking about learning from other writers, while Egan demonstrates concrete ways in which she has done so. Nonetheless, the rhetoric into which all these writers fall remains noticeably different from Lethem's much more determined bid to place such source materials in the foreground of discussion. An especially revealing statement in this regard is his Preface to *The Ecstasy of Influence*. Exploring and justifying Lethem's self-consciousness as a writer, this piece addresses the typical rhetorical status of the novelist, and the cultural and journalistic norms governing what they should and should not say. Thus: 'Many people prefer artists to make statements along the lines of: "I don't know what I'm doing, I just go into a small, badly furnished room and out come these stories", "The songs write themselves", "The paint tells me where it wants to go", etc' (Lethem 2011: xvii). He goes on, a page later, to note that despite the discursive privileges afforded the novelist,

> it's often weird what the polite novelist lately *isn't* supposed to say aloud. We're not meant to refute critics […] we've renounced, after a brief, misguided sally, entering our names on search engines. We don't rank ourselves among our contemporaries, or attack other novelists for being overrated […] We don't know why we do what we do, but we're not *too* amazed with ourselves for being the lucky keepers of this universal flame. […] Influence is semiconscious, not

something to delineate too extensively, except when we've patterned our latest book on a literary monument of the past, at least a half-century old, by a master with whom we'd never dare compare ourselves, only hope to be 'worthy of'. We don't speak of our own career's arc, let alone of crises encountered therein, because we'd never think of what we're doing in crass terms of a career. Rather, blinkered devotionally, we 'serve the needs of the book at hand', and besides are permanent amateurs, born anew each time we start writing […] (2011: xviii–xix)

Though not promoted with much fanfare, this passage is almost as significant a guide to Lethem's aesthetic as 'The Ecstasy of Influence' itself. It proceeds by negation: Lethem outlines an outlook by its implied dissent from what his text actually says. If this is what the polite novelist is *not* supposed to say, we may find our way across to its opposite and view it as an alternative stance that Lethem would like to entertain. What if the novelist *did* refute critics? Then we would see essays like 'My Disappointment Critic', his riposte to James Wood published in the same volume (2011: 384–9). What if novelists *do* have some idea why they do what they do; or influence is in fact fully conscious, something to delineate extensively; or the writer goes into a small, badly furnished room and produces stories there through the careful deployment of pre-existing aesthetic resources? Implicitly, Lethem poses his own career as the answer to these speculative questions. If this is a refreshingly different way to see artistic creation, he also dares to say that it might have a hidden political implication: 'For if we consent that what appears natural in art is actually constructed from a series of hidden postures, decisions, and influences, etc., we make ourselves eligible to weigh the notion that what's taken as natural in our experience of everyday life could actually be a construction as well' (2011: xvii).

Art and Theft

This chapter has demonstrated Lethem's avowal of the value of influence, and his readiness to accept the presence of other artists and works as part of his own creative process. Let us finally consider some instances of how these ideas are played out in Lethem's own fiction.

The story 'K for Fake' is part of a series of writings on Franz Kafka that Lethem undertook in the 1990s. It closes *Kafka Americana* (1999), in which volume Lethem's two contributions are matched by two from Carter Scholz and another, 'Receding Horizon', is a collaboration between the two writers. The collaboration with Scholz enhances the sense of creativity as a shared, not necessarily individual matter – a sense that Lethem has encouraged with other collaborative works, including the Nebula-nominated 'Ninety Per Cent of Everything' (with John Kessel and James Patrick Kelly, 1999), and the additional Kafka piece 'The Elvis National Theatre of Okinawa' (with Lukas Jaeger, 1992), and in a different way with the cut-up work 'Always Crashing in the Same Car' (2007), where his own words are edited into a series with those of David Bowie, J.G. Ballard and others. In *Kafka Americana*, Kafka is openly acknowledged as a source, and to make 'second use' of him is the authors' professed task. 'K for Fake', last in the volume, offers a kind of crescendo.

The story is primarily a compressed rewrite of Kafka's novel *The Trial* (written in 1914–15). The protagonist K. moves through a late twentieth-century cityscape, with Kafka's Central European streets replaced by Brooklyn. The painter Titorelli, who sells Josef K. his works in *The Trial*, is here K.'s art dealer, and takes his advice to hang a monotonous series of landscapes upside-down. On the strength of this, he asks K. to sign each work with his initial, then casually reveals that they were painted by his assistant Lilia. She has already played the Kafka role of *femme fatale* with K., but at the story's end takes him to court for falsely asserting his authorship of her paintings.

The tale is narrated principally in a pastiche of Kafka's style, in its canonical English translation by Edwin and Willa Muir. Lethem captures the air of innocence and naiveté with which the protagonist encounters each new, confounding or seemingly impossible situation, and the bewildering yet uncompromising assertions thrown at him at each turn. Most of *The Trial*'s events are omitted, and those that remain are moved around, in this collage of pieces of Kafka. As importantly, the direct relation to Kafka is complicated by other borrowings. Orson Welles' film of *The Trial* (1962) is almost as much a source as the book. Welles' own words from interview are interpolated into the story (Lethem and Scholz 1999: 82, 92, 99), and 'K for Fake' varies his title *F for Fake* (1973). His screen performance as the Advocate is reprised here as the Advertising Pitchman, 'advocate for certain commercial products: wine, canned peas and pears, a certain make of automobile' (86). While the character remains almost identical to Welles's film role, it also takes on the extra-diegetic status of the late Welles's career as a voice for commercial hire: Welles appears at once in and out of character. Lethem's rendition of his screen persona – chuckling, gesturing histrionically, 'arching an eyebrow dramatically' (95), dismissing the painting contest with the judgement 'A hot-dog eating contest would be more exalted' (97) – is a skilful cameo akin to the lengthier rendition of John Wayne as Efram Nugent in *Girl in Landscape*. Another Lethem standby is also in play: Rod

Serling's *Twilight Zone*, implicitly posited here as Kafkaesque TV as Lilia calls K.'s experience 'practically Serlingesque'. The alternative, more familiar adjective is beyond K.'s recall (88–9).

The story's theme is significant, and congruent with that of *F for Fake* itself: artistic forgery and the contestation of authorship. These themes are indicated in K.'s charge sheet – 'Impersonation: Forgery, Fakery, Ventriloquism' (87) – and become charges made against Kafka, perhaps by Kafka himself: 'Impersonation of the Gentile, Impersonation of the Genius' (87). Lilia, prior to her day in court, dismisses the rights of the author: asked about the rehang of her own paintings, she avers that 'The artist's intentions don't matter [...] Anyway, the artist is dead, and his intentions are unknown' (89). It cannot be said that such talk provides a coherent, explicit position on such issues. Rather, if anything, the story's stance is performative, enacting a daring, comic plagiarism; and its thematization of such plagiarism does not so much invite the accusation as neutralize it, making claims of authorial ownership into a dark courtroom farce.

This is parallelled in another, slightly earlier story: 'The Insipid Profession of Jonathan Hornebom' (1995). The scene is once again laid in contemporary New York. Detective Harriet Welch is employed by the elderly painter Jonathan Hornebom to trace his movements, as he has been entering a fugue state and finding his own work marred by images of giant birds. Harriet trails Hornebom to the Museum of Modern Art, where he is transfixed by Max Ernst's Dada object 'Bird Camera', 'a combination printing press and toy cannon' (2006a: 55). During these trances, a second Hornebom paints the gruesome birds on his otherwise saccharine canvases. Harriet and the art student Richard DeBronk steal 'Bird Camera' from the museum and produce 'Maxographs' in which real-life scenes are also populated by the giant birds. This is plainly not a mere artistic technique but a metaphysical revelation: a fact corroborated by the menacing appearance of giant birds with the names of Dada artists (Eluard, Breton, Tzara) through the television set. Resolution arrives when Ernst's spirit, in the form of a bird, materializes and announces that he is Hornebom's father.

A first-time reader might not realize how closely the tale is based on another work: Robert Heinlein's story, 'The Unpleasant Profession of Jonathan Hoag', published in *Unknown Worlds* in 1942. Much of Heinlein's structure is replicated: the client's fugue state; the pair of detectives (Heinlein's married couple, Ted and Cynthia Randall, are replaced by Lethem's investigators who pair up during the story); the fantastic perils offered by mirrors in one story and televisions in the other; the interest in art (Hoag turns out to be a critic who is assessing life itself as a work of art); right down to the ending where Lethem closely mirrors

Heinlein's statements, yet modifies them into a more reassuring denouement. Crucially, the bird motif is also present in Heinlein, and indeed is a major reason for Lethem's decision to work Ernst's characteristic avian imagery into his story.

This story is among Lethem's most extensive replications of another's work. Looking back from 2005, he recounts:

> an editor, in the process of rejecting the piece, wrote me a worried letter to say I'd either consciously or unconsciously plagiarized the Heinlein. I retitled it to make the homage self-evident, but the incident was jangling, one of my earliest brushes with a confusion over the shades between 'parody', 'appropriation', 'influence', 'quotation' and 'theft' that, in a world which makes room for Andy Warhol, Walt Disney, and Borges' 'Don Quixote by Pierre Menard', still bedevils me. (2006a: 106)

This account clearly approaches the concerns of 'The Ecstasy of Influence', and finds their origin over a decade earlier. Yet the effect of the story is rather different from that of 'K for Fake'. That story would seem to make little sense without Kafka, whereas this one stands, eccentric yet seemingly self-contained, in its own right. 'K for Fake' incorporates increasingly brash, frame-breaking slogans (99–100), where 'Insipid Profession' retains its own narrative integrity, albeit a stylized world which Lethem can later perceive as 'cute' (104). Nonetheless, the two stories share another key feature. Both do not simply replay a single prior model, but combine multiple sources, producing interference in the transmission of 'influence'. Kafka, Welles and Serling are here matched by Heinlein, Ernst, Hitchcock (*The Birds* most obviously) and The Trashmen's rock song 'Surfin' Bird'. Lethem's verb for the process here is 'smash it together' (106). His practice could also be described by Lawrence Lessig's theorization (2008) of remix culture, in which existing resources of image, sound or text can be creatively combined. Lessig's emphasis is on the extent to which digital technology has now encouraged this across a range of media, but he notes that its most intuitive origin is in text, in which 'The freedom to quote, and to build upon, the words of others is taken for granted by everyone who writes' (2008: 53). Building further upon the textual creations of others, Lethem's story also adds another pre-existing character, the children's heroine Harriet the Spy: now an adult private eye, but with memories of her childhood (61). Besides the resemblance to Heinlein's story, another striking case of 'influence' is the extent of the tale's reference to visual art, which Lethem admits provides a connection to 'K for Fake' among other texts (104). Both stories replay, borrow and repeat with variation others' work; both also depict and describe art being made, contested or collaborated upon. Hornebom's canvases are uncannily altered by spirits beside his own. Ernst's bird camera allows Harriet to make new images. Her professional reputation is eventually founded on her theft of the camera, and thus its 'celebrated rescue' (101). Art in both stories is a shifty space, close to crime. Lethem's stories that most flagrantly borrow others' art seem compelled also to be *about* borrowing others' art.

His longest fictional meditation on these themes is the novel *You Don't Love Me Yet* (2007). In the early 1990s, Lucinda Hoekke, bassist in a nameless band, is participating in an installation art project in which Los Angeles citizens call with complaints. Lucinda becomes fascinated by an insistent caller, Carl, and writes down some of his phrases, which she takes to the band. His phrase 'monster eyes' gives a title to the band's most popular song, then becomes their de facto name. Lucinda gives more of Carl's phrases to their songwriter, Bedwin, who successfully weaves songs from them. The band tastes brief local success. On the grounds of his unwitting contribution, Carl presumes to become part of the band, inveigling his way in as keyboard player and then, with his self-indulgence and presumption of ownership, ruining their big break on local radio.

At the band's first concert, the audience is intrigued by 'the mystery of authorship', wondering how far the songs depict an individual's experience (107). Questions of authorship indeed become crucial. When a disc jockey asks the band who wrote their song, three members simultaneously name three different people (184). How much right does Carl have to the band's new songs? One reason he assumes this right is that his own job is to produce slogans – 'pour love on the broken places', 'all thinking is wishful' (86) – which gain him inordinate amounts of money. He thus believes that coining 'itchy' or 'gummy' phrases is of great worth. Hearing his own phrases used in the songs, he comments: 'I usually collect hundreds, if not thousands, per verb or noun' (119). Yet he has not truly written the songs, only fed some verbal material into them. Music and melody are beyond him, supplied by Bedwin, while the rest of the band might also claim their own part in forging the arrangement. After their first performance of 'Monster Eyes', the band already feel it to be 'a fixture in their lives, a given. [...] the song was there all along, waiting to be given the air' (108). Carl can only truly claim to be a source of inspiration, or one of multiple collaborators. Drummer Denise refuses to accept his authorship as the dominant factor: 'The lyrics you wrote, they wouldn't amount to anything at all if we hadn't played them onstage. They wouldn't be worth ten cents if they weren't coming out of [lead singer] Matthew's mouth' (154). This form of art is shown to be collective, not necessarily susceptible to a single author's claim. Lethem might say that the same applies to writing.

Carl's arrival in the band produces a kind of collaboration – of a kind plainly interesting to Lethem – yet is also destabilizing for the band. Lethem is alive not only to the concept of creativity but to the practical consequences of jealousy and exploitation. Denise tells the ageing roué Carl 'You see us as a fund of young new friends' (152), including his new sexual partner Lucinda. Whatever his claim on the songs, his uninvited insertion of himself into the unit, making a four-piece into a quintet, has no ethical warrant; it succeeds mainly because of the docility of the band members.

Yet Carl finally does the decent thing: in discussion with Bedwin, he abruptly agrees to give up all rights to the songs. What has seemed a delicate negotiation – 'we could just divvy them up, you get some, I get some. Or we could split them down the middle, lyrics and music. [...] Maybe we should split them the other way, you take the words, me the tunes. That way we've each got what we didn't have before' (211) – is interrupted by Carl's realization that Bedwin, unlike himself, sees himself as an artist: 'you're looking at someone without a creative life, let alone one with significant chapters' (212). Carl has been viewing the negotiation as an interesting financial matter; realizing that to Bedwin their ownership has another dimension, he is happy to declare: 'You should help yourself. Take them outright, no charge. [...] If they mean that much to you. Truth is, I was never so into music in the first place' (212). Despite his presumptuous behaviour, Carl shows himself able to step out of a financial exchange, into another framework where judgments are made on the basis of emotion or the investment of time or personality. Abruptly transferring the discussion from cash nexus to artistic value, Carl turns his claim into a gift.

The novel is interested in such transfigurations of value. A crowd that has gathered for a party becomes, once the band starts playing, an audience, subject to a different behavioural pattern. By the same token, the band members are suddenly elevated, 'a thousand percent less ordinary than at the retail outlets or previous social gatherings from which these men are fairly certain they recognize them' (106). The obscure band has suddenly become an 'enclave' which others yearn to penetrate (107). The discrepancy is analogous to the one that Lethem, in this 'Ecstasy' era, identifies between work sold at high cost and given away free (Clarke 2011: 135, 147). Some values might not come down to money. Lucinda, newly happy after encountering Carl, thinks of her mood as 'all one thing', to be shared with her friends: 'the source of her happiness was a stream through all their lives' (90). In a related insight, the conceptual artist Falmouth Strand's plan for a party comes unstuck because 'Falmouth had tried to appropriate other people's happiness, and been met with that property's devastatingly blithe resistance. Happiness was disobedient, had its own law' (99). Happiness, on this account, belongs to what Lethem had come to call the Commons.

Lethem would revisit this paradigm from the opposite end in *Chronic City*, where a 'Note' at the end indicates borrowings from seven different writers. Most of them are individual sentences: for instance, an initial description of Perkus Tooth's cultural ramblings contains the complimentary statement, 'In the midst of these variations the theme was always ingeniously and excitingly retrieved' (2010: 13), which turns out to be taken wholesale from Saul Bellow's novel *Humboldt's Gift* (1975). Lethem's listing of sources here is structurally akin to the 'Key' at the end of 'The Ecstasy of Influence' itself, with the quantitative difference that unlike the essay, most of the novel is not composed in this way. His note makes a point of saying that he 'returns' these borrowings to their sources, as though nothing has been lost: any crime has been victimless. Having made this brief list, he adds a last note that envelops and transcends it: he also returns 'everything else to everywhere else forever and ever amen'. The gesture is sing-song and playful, but also accords with the ethos that Lethem has been cultivating: that at some level, everything is borrowed and reused, and could be returned to a common source. It recalls his reference, late in 'The Beards', to Steven Wright's mind-opening joke: 'I keep my seashell collection scattered on the beaches of the world' (Lethem 2005: 148–9).

A more recent example of such borrowing is Lethem's composition 'Nancy, All Too Nancy', published in *McSweeney's* in 2018. The piece contains fifteen images from the *Nancy* comic strip created by Ernie Bushmiller in the 1930s, each captioned by a sentence or two from Lethem. The words look like quotations from existing works of philosophy or psychology – 'Most of us have experienced the inkling that there is a world behind the world' (Lethem 2018a), runs the first caption – yet they are uncredited and appear to be Lethem's own. Each caption corresponds directly to the image above it: thus the line just quoted captions an image in which a character lifts the carpet and shows Nancy the mess beneath it, and a caption containing the words 'when peering out from behind a mask, we can only guess what faces others have drawn for us' accompanies an image of Nancy holding up a picture of her own head in front of another girl's face. The relations between word and image may be ambiguous, but are unmistakably intended. This slight, occasional piece exemplifies Lethem's continued interest in using 'found' material. The effect may be to make *Nancy* seem stranger than it normally does, but the corollary of this is that the piece reminds us of this comic strip's own penchant for strangeness.

This chapter commenced by noting that art indeed draws from life. But we have subsequently seen that for Lethem, the two terms can become inextricable. Writing about life might also involve imbrication in another's art. To illustrate the point, let us finally consider the example of Lethem's time at Bennington College.

Lethem's brief Bennington generation generated literature: fiction not just from, but about, the college. Bret Easton Ellis, who had published *Less Than Zero* (1985) at just twenty-one, located his second novel *The Rules of Attraction* (1987) at a fictional Bennington, named Camden College. The name had already appeared in the margins of Ellis's debut, and Jill Eisenstadt, another classmate, reused it in her first novel *From Rockaway* (1987). Ellis's rendition of Camden is Brat Pack writing, a long sequence of beer-keg parties, drugs and casual sexual encounters. When a character refers to a 'weird Classics group [...] probably roaming the countryside sacrificing farmers and performing pagan rituals' (Ellis 1987: 179), it is a fractional preview, uninterpretable as such at the time, of Donna Tartt's first novel. *The Secret History* (1992), ten years in production, rebrands its fictional campus as Hampden: a slight swerve from Ellis's version that nonetheless keeps it in view.

Tartt's version of college life, though, is substantially different from Ellis's, centring on an eccentric group of students devoted to the classics. Bibulous though they are, Ellis's ultra-hedonism is replaced by a milieu closer to a reprise of Evelyn Waugh: more centred on Europe (notably the classical world) and styled after an idea of upper-class England. Tartt's narrator, installed at Hampden (like Lethem) on a special grant for poorer students, also notices more of his physical environment:

> A group of red-cheeked girls playing soccer, ponytails flying, their shouts and laughter carrying faintly over the velvety, twilit field. Trees creaking with apples, fallen apples red on the grass beneath the heavy sweet smell of apples rotting on the ground and the steady thrumming of wasps around them. Commons clock tower: ivied brick, white spire, spellbound in the hazy distance. (Tartt 2007: 13)

Lethem was working in a bookshop when Tartt's debut appeared: he recalls selling many copies and looking for himself in its fictional world (Lethem 2011: 25). He finally delivered his own fictional version of Bennington in 2003, mixing

Ellis's darkly hedonistic party with Tartt's greater appreciation of its pastoral setting. Dylan Ebdus, narrating the latter part of *The Fortress of Solitude*, recalls:

> the idyllic walled preserve, the bucolic acres of the campus [...] an environment one part New England farmland, complete with white clapboard dorms, twisted apple trees bearing inedible fruit, low lichen-covered Frostian stone walls wending nowhere through the woods, and tattered cemetery plots with burial dates in the 1700s. (Lethem 2003: 383)

Lethem, like Eisenstadt, directly follows Ellis: his fictional college is called Camden. The gesture is very deliberate. In writing himself into this piece of literary history, twenty years on, Lethem elects to follow the contour that this time and place have already been given in fiction. The use of the name is a homage to Ellis (and Tartt, as Hampden remained verbally close to Camden); an acknowledgement of Lethem's comparative belatedness as a successful writer from their generation; and a gesture that places his own fiction unmistakably into an intertextual relation with that of his peers.

Lethem would even recreate the college yet again, under a fourth name, in the story 'Super Goat Man', which appeared in *The New Yorker* seven months after *The Fortress of Solitude*. Now it is 'Corcoran College, in Corcoran, New Hampshire'. The ageing superhero-cum-professor of the title is spotted 'moving across the Commons lawn on a September afternoon, one with the scent of fallen and fermenting crab apples on the breeze' (Lethem 2004: 127). The story echoes John Barth's *Giles Goat Boy* (1966), a novel centred on a university campus; its echo of Lethem's own contemporaneous novel is equally clear, from the landscape to the parties held in dormitories. Super Goat Man is called to assist two 'reviled frat boys' (Lethem 2004: 132) who have climbed the college's clock tower. That location has its own analogue in 'the stopped clock on the Commons tower' in *The Fortress of Solitude* (Lethem 2003: 391).

Bennington has thus proliferated into several textual versions, including Ellis's Camden (1987), Tartt's Hampden (1992), Lethem's Camden (2003) and Corcoran (2004), and ultimately (in 2011) Lethem's brief memoir of Bennington itself. This might complete the circle by restoring us to fact, though in Lethem fact and fiction can be enduringly hard to disentangle. He ends with a recollection of serving food to students alongside Tartt, which he admits may or may not be genuine: 'If it is a fantasy, it was surely induced by rereading the brilliant first pages of Donna's novel' (Lethem 2011: 28). He closes by hinting that he thinks he is the model, not for Tartt's murdered farmer, but for her scholarship-funded protagonist. It is apt that Lethem's memory of such a heavily fictionalized period should ultimately lead back into fiction. The variation of names into Corcoran might seem to break the chain of inter-fictional connection. In fact it tacitly but firmly strengthens that link, for the new name is that of the student, Bunny Corcoran, whose murder is central to *The Secret History*.

Lethem's choices, in writing Bennington College into his own fiction, are characteristic for their evident desire to entwine that fiction with others'. His Camden and Corcoran are, in a sense, invitations to connect, sent out not so much to Ellis and Tartt as individuals, but to their writing itself. The result is a fragile web of fictional Benningtons, overlapping and homologous yet also different – each one closely tied to its author's particular literary persona and aesthetic. It is a happy semantic accident that one feature that all these fictions share is reference to 'the Commons' – the grounds in the centre of the campus. For these texts' tenuous network has itself created a kind of Commons, in the sense outlined above: a cultural sphere that is open to be entered and repurposed by multiple artists and recipients.

Then again, if the Bennington writers' worlds overlap, they also subtly differ, and hence arguably represent alternate fictional zones. Chapter Three below will explore fiction's power to make and break such worlds. That power was a theme for Philip K. Dick, who – four years before Ellis, Tartt and Lethem arrived in Vermont – described the 'astonishing power', shared by ideologies and fiction writers, of 'creating whole universes, universes of the mind' (Dick 1978). The multiple Camdens, Hampden and Corcoran might be pictured as belonging to a patchwork fabric of fiction, or as adjacent realities in a multiverse. To reprise one of Dick's aphorisms: if you think this Bennington is bad, you should see some of the others.

The work we have reviewed in this chapter shows that intertextuality, for Lethem, is not an optional extra, nor a gimmick to be briefly deployed and then dispensed with. The abiding sense of his writing is that not only an artist's work, but their self, is intertextual: composed of source texts and artistic experiences that are themselves transfigured by the contingency of time and place. Foucault's statement, quoted earlier in this chapter, may be gently rewritten: '[N]o-one can exist by themselves; they are always in a relationship of support and dependence in regard to others'; All of us 'refer [...] explicitly or not [...] to other books, other texts, or other sentences'. Nudged this way, Foucault's statement may be seen to shift from a declaration of intertextuality to a declaration of intersubjectivity. As a utopian statement about human interdependence, it chimes plausibly with Lethem's emphasis on common ground: that which 'belongs to everyone and no one', its use 'controlled only by common consent' (2011: 108). If it was not evident from his earliest fiction, Lethem's later work would make plainer such a political imperative.

Lethem's tendency to make writing from his reading will be recurrent in the chapters ahead. We can turn next to a particularly systematic and significant form of artistic repetition and citation: genre.

2

Genres

If one literary term has been associated with Jonathan Lethem above all others, it is genre. For the first decade or so, genre seems virtually the key to his body of work. Over subsequent years it gradually loses exclusive traction and becomes one relevant theme among others. This corresponds to Lethem's own commentary on his work. In 1997, he could openly declare: 'I think that I have a propensity or weakness for writing meta-fictionally about genre. All of my stories tend to be, at one level, interrogations of the genre they inhabit' (Clarke 2011: 6). In 2001, he averred that 'I'm almost always (half-consciously) hiding one apparent "genre" under another, or under several' (35). But by 2016, Lethem could tell an interviewer: 'If you look at the interviews from the first four or five years of my publishing life [...] you'd see me endlessly discussing "genre boundaries" and how to disrupt them. How silly it looks to me now, and also exhausting' (McIlvain 2016). This statement is not a dismissal of genre writing itself. It is primarily a piece of self-mockery, from an older writer impatient with his younger self. Different phases of Lethem's fiction will respond to differing conceptual tools. But notwithstanding Lethem's own shifts, the present book needs to engage with the claims of genre.

The following discussion will first establish a working idea of genre, tracing the logic of Lethem's own statements about it. The chapter will then turn directly to Lethem's fictional work with genre. After a consideration of one story's use of science fiction, it will closely consider Lethem's work in the detective genre in the 1990s, before a synoptic consideration of how far Lethem's work with fantastic genres has shifted across his career.

Ideas of Genre

In the discussion of fiction or narrative, a genre is a way of gathering a group of texts, and describing their coherence as a group. The group may be very large, encompassing many thousands of narratives. To form a genre, the texts must possess significant elements in common, even though, across many texts, they will naturally diverge and differ in numerous ways. There is not one single set of genres that can be conveniently applied across all narratives. Rather, a number of different sets of genres have emerged through cultural history, sometimes superseding each other, sometimes continuing to exist and overlapping with new arrivals.

Thus one plausible list of the primary genres of literature, at least since the eighteenth century, would read simply: fiction, poetry, drama. This is to consider genre as a discursive format, implying a particular relation between author and audience. Alternatively, generic terms can refer to the range of genres found within one of those textual formats. A major instance of this is the classical set of tragedy, comedy and their companions like romance and satire, inherited from the ancient world and still in use. Other groupings that have developed during the history of the novel may also be considered genres: the *Bildungsroman* or novel of development, usually showing a youth coming of age and venturing into the world; the Picaresque, or episodic tale of travel and adventure. These two groupings, in fact, can also be found in Lethem, for instance in *The Fortress of Solitude* and *Amnesia Moon* respectively.

But the heart of the matter, in Lethem's case, is the use of genre to refer to the varieties of *popular* narrative which have developed in the era of mass culture, from the paperback and comic book to the radio serial and Hollywood film. The relevant genres include Gothic and horror; science fiction; fantasy; crime and detective fiction; romance; the Western. To different degrees, Lethem has engaged with all of these. For convenience, science fiction, fantasy and Gothic can all be grouped as varieties of 'fantastic' genres, while other genres such as the Western or crime are more typically set in versions of the historical world. Both options will be considered during this chapter.

To confront a list of popular genres is to be reminded of the complexity of genre classification. For one thing, each of these genres has its own sub-genres – the space opera, the cavalry Western, the hospital romance – which may, in practical usage, be referred to as genres in their own right. For another, the boundaries of genres are not absolute. They overlap, blend and combine. A notable example is the relation between science fiction and fantasy. While the influential theorist Darko Suvin (1979) has defined science fiction precisely in opposition to genres like fantasy, which lack science fiction's 'cognitive' and scientific rigour, many writers and readers have found the two genres to be more of a continuum than a diametric opposition, and in the twenty-first century the term compound 'SFF' (science fiction and fantasy) is often used. This too is relevant to Lethem, whose work in science fiction is often best located along such a broad spectrum of fantastic narrative.

To talk of 'genre fiction' is often, in practice, to introduce particular connotations of cultural value. Ray Davis (2009) has shrewdly pointed out how different criteria have typically been applied to different forms of cultural production, with the individual author of literary art not always commensurable with the collective processes that have produced genre narratives such as comic books and much Hollywood film. In terms of generic content, meanwhile, Gary K. Wolfe posits a long-standing 'devaluation, or at least devalorization, of the fantastic' during and since the Romantic era, even as 'the outlines of the modern popular genres of the fantastic were first being laid down in a series of seminal works': Poe and the Gothic novel for horror; *Frankenstein* for science fiction; 'extended fairy-tale narratives' offering 'the portaled alternate realities that became a key element of modern fantasy' (2011: 7). Eventually, Wolfe asserts: 'The act of reading fantastic literature became marginalized not only ideologically, by virtue of its content, but commercially, by its venues of publication' (9). The fantastic was associated with the popular, and further, with 'the rise of the pulp magazines and the attendant culture of pulp' (9).

'Pulp' derives from the material properties of the publication of genre fiction in a certain historical period. Magazines printed on wood pulp paper were cheaper to produce than those on 'slick' paper such as the *Saturday Evening Post*, *Life* or *New Yorker*. Without those titles' expensive advertising, pulp magazines relied primarily on the proceeds from large readerships to derive profit. The pulp medium has become most closely associated with the short fiction that dominated dozens of magazines between the 1890s (when *The Argosy* appeared in this format) and the 1950s (when the magazine market diminished and was replaced, in particular, by cheap paperback novels). Genre was important in the production of fiction for the pulp magazines. Some magazines featured an eclectic range of story types, while many others majored unashamedly on single genres or sub-genres. By the 1920s and 1930s these included, to cite just a tiny indicative selection of titles by genre, war stories (*Over the Top*), the sub-genre of air war fiction (*Sky Birds*), gangster fiction (*Gun Molls*), science fiction (*Amazing Stories*), Westerns (*Lariat*), detective fiction (*Dime Detective*), horror (*Horror Stories*), romance (*Love Story Magazine*), college fiction (*College Stories*) and titillation (*Bedtime Stories*) (Blackbeard 1982: 300–1). Genres were stratified – it was important for a potential reader to know that a magazine would contain detective stories – yet also, on commercial grounds, pragmatically open to combination and ambiguity.

Genres associated with pulp magazines often had substantial histories before this particular format. Yet the magazines did much to codify these genres as they would become known to the twentieth century. Science fiction is a major instance: though it was significantly pioneered by Jules Verne, H.G. Wells and still earlier creators, a large proportion of the genre's iconography and typical contents was laid down in the 1920s and 1930s by writers and artists in *Amazing Stories* and *Astounding Stories*. The term 'science fiction' itself was codified by Hugo Gernsback in 1929 after he lost the rights to *Amazing Stories* and his own neologism 'scientifiction' (Westfahl 2015: 18). The detective story, meanwhile, clearly predated pulp magazines (its history is typically traced to Poe, Dickens and Wilkie Collins, and Arthur Conan Doyle's Sherlock Holmes appeared in the *Strand* magazine in the late nineteenth century), but it was in pulp magazine stories that the definitive American sub-genre of the 'private eye' emerged, notably through Dashiell Hammett's contributions to one of the most influential magazines of the 1930s, *Black Mask*. In turn, these genres would profitably move from magazines into other media: novel (which after 1950 took over as a major publishing site for science fiction and crime), comic book, radio and cinema. Eventually the most widespread public image of many popular genres would be a memory of Hollywood: Humphrey Bogart in a black-and-white *film noir* adapted from a hard-boiled novel; Robby the Robot in *Forbidden Planet*; Boris Karloff as Frankenstein's Monster; a big-screen Bat-Man.

Genre fiction as a whole is defined in part by that which is contrasted to it. This is a body of work comparatively bereft of the iconography of the popular genres, and often considered, at least on average, to be better written and more fully achieved as art. Terms for such work include 'literary', 'realist', 'mainstream' or even 'serious' fiction (Eaglestone 2013: 1098). All these labels have their particular connotations and problems. In recent times, it has been argued that 'literary fiction' itself is a genre, as comfortably convention-bound as the Western, and that to distinguish it from genre is thus misleading. Jonathan Lethem himself has asserted as much, referring to 'the persistent, oppressive shorthand that mainstream and literary, etc. aren't genres' (Davis and Lethem 1998). Yet for practical purposes, it is difficult to relinquish reference to 'literary', 'mainstream' and related terms in discussing popular genres and what lies beyond their borders.

By the time Lethem's literary career commenced, the boundary between fictions considered as 'genre' and as 'art' had already been ostentatiously crossed a number of times. In the late 1960s the maverick American critic Leslie Fiedler had urged that writers should 'turn frankly to Pop forms' to revitalize US fiction.

He included the Western and science fiction as good sources of inspiration, but already, thirty years before Lethem published *Motherless Brooklyn*, considered detective fiction 'hopelessly compromised by middlebrow condescension' (Fiedler 1972: 69). In the decades from Fiedler to Lethem, numerous ventures were indeed made into genre territory by writers who had started outside it. William S. Burroughs' *Red Night* trilogy (1981–7) brought elements of different generic types (gunfighters, pirates, detectives) into its fractured montage; Robert Coover's *A Night at the Movies* (1987) offered a collection of gross parodies of Hollywood film. Angela Carter's *The Passion of New Eve* (1977) portrayed a science-fictional dystopia while also offering elaborate conceptual arguments about gender; Paul Auster's *New York Trilogy* (1985) staged a cool encounter with the mystery genre. Brian McHale (2009) has argued that all of Thomas Pynchon's work after *Gravity's Rainbow* (1973) reworks forms of popular narrative.

Much of this work has been discussed under the rubric 'postmodernism'. It is evidently consonant with the assertions of Fredric Jameson, in a key document of that term, that postmodernism is typified by 'the effacement [...] of the older (essentially high-modernist) frontier between high culture and so-called mass or commercial culture, and the emergence of new kinds of texts infused with the forms, categories, and contents of that very culture industry so passionately denounced by all the ideologues of the modern' (1991: 2). The periodizing analysis is clearly suggestive. Lethem's work arguably falls within the period delineated as 'postmodern', albeit a generation later than some other writers most typically associated with this term (Pynchon, Coover, John Barth, Don DeLillo). Yet as Rivka Galchen (2009) avers, the word 'postmodernism' itself offers little additional illumination here. Over its storied career, the term has tended to collect a baggage of controversy and connotation that may distract attention from the particular work done by writers. By the same token, it has been associated with a range of practices so wide as to be contradictory. These misgivings are voiced by Lethem himself, who proposes that 'all of the modes denounced under the banner of "postmodernist" are incompatible' (2011: 79) – in part, as a way of defending those diverse modes themselves. His own suggestion, which the present book endorses, is that many of the vitally interesting works and ideas that have sometimes been associated with this word are, at this point, not much clarified by their subsumption under it. In Lethem's succinct, teasing phrase: 'What postmodernism really needs is a new name – or three of them' (2011: 80). The present book attempts to offer more specific analyses to describe the effects of his work. Conceptually, one route to greater conceptual specificity is offered by Martin Paul Eve, who proposes the new term 'taxonomographic metafiction' to describe 'fiction about fiction that deals with the study/construction of genre/taxonomy' (Eve 2016: 163). For Eve, such 'taxonomographic' activity is often performed with the attention of academic literary criticism in mind, but can perform for a wider audience receptive to the signs of genre. Taxonomographic fiction can be expected to play with this audience's knowledge of genre: 'as the text temporally unfolds, it must anticipate the process through which its target discourse communities – whether academic or popular – will systematise its contents; it must guess what the reader will guess' (Eve 2016: 183). This is a fair description of the way that Lethem's fiction works with the knowledge embedded in its implied readers.

Lethem himself has reflected on the place of genre in literary history. He recalls spending his apprentice years attending science fiction conventions and perpetually appearing on panels discussing 'Science Fiction and the Mainstream'. Lethem himself could claim the privilege of a liminal role, one who knew science fiction better than mainstream critics but also 'knew more about contemporary writing than anyone else' in the seemingly hermetic zone of science fiction (Lethem 2011: 68). The 'quarantine' of science fiction from the mainstream seemed antiquated to Lethem, whose tendency in such discussion is consistently to run the two lineages together. Thus, in a retrospect on the discussions of the 1980s, he poses the indignant, imploring rhetorical question:

> After Pynchon, Joseph McElroy, DeLillo, and others had made ready use of the technological NOW that had swallowed the future, after Doris Lessing and Stanley Kubrick and Haruki Murakami, after Delany, Ballard, Angela Carter, Thomas Disch, Russell Hoban, James Tiptree Jr., and others had etched their beauties into literary history, what did the quarantine mean to any thinking reader? (2011: 68–9)

The gesture is very characteristic, in its capacious opening into literary history. Similar invocations recur across Lethem's critical writing and memoirs, as in the recollections that his early work was intended to *triangulate between DeLillo and Lem, or Steve Erickson and Ballard* (2011: 35) or that his original intention was to 'prove that Patricia Highsmith and Charles Willeford and especially Philip K. Dick [...] were the exact same thing as Faulkner or Pynchon' (2011: 34).

As all these instances suggest, in Lethem's presentation of the issue, the emphasis is often on a single space of imaginative writing, which has been unnecessarily complicated and fenced about by genre distinctions. In such a space Kafka and Dick, Borges and Ballard could belong together, perhaps under the capacious roof of 'the fantastic'. Such an ecumenical approach fuelled

Lethem's 1998 polemic 'The Squandered Promise of Science Fiction', which argued that the genre had gone wrong the day in 1973 that Pynchon's *Gravity's Rainbow* was not awarded the Nebula award. Pynchon's nomination, Lethem declared, 'now stands as a hidden tombstone marking the death of the hope that science fiction was about to merge with the mainstream'. Ideally, Lethem (1998b) proposed, 'the notion of science fiction ought to have been gently and lovingly dismantled, and the writers dispersed'. By these lights, much of his own early fiction was ideally intended to belong to a realm in which the reifying labels of genre would not apply.

Yet the aspiration occludes the way that Lethem's own fiction was fired and given definition by its roots in science fiction, rather than in a vaguer literary space. One can recognize the spirit of Lethem's protest against literary 'quarantine', while also observing that the visibility of such barriers has been of creative use – to him, as to many others. When Lethem describes 'writing meta-fictionally about genre' such that his stories effect 'interrogations of the genre they inhabit' (Clarke 2011: 6), the logic of the statement is not to eliminate genre but that genre is – at least at this particular point – crucial to the work's substance. Boundaries can be productive, as the Oulipo would insist. (In 2013 Lethem would corroborate this view, in a science-fictional context, by contributing a cyberpunk parody to a neo-Oulipan anthology [Lethem 2013b].) Roger Luckhurst has noted that declarations of the dissolution of genre are rarely convincing: games played at generic margins take their force from the power of genres, rather than from their weakness (2005: 243). In a rapid response to Lethem's *Village Voice* polemic, Ray Davis noted that its revaluation seemed ultimately to work in favour of the mainstream and against the genre (Davis and Lethem 1998). Lethem's ecumenical aspiration seems laudable, especially in bidding for greater respect for science fiction writers, but some of the most dynamic gestures of his own fiction were predicated on the barriers whose dismantling he urged. That his own early fiction sometimes collided multiple genres exacerbates rather than diminishes the point. As we shall see shortly, the effect of *Gun, with Occasional Music* (1994) requires the legibility of the two primary lines of influence shaping it, rather than their dissolution.

Since Lethem's debut the claims of genre have increased, both on contemporary fiction and in discussion of it. As Rob Latham notes, generic hybridity 'has only served to spawn a host of efforts to coin fresh terms to describe new kinds of cross-border fictions: "new wave fabulism", "interstitial fiction", "transrealism", and what the cyberpunk writer Bruce Sterling called 'slipstream' writing, deliberately rippling the term 'mainstream' (2015: 107). Gary K. Wolfe ponders the 'evaporation' of genres – such that fantasy, for instance, is 'growing more diffuse, leaching out into the air around it, imparting a strange smell to the literary atmosphere' (Wolfe 2011: viii). For Wolfe here, the evaporation of a genre means not its extinction but its increased pervasiveness. As Latham points out (2015: 104–5), Lethem and his contemporary Michael Chabon have accepted nominations for genre awards as well as mainstream prizes. And a genre may be enlivened, rather than diminished, by writing that cuts athwart its borders. In 1997 Lethem's interviewer Fiona Kelleghan suggested that science fiction should thank him 'for being a crossover writer. It makes the whole field look good' (Clarke 2011: 5).

The shift in attitudes to genre is attested by a dialogue which in 2015 the fantasy author Neil Gaiman conducted with Kazuo Ishiguro: a 'literary' author and past Booker Prize winner who yet recounted his increasing ventures into territories that seemingly belonged to popular genre. Earlier in his career, Ishiguro reflected, he would not have cast *Never Let Me Go* (2005) in the science fiction mould it assumes. But: 'Some time in the Nineties I felt a change of climate in the mainstream literary world. […] I sensed that there was a whole generation of people emerging who had a very different attitude to sci-fi, and that there was a new force of energy and inspiration because of that' (Gaiman and Ishiguro 2015). Lethem's endeavours made a significant contribution to this situation. Indeed it is relevant that he is a long-standing enthusiast for Ishiguro's work, and has repeatedly praised him for a boldness that Lethem thinks belies Ishiguro's respectable reputation. 'Kazuo Ishiguro is much weirder than I think you think he is', Lethem begins a 2000 review which suggests that 'pop-cultural archetypes murmur under the surface' of his work (Lethem 2017: 170). In effect, Ishiguro eventually decided to accept and explore this description.

Another Dimension

Let us consider a particular case of Lethem's engagement with fantastic genre, which also implicitly comments on the question of genre itself. The story 'Light and the Sufferer' was published in 1995, included in Lethem's first collection of stories the following year, and republished in an anthology of slipstream writing in 2006. The tale depicts two brothers in New York City: one, Donovan, a drug addict, the other, Paul, earnestly seeking to take his brother away from the city's corrupting influence and fly to a new life in California. They steal drugs from a pair of dealers in Greenwich Village, and are finally picked up by the drug kingpin Randall, whose hirelings kill Don and leave Paul alive. The story is thus a piece of gritty urban fiction of the contemporary city: alive to class and racial tension (the gangsters are all black, and are the source of Don's nickname 'Light'), drug addiction and violence, and mostly written in a clipped, functional first-person style, set by its opening lines: 'My brother showed me the gun. I'd never seen one up close before' (Lethem 1996: 123).

Yet the story also features another element. The brothers find themselves accompanied by an alien being, a 'Sufferer', which lopes after their taxi and follows them everywhere they go, before finally departing after Don's death. The understanding is that Sufferers follow people in trouble – 'That was what they liked to do' (128). Its insistence on following Don is thus ominous. The Sufferer is the source of speculation, especially from the gangster Randall who is followed by a Sufferer of his own. Perhaps it wants to cure Don of his addiction ('Where'd you read that, *Newsweek*?' [138]), or is trying to use up his supply (145); perhaps it simply likes taking drugs ('It just wants to hang. [...] Came from space to party with me' [143]). Some people, warns Don's girlfriend Annette, will 'beat you up just because you've got one of these things following you around. It's a reactionary thing, like AIDS-bashing, you know, blaming the victim' (145). Another character tells Don that the Sufferer is 'following you because you're dead, you loser [...] it's like your death angel' (150), while Paul desperately insists on a more optimistic rationale: 'It's an empathy thing, it's responding to the *life* in Don' (150); 'It's like a guardian angel' (161).

To adopt Farah Mendlesohn's classification, the story may be viewed as a piece of 'Intrusive' fantasy, in which 'the base level is the normal world'; the text maintains 'stylistic realism' while seeking to describe an element of the fantastic that has arrived unexpectedly in an otherwise naturalistic fictional universe (Mendlesohn 2008: xxi–xxii). Yet the Sufferers' existence is also accepted as a fact of the world. While strange enough to be remarked upon, they do not prompt what Mendlesohn calls 'constant amazement', an 'awestruck' tone in which 'the protagonists and the reader are never expected to become accustomed to the fantastic' (2008: xxii). They are rapidly transferring from the status of fantastic 'intrusion' to being accepted as a piece of quotidian reality, and this liminal status is one of the phenomena subtly depicted by the story.

Sufferers are specifically identified as 'aliens', from 'space'. Lethem goes out of his way to make the Sufferer an insistently physical presence, with its dog-like behaviour – 'The Sufferer seemed to like the park. Several times it roamed wide of us, disappearing briefly in the trees' (155) – and a series of zoological comparisons: 'giant panther' (128), 'obedient dog' (136), 'hunting cat' (137), 'perky cat' (138), 'giant snake-skinned cougar' (148). As this shows, the animal's appearance also remains uncertain: at each glimpse, it is described slightly differently, in an echo of a dog in James Joyce's *Ulysses* (1922) which is successively compared to a range of animals: 'a bounding hare', 'a rag of wolf's tongue', 'a pard, a panther' (Joyce 1993: 38–9). The reader's working assumption is deliberately undercut: 'Now that I could see it up close, it really didn't look so much like a cat' (Lethem 1996: 145). The Sufferer is at once bluntly present on the scene, and ineffably mysterious. If its physical character is hard to pin down, its motives are still more unfathomable. It adds a dimension to a story that would otherwise be thoroughly rooted in the real, complete with specific Manhattan addresses. Indeed Don literally, though vaguely, evokes the idea of 'dimension' in describing the alien's presence: '"Of course it's weird […] That's why we love it, right, Paul? It's from another dimension, it's fucking weird, it's science fiction"' (145).

Don's words are characteristically careless, but as Lethem's construction they are surely more carefully considered. At this point, a notable proportion of his work had appeared in science fiction magazines. The status and powers of science fiction in relation to mainstream literature were prominent in Lethem's thinking at the time. Don's statement, then, prompts us to consider how far 'Light and the Sufferer' is itself a work of science fiction. Following Don's words literally, we may consider that the Sufferer itself is a piece of science fiction, unleashed in a mainstream world (or even the world of another genre, crime fiction). A Sufferer is a message of warning, or a symbol of trouble. In this sense 'science fiction' is a way of commenting on the real through other means. A piece of radical alterity – a being from another dimension – the Sufferer occupies the (variously indifferent, interested or resentful) empirical world of the present, and comments sagely yet enigmatically upon it. In this it may be taken as a figure for the operations of science fiction itself. By extension, 'Light and the Sufferer' undertakes a characteristic move of Lethem's – bringing the realistic and fantastic into collision or combination – while also standing as an allegory of that very strategy.

Our discussion has focused primarily on science fiction and fantastic literature. But Lethem also ventured boldly into genre territory through his use of detective fiction. Let us now consider in turn his two major forays into this genre in the 1990s.

Ugly Punctuation

Gun, with Occasional Music is narrated by Conrad Metcalf, a private investigator working in a version of San Francisco in the twenty-first century. The novel occupies two slightly different periods: Part 1 (200 pages) is followed by a much briefer Part 2 subtitled *six years later*, in a world that has become still more repressive. The novel uses the methods of hard-boiled detective fiction, a mode brought to its apotheosis by Raymond Chandler between the 1930s and 1950s. Chandler can be considered the most significant precursor for *Gun*'s work with the genre, not least because he is explicitly named by Lethem as a crucial model for the book's project (Clarke 2011: 51).

The hard-boiled mode historically represents a shift from the 'Golden Age' of country-house detection exemplified by Agatha Christie and Dorothy L. Sayers. The hard-boiled detective of the 1930s and 1940s moves the pulse of the genre to the United States, and to urban and suburban locales where the profession of detection involves not merely intellect but violence and danger, even as the puzzle element of detection endures (Rzepka 2005: 186–9). Dennis Porter sees the private eye as belonging to an era of '[u]rban blight, corrupt political machines, and de facto disenfranchisement of significant sections of the population through graft and influence-peddling', and like other historians he points to the policy of Prohibition of alcohol as encouraging organized crime, another significant element in the hard-boiled landscape (2003: 96). Charles J. Rzepka adds that the mode idealizes 'personal autonomy' – specifically that of the lone male detective, like Chandler's Philip Marlowe – in the face of these 'shadowy coercive forces', in a 'quintessentially American' fashion (2005: 180). Walter Mosley, a practitioner himself, writes that the mode poses the question: 'Can I do right in a world gone wrong?' (Mosley 2009: 601). The 'hard-boiled' attitude is a laconic response to this degraded and perilous setting.

Certain elements became standard in the hard-boiled detective story. These are what John Frow terms a genre's 'metacommunications': those 'cues' that make 'reading or viewing [...] a process of progressive refinement and adaptation of the sense we have of those cues' (Frow 2006: 104). In the hard-boiled genre, such cues have included the solitary male detective: often, as John G. Cawelti says, 'a traditional man of virtue in an amoral and corrupt world' (1976: 152), committed to a form of chivalry despite his cultivation of a tough, hardened attitude to crime and to the world in general. With this comes the deployment of humour or wryness, whether in dialogue between detective and others or in a first-person narrative voice offered by the detective. A range of typical scenes and characters are also available to the hard-boiled writer. The detective is approached by a client in his office: 'the dusty and sordid atmosphere', Cawelti observes, 'of an office located in a broken-down building on the margin of the city's business district' (1976: 144). Typically, at some point the hard-boiled detective is knocked out by a blow to the head from a thug; encounters a criminal kingpin in his lair; or navigates an encounter with a seductive and dangerous *femme fatale*. More concrete details, like the detective's trenchcoat and hat, also serve as cues of genre.

All of these appear in *Gun*, as part of what Eve would term its 'taxonomographic' strategies. Conrad Metcalf wears a 'hat and coat' which are verbally paired (4, 11). He is approached at his shabby office by his client Orton Angwine (7), and finds that the initial case leads him into a much larger labyrinth of corruption. He is knocked out by a blow to a head from a hired goon ('something dull and heavy had found smashed itself into the back of my neck [...] the floor peeled up in a curl to embrace the sides of my head, and the weave of the carpet spiraled up to tickle the inside of my nose' [121]). He encounters the obese kingpin Danny Phoneblum in a mysterious underground complex (111), and discovers the dismaying extent of Phoneblum's power of an underworld racketeering network (in effect metaphorically corresponding to his literal lair). Metcalf tangles with the glamorous Celeste Stanhunt (24), precisely replicating Cawelti's description of sex in the genre as 'an object of pleasure, [with] a disturbing tendency to become a temptation, a trap, and a betrayal' (1976: 153). Even more marginal figures in *Gun* correspond to a generic logic. Thus Doctor Grover Testafer, with his fine house in the hills and secret association with the criminal network, is one of 'those who seem respectable at first, but turn out to be involved in the pervasive corruption of society if not directly in the crime itself'; such characters 'confront the detective with the various threats and temptations to "lay off" that he must resist in order to carry out his mission' (Cawelti 1976: 152). So, too, Metcalf must cope with interference from the official police (known in his world as the Inquisition), in a struggle between the invasive state and the private professional who has left its employ in the name of honour.

The detective's office is another generic motif. Metcalf and a dentist share a waiting room formerly used by a pair of psychoanalysts. As Cawelti notes: 'We see the detective as a marginal professional carrying on his business from the kind of office associated with unsuccessful dentists, small mail-order businesses, and shyster lawyers' (1976: 144). Metcalf arrives at his office in *Gun*'s first chapter:

I'd been away for a week, but the room hadn't changed any. The lights flickered, and the dust-bunnies under the furniture pulsed in the breeze when I opened the door. I couldn't see the water stain on the wall because of the chair I'd pushed up against it, but that didn't keep me from knowing it was there. I burdened the hunchbacked hat tree with my coat and hat and sat down behind the desk. (4)

The primary sense here is of reduced circumstances, as the private detective's proper sphere. A visitor to Marlowe's office 'stood looking at the five green filing cases, the shabby rust-red rug, the half-dusted furniture, and the not too clean net curtains' (Chandler 2010: 91). The physical environment is morally pertinent: the shabbiness of the detective's circumstances is a kind of testament to his honesty, in a way that a slick and expensive office would not provide.

Voice is fundamental to the genre. Here the comparison of Lethem and Chandler is especially instructive. A line like Metcalf's 'Murder doesn't get publicized much anymore' (3), dealing so briskly with the grimmest of material, is comparable to Marlowe's cold report in *The Lady in the Lake* (1944): 'I bought a paper and looked through it to see if there were any interesting murders. There were not' (Chandler 1952: 178). The following paragraph from Lethem is also tonally suggestive in conveying the bathetic, rough life of the solitary detective: 'So I showered and shaved and got my gums bleeding with a toothbrush, then stumbled into the kitchen to cauterize the wounds with some scalding coffee. [...] By the time I was done with it, the morning was mostly over. I went down to the office anyway' (3–4). Compare Philip Marlowe's morning: 'I got up at nine, drank three cups of black coffee, bathed the back of my head with ice-water and read the two morning papers that had been thrown against the apartment door' (Chandler 2010: 89). Metcalf's attempt to find out about a murder on the radio – 'I switched stations, hoping to pick up some other coverage, but it must have played as the lead story all across the dial [...] there wasn't any more' (5) – directly resembles Marlowe's casual references to the sporadic progress of a crime through news media: 'There was a paragraph and a bit about Moose Malloy [...] but [police detective] Nulty didn't get his name mentioned. There was nothing about [murder victim] Lindsay Marriott, unless it was on the society page' (2010: 89).

Lethem recurrently uses specific motifs from Chandler's narration. Marlowe has a tendency to close a chapter with an exit, flatly denoted: 'I shut the door again and went away' (2010: 40); 'I left the office again in time for an early dinner' (2010: 46); 'I didn't have any more. I went out' (Chandler 1952: 126). Across *Gun*, Metcalf can be seen establishing a similar rhythm of blunt scenic closure: 'I wiped the desk clean with my sleeve and put on my hat and coat and went out' (11); 'I rolled up the windows of my car and drove back downtown' (80); 'I couldn't think of anything nice to say, so I left without saying anything' (94); 'I laid my business card on the dresser and went out into the dying minutes of the day' (164). These sentences are usually functional, in giving the author a clear note on which to close a chapter while also pointing ahead to the next phase of action. Their typical matter-of-factness, highlighted the more when closing a section of prose, also helps to form the detective's voice.

When Metcalf announces 'I bustled past the dentist's midday patients and into my office, where I lowered my collar and relaxed my sneer' (4), he adds a note of self-awareness, in the rhythm and balance of 'lowered my collar and relaxed my sneer' and in the sense that Metcalf can 'relax' the facial expression that we now learn he has been wearing on the way in. Such self-consciousness is already present in Marlowe's highly deliberate manipulation of facial expression: 'She made an impatient gesture, so I stopped fooling around and got my battle-scarred frown back on my face' (2010: 97); 'Miss Fromsett gave me a sweet sad smile and I gave it back to her in the form of an obscene leer' (1952: 7); 'I made a face like a man from the finance company coming about the car payment' (1952: 98).

In numerous ways, then, Lethem in *Gun* produces an acute derivation of Chandler's fiction. What does this achieve? A first answer is homage, and an accompanying satisfaction. We can recall Lethem's insistence on the 'somatics of influence' – 'I felt influence, and thrilled to it, with my body, and did so before I knew it had a name' – and the urge to construct one's own canon of revered ancestors, 'and wear it, an exoskeleton of many colors' (2011: 123–4). To produce a delicately precise remake of Raymond Chandler's prose is a pleasure in its own right. By the same token, the reader too derives pleasure from the work. Part of Lethem's 'somatics' concerns the experience of reception – 'how it felt to surmise the existence of Edward G. Robinson from a Bugs Bunny aside', or 'what a throb of quote-recognition could do to you' when listening on headphones to a pop song (2011: 123). In this way, his first novel is strongly consistent with the purposes and values of his later manifesto.

The use of Chandler is also a formal strategy that creates possibilities for the writer that would not otherwise exist, rather as the choice of particular materials would for a painter. To proceed by such deliberate strategy immediately, defiantly sets Lethem apart from a standard aesthetic assumption, in which the expectation might well be for him to commence by writing about his Brooklyn upbringing. To recall Lethem's querying of literary norms in his later Preface: 'We don't know why we do what we do'; 'Influence is semiconscious, not something to delineate too extensively' (2011: xviii). As a debut, *Gun* blatantly inverts these implicit rules: it seems like the work of someone who knows just what he is doing, and who could delineate his influences as extensively as one could wish. Lethem's 2003 description thus remains peculiarly telling: '*Gun, with Occasional Music* is a piece of carpentry. I wanted to locate the exact midpoint between Dick and Chandler' (Clarke 2011: 51). To talk of carpentry is clearly to imply craft, figuring the literary work as a piece of material on which one could measure the 'midpoint' between two other objects. This attitude to creativity was a salutary one for Lethem to adopt at his career's outset.

This discussion has not yet accounted for the second element of Lethem's measurement: his invocation of Philip K. Dick. In numerous respects, the novel's future world is different from the 1990s in which it was written, let alone the 1940s from which the genre norms described above derive. Most strikingly, the human population coexists with 'evolved' animals that have been bred according to 'Dr Twostrand's evolution therapy'. Animals thus 'stand up and talk', wear clothes and compete in the labour market, though usually at a disadvantage to the more privileged humans. In this way we rapidly encounter a sow, a dachshund, a kitten, a ewe, and, in more crucial roles, a kangaroo and a gorilla. Meanwhile 'the scientists decided it took too long to grow a kid' (Lethem 1994: 19), and the same scientific advances have thus been applied to human babies, resulting in 'babyheads': large babies, mentally developed yet eccentric and tending to occupy their own social niche.

Conrad Metcalf's urban world is also one profoundly addicted to drugs, bought from the professional Makery with a 'blend' adapted to each citizen. At any point, large parts of the population are thus affected by particular chemical compounds, with components like Believol, Regrettol and Forgettol. Official control is maintained by the Inquisition: a police department with powers vastly enhanced, and the standard penalty of putting a criminal in a cryogenic freezer – or to work in a slave camp with a box to deaden their consciousness (120). The Inquisition monitors and manages citizens' karmic levels, which are stored as electronic data on a card. Although Metcalf knows that such karma is a mere construct, he also understands its practical power, and is eventually frozen himself when a police officer reduces his karma to zero. A further new development is found in the book's last section, set six years on into the future. Citizens now outsource their memory to machines, which answer questions with blandly reassuring answers. 'Memory', Metcalf perceives, 'was permissible when it was externalized, and rigorously edited. That left you with more room in your head for the latest pop tune – which was sure to be coming out of the nearest water fountain or cigarette machine' (Lethem 1994: 224). This in turn refers to another technical development: a turn to abstraction and music in media, with 'musical news' displacing verbal analysis (3); abstract television programmes in place of drama (67); and, in the later world, everyday objects (a cash register, a gun) that play musical themes as they are used (219, 226).

Gun is therefore a work of science fiction as well as a hard-boiled detective novel. But what is the meaning of their coincidence, and how do they interact?

Once more, a simple answer applies first. If one is essaying genre, then two genres might be better than one. The technical achievement – managing Chandler's tone against a backdrop of social realities beyond Philip Marlowe's imagination – is greater. The 'somatic' pleasure that Lethem ascribes to being 'influenced' is redoubled in producing a remix of two potent influences, and the sense of the remix as a model for creativity comes into focus here in a way that it would not with a simple imitation of Chandler. Again, what goes for the author goes also for the reader: the challenges and pleasures of cognition and recognition are multiplied by the encounter of two sets of source materials being in play simultaneously. The novel clearly chimes with Jacques Derrida's sense of the productivity of what he also portrays as a forbidden act: 'Genres are not to be mixed' (1980: 55).

Yet the question abides of what is specific about the encounter of these two genres. A first answer is that the encounter demonstrates a convergence in fictional world. The sense of the hard-boiled universe as a dystopian world, cited above by Walter Mosley, appears to have been a way to encode real experience: 'I've come to understand that it had to do with Watergate [...] with New York City in 1971 – the crumbling infrastructure [...] That's where I came of age. My appetite for reading tales set in dystopian cities, my pleasure in Orwell, my pleasure in Ballard, was a pleasure of recognition' (Clarke 2011: 53). Lethem in fact says this about his second novel, *Amnesia Moon*, which was commenced earlier. But the point about dystopian cities applies to both; of *Gun*, he comments, 'That's a degraded world, all right' (Clarke 2011: 36). In 2001, Lethem would comment: 'Paranoia is frequently justified: yes. As a young reader I found confirmation for these intuitions in dystopian science fiction and in noir crime fiction and films' (Clarke 2011: 35). Here two genres converge on the same territory. *Gun* actualizes this meeting, asking what it would mean for Chandler's 'mean streets' to be those of a dystopia proper.

Second, detection offers a particular method of approaching this future world. In the terms offered by Mendlesohn's *Rhetorics of Fantasy* (2008), *Gun* is an immersive fantasy: a self-contained world in which we are present from the start, rather than an alternate universe to which we journey. In Mendlesohn's words, 'it presents the fantastic without comment as the norm both for the protagonist and for the reader: we sit on the protagonist's shoulder and while we have access to his eyes and ears, we are not provided with an explanatory narrative' (2008: xx). Thus, for instance, Metcalf's first encounter with an 'evolved sow' draws a particular remark from Metcalf about her smell, but no explanation to a reader who has never previously heard of such a being (Lethem 1994: 12). Granted this restriction, Metcalf is then a useful tool for exposing the reader to the novel's strange world; for as a detective he is inherently inquisitive and observant. As Mendlesohn acutely observes, immersive fantasy benefits from a protagonist who is *antagonistic* to its world, thus allowed 'to question it while staying within the shell of immersion' (2008: 67). This character 'must be able to challenge the world in some way, to step aside from it, and judge it' (113). Such a figure is 'our surrogate questioner' (72), an apt label for Conrad Metcalf, who is deeply dissatisfied with the political and moral state of his world, notwithstanding his inescapable 'immersion' in it. It is also pertinent to *Gun* that, as Mendlesohn says, the immersive form tends towards an urban setting: 'the city becomes the world, and one can only ever go deeper into the urban labyrinth' (90).

These insights lead to another. The detective genre has a history as a means of social investigation. The private eye is a figure who can cross from one area of society to another: from ghetto or housing project to mansion or boudoir, from casino to police station, and so on. Hence Jameson's intuition (2016) that Chandler offers a 'detection of totality', a narrative mode for making connections and perhaps, ultimately, seeing society whole. This role is subtly adapted in Lethem's science-fictional dystopia. On one hand it becomes simply a means of disclosing the world to us: the detective, travelling across San Francisco, is an efficient narrative mechanism for relaying considerable social novelty to the reader. Yet more than this, the detective's proto-political role becomes hypercharged as he confronts a society of radical corruption and repression. The oppressive structures of Lethem's fictional world – the Inquisition, the shutdown of democratic debate or ultimately of any public discourse, the use of karma points, the universal drug dependency – come into sharper focus under Metcalf's questing, sceptical gaze than they otherwise would.

A particular feature of the novel is relevant here: the prohibition on asking questions, which emerges gradually for the reader as a major feature of social interaction in this future society. As a private professional sleuth, Metcalf is licensed to ask questions in a way that other citizens are not, such that Celeste Stanhunt, in an ingenious linguistic estrangement on Lethem's part, accuses him of 'using a lot of ugly punctuation' (1994: 21). The scenario is heightened when Metcalf emerges from the freezer, to be told to 'Forget questions' (216). The question is fundamental to the detective's role and to the progress of a narrative in this genre, and in making it a fragile, suspect convention Lethem draws our attention to this anew. In this sense science fiction reacts upon and reframes the detective genre, as well as the reverse. It does so too in the literalization of karma, brutally codifying something that remains implicit in such a writer as Chandler: the quality of the detective's relations with the police, and the status of those (like his clients) whom he meets and judges.

Two more related themes provide crucial ground for the productive meeting of the two genres. Charles J. Rzepka proposes that detective fiction significantly derives from the development of modern science and the displacement of religious worldviews by secular ones insistent upon 'the physical "clues" of history' (2005: 35). For Rzepka, the history of science in turn feeds the science of history, in which detective fiction is deeply rooted. This means that detective fiction is a genre with a strong investment in reason and cognition: faculties of which Sherlock Holmes is exemplary, but which are not unknown to Marlowe. But the same has been said of science fiction. On Darko Suvin's influential, albeit contested account, it is distinguished from the imaginative forms of fantasy or Gothic by its foundation in the cognitive. In Roger Luckhurst's summary, 'an SF future is one that is meant to extrapolate rationally or scientifically from tendencies within the "empirical environment"' (2005: 7). To bring the two genres so directly into contact, then, is to bring two forms of 'cognition' into relation, whether productive or rivalrous. In *Gun*, the detective's cognition dominates: scientific explanation of each new phenomenon is sketchy and brief, though its implicit presence remains important as a generic anchor.

Deduction depends on memory, which is the last site where the two genres productively collide in this novel. A Philip Marlowe needs to build a coherent narrative account of the crimes that he is investigating, holding together evidence and possibilities in building an account of the past. The memories of others – suspects and witnesses – are important raw material. Yet in *Gun*, memory is progressively at a discount. The drug Forgettol already threatens it at the start of the action: Maynard Stanhunt, the murder victim, is so addicted that he does not recognize Metcalf despite having hired him (5). This turns out to be a central plot point: Stanhunt's ability to generate amnesia creates the scenario of his murder (250). Metcalf can stand aloof from this, but the outsourcing and sanitizing of memory in the book's second phase threaten virtually to erase the concept of evidence. Metcalf wryly tells his ingenuous interviewee Pansy Greenleaf: 'I have the new kind of memory [...] It's a cranial implant. You don't have to speak out loud. You just think, and it talks to you in a quiet little voice in your head' (225). This is really, of course, the old kind of memory. Its marginalization threatens the process of detection, not to mention human identity itself.

The fate of psychoanalysis is thus, aptly enough, symptomatic. Psychoanalysts have been put out of business by Metcalf's trade (4). Their doctrine makes another appearance when Metcalf encounters a pair of door-knockers, equivalent to Jehovah's Witnesses in the real world, who explain: 'We're students of psychology. If you're not too busy, we'd like to read you a few selections from Freud's *Civilization and Its Discontents*' (78). Metcalf declines – 'I'm not a believer myself' – and they move on to the next house; when he emerges, 'I looked up and down the street, but the Freud nuts had given up and gone home' (80). The scene is in part an audacious joke on psychoanalysis as a cult: the future world can see it as a set of myths as implausible as any religion. Yet in this particular dystopia, such a view may also be an ominous sign. The body of human inquiry most profoundly devoted to asking questions and to plumbing memory is no longer taken seriously. We can be confident that six years later, the Freud nuts have gone for good. So have detectives.

Reviewing the case, we can note the following. Lethem's treatment of Chandler's paradigm is thorough: the work of a dedicated student of the form. More than this, it works as an example of the form, rather than merely imploding or mocking it. A significant fact about Lethem's practice is visible here: the use of an extant form in a way that does not merely exploit it but produces a substantial instance of it. The combination of two major genres has particular effects. It produces interference, so that neither genre is wholly experienced in the customary way. Each genre is reconditioned by the shaping force of the other. The detective genre offers a way of exploring the science-fictional world as a corrupt and criminal society, a site of conspiracy. Equally, the dystopian mode takes the degraded world of the private eye to a new extreme, while this world's peculiar conditions also foreground elements that are important to the detective genre: the prohibition on questions is a significant instance. If both modes are implicitly 'cognitive', dystopia also undercuts the capacity for cognition by placing memory under threat. All these effects of generic collision, seen more broadly, announce from the outset of Lethem's career an aesthetic of borrowing, appropriation and recombination, in which genre will be a crucial element.

Just Say Detective

Lethem records that various readers were disappointed to learn that there would not be a shelf of Conrad Metcalf novels to follow *Gun, with Occasional Music*. What had seemed the brilliant beginning of a career in the detective genre turned out to be a deliberate false start, a one-off. His next few novels essentially turned from the genre, while demonstrating his deeper connections to science fiction. Yet he was not finished with it after all, as his fifth novel was a detective novel that would be – with Lethem's career a few years better established – still better received than *Gun*. Now readers would ask when they would see the next Lionel Essrog novel, to similar disappointment (Clarke 2011: 160).

In certain ways, *Motherless Brooklyn* can definitely be labelled a detective novel. It commences with a murder; it involves the search for the killer and the complex dealings that led to the crime. It is heavy on plot, and driven by a quest to uncover secrets and connect them. The 'puzzle element' that Rzepka (2005: 186–9) sees as enduring in the hard-boiled mode is discernable. Certain clues connect to the underlying criminal plot, and the reader sometimes witnesses the reaction to them of the protagonist, Lionel Essrog, as his cognitive processes whir. The recurrent motif of the last joke mentioned by Frank Minna ('The High Lama will see you now'), directing Lionel to his brother the Zen tutor, is an example, compounded by the visiting monk's reference to 'Jerry-Roshi' who turns out to be Gerard Minna (199–200). More strikingly, Kimmery's leaflet advertising a 'Place of Peace' (208) triggers the memory of Julia Minna's flight for such a place: Lionel's mental response ('Pleasure police. / Pressure peas') reprises two of the ticcing distortions that he makes of the phrase upon Julia's first use of it (105, 107). Resolving all this, the novel's penultimate chapter commences with a large passage of revelation, representing what Julia tells Lionel, but also offering this crucial information to the reader. After this epistemological climax, the novel ends with vice seemingly punished and a new equilibrium restored.

In other ways, though, the novel differs from the expectations of a detective novel. It centres on a group of four orphans plucked from St Vincent's Home for Boys by their mentor Frank Minna, who puts them to work as his Minna Men around Brooklyn. We join the action twenty years after this apprenticeship begins, and the second, eponymous chapter contains much back-story covering this intervening period. The orphanage and the quartet make for a different starting point from the lone private detective, whose childhood is usually out of bounds, irrelevant to the hard-bitten man he has become. Then there is the question of what the Minna Men actually do. They begin as servants of L&L

Movers, loading and unloading goods, stolen or otherwise. After Frank Minna's trouble with his secretive Italian-American bosses Matricardi and Rockaforte ('The Clients') and his three-year absence in Maine, he returns to set up L&L as a car service, run from a shop in Cobble Hill. But this is a front for a *'detective agency'* (88).

L&L has done some of the work a detective agency might do: it 'tracked a wife for a husband or watched an employee suspected of pilferage or cooking the books', gathering information with 'bugs and cameras', keeping files (167). But the Minna Men have also been 'as much errand boys as detectives', and many of the errands – such as minding a van until it is towed away, and wondering whether it contained money or a body – have been done on behalf of Matricardi and Rockaforte themselves. In Julia Minna's account, 'most of [Frank's] detective work was on [the Clients'] behalf': 'she wished he genuinely ran a car service' (291). Lionel often cannot tell whether the work – 'Seize a given piece of equipment from a given office […] Collect this amount from such and such a person […] Unseal this envelope, tap this phone' (169) – is done on the Clients' behalf, but either way it does not all sound like 'detection'; more like intimidation. As another brisk passage puts it: 'Minna Men stand behind Minna, hands in their pockets, looking menacing' (90). In short, the supposed detectives seem closer, much of the time, to the world of organized crime than to the dogged exposure of wrongdoing and upholding of the law.

The novel as a whole also swerves from the detective novel in having other preoccupations, or fitting other categories. Thus Lethem says that 'it's really a Bildungsroman, a family romance, a coming-of-age story, whatever' (Clarke 2011: 35–6), emphasizing the novel as the story of Lionel Essrog's development rather than of the crime plot. As well as tracing the origins of the Minna Men in the orphanage, the novel also stages a rapid acceleration in Lionel's development, to autonomy and understanding, across the brief period of its events. So too, ingeniously, Lethem locates it as a 'geek novel', comparable to *The Catcher in the Rye*, in which the reader is to sympathize with the downtrodden protagonist's intelligence and wit (Clarke 2011: 36, 107). But most obviously, Lionel's defining characteristic, his Tourette's syndrome, is spectacularly ill-suited to work in this genre. Where the private detective should be cool, withdrawn, reserved, sardonic, in control, Lionel lacks control of his own speech and gestures. In a scene like the Zen meditation session which Lionel finally disrupts with his tics – 'Ziggedy zendoodah […] Zazen zaftig Zsa Zsa go-bare' (201) – we see at its most extreme the collision between the detective's need for discretion and Lionel's inability to achieve it. But even through most of his other encounters, with colleagues, police or suspects, Lionel's detective discourse is warped by his syndrome. Lethem, then, has set in place a 'detective agency' that shades into criminality, and made his protagonist seemingly the last person who should be working as a detective.

It would be most accurate to say that the novel nonetheless *becomes* a detective novel despite these carefully engineered complications. Across the narrative, Lionel increasingly convinces himself in the role. When, around a third of the way in, Lionel tries 'to let the day settle over me, to try to make some sense of it' (118), it allows a lengthy reprisal of pertinent events and questions thus far ('I lingered over my paltry clues'), in the manner often periodically offered by Philip Marlowe, sometimes with an interlocutor like a police detective. Dismissing his colleagues from his mind, Lionel tries 'to pretend it was my case alone': at once, evidently, adopting the detective's way of thinking about such a complex set of events as a 'case' (the agency's previous work seems hardly to have involved such cases), and asserting his solitude in the lone role of 'private eye'. He wakes the next morning with a heightened sense that 'the city shone with clues': 'It seemed possible I was a detective on a case' (132).

Several times after this, we witness Lionel assert or grasp for this role. Working alone, he realizes again, allows 'playing lead detective instead of comic – or Tourettic – relief', even if he has been characteristically distracted into examining biscuits in what he self-deprecatingly calls 'the Oreo conundrum' (143). The Clients flatter him by appealing to 'your talent for detection. The training instilled' (176). Talking to a real detective, Lucius Seminole, Lionel defensively insists that L&L is not a car service but a detective agency (188). Seminole informs him: 'I looked into that rumor [...] None of you carry investigators' credentials'. Lionel insists that 'We assist a detective. We're, uh, operatives', making his way through cognate terms in a search for credibility; Seminole redefines the role as 'stooge work for a penny-ante hood' (189). The exchange is revealing about the discrepancy between L&L's self-image and its legal reality. It also demonstrates Lionel's desperation to believe in his role as detective, and Frank's by extension. It is deeply telling that when he files an obituary notice for Frank Minna and is asked for a title that would summarize the dead man, Lionel replies: 'Just say detective' (165). This validates Minna's dubious history as owner of a 'detective agency' by projecting Lionel's more virtuous current activities back onto it; correspondingly, insisting on Frank's role as detective makes him the acknowledged precursor to Lionel. As the novel progresses, Lionel noticeably takes on Frank's mantle. He wears Frank's watch and beeper; as he approaches the villain's lair again, he presents his image as 'collar up against the cold like Minna, unshaven like Minna, now, too'; 'that black outline of a man in a coat, ready suspicious eyes above his collar' – even as he immediately admits how his Tourette's mind complicates this image in reality (226–7).

We could say that Lionel is trying to assert his claim to belong to a certain genre. This notion is made more literal by his familiarity with actual detective fiction. Hence his remarkable query to the reader, who is normally only fed with one-way information: 'Have you ever felt, in the course of reading a detective novel, a guilty thrill of relief at having a character murdered before he can step onto the page and burden you with his actual existence? Detective stories always have too many characters anyway' (119). Lionel is reacting to news of the death of Ullman, a bookkeeper who had been in league with Frank Minna: he is relieved at the loss of this complication while simultaneously troubled that 'the world of the case was shrinking'; 'My clue had been murdered' (119). To the reader, Ullman really is just an unknown literary 'character': Lionel thus tells us in advance what our response might be to the news, while (in accordance with a certain convention of first-person narration) not really acknowledging that we are reading a novel, which would make him also merely a character. At another level again, the reader can sense Lethem's own acknowledgement of the genre: talking self-consciously about a detective novel is in one way a frame-breaking device, but it also confirms that this *is* a detective novel.

Lionel, who 'grew up in the library' of the orphanage (36), has an extensive range of literary and screen reference, and Lethem has admitted the process in which he decided that the character, obsessive about many things, would logically also be fascinated by stories of detection, the profession he is so keen to occupy: 'Why would someone like him want to be like him *unless* he'd read Raymond Chandler?' (Clarke 2011: 88). That is the rationale for Lionel's direct references to Chandler, who is again the most important resource for this novel. He twice quotes *The Big Sleep* directly in his address to us, both times wrapping it in a larger disquisition on fictional detectives: their tendency to be knocked out and to fall 'into such strange swirling darknesses, such manifold surrealist voids' (205), their tendency to sweeping assertions ('in detective stories things are always *always*' [307]). In both cases the reference confirms Lionel's own relation to the genre, while he also takes a distance from its norms: he says he has nothing to add to the tradition of surrealist voids, and casts some suspicion on the tendency to assertion by likening it to a symptom of Tourette's.

The references reassert Marlowe's centrality as Lionel's precursor, not least in his own mind, but briefer references also appear to other fictional models.

Lionel's reflection '*The quieter the monk, the gaudier the patter*' (215) puns on the words of Dashiell Hammett's fictional sleuth Sam Spade: 'The cheaper the crook, the gaudier the patter' (Hammett 2005: 116). One of the subtlest references is to the same novel, when Lionel is talking of cinematic calendar pages flipping and goes into a Tourettic tic: '*Flip-a-thon! Fuck-a-door! Flipweed! Fujisaki! Flitcraft!*' (230). Flitcraft is the name of a man recalled by Sam Spade, who transforms his life in response to the existential randomness of just being missed by a falling beam in the street (Hammett 2005: 59–62). Lionel is plausibly falling back on his own reading here, though the brevity of the unsignalled reference makes it more of a game with the reader on Lethem's part. More explicit references proliferate elsewhere. Immediately after calling Lionel 'Marlowe', the rogue Minna Man Tony Vermonte also scornfully adds: 'You think you're Mike fucking Hammer. You're like the Hardy Boys' retarded kid brother' (179). Working through the range of fictional detectives, on the same page he calls Lionel 'McGruff' (the name of a trenchcoated cartoon 'crime dog' used in public information films since the early 1980s) and 'Shitlock Holmes', and shortly after adds, 'You're Sam Spade' (179, 183).

Part of the dynamic here is Tony's scorn for the very role of the detective: though he wants to take over Minna's role, his aspiration is for crooked property deals rather than the role in which Lionel keeps trying to reinsert Minna. Tony wants the investigation closed down, the story to dispense with the detective genre; he wants, in effect, to occupy a crime story by Mario Puzo, in which the Mafia are the lead characters. Lionel openly tells Tony that everything they both know came from 'Frank Minna or gangster movies' (184). But he has no interest in claiming that part of Minna's legacy, and increasingly finds his identity and sense of honour in rehearsing the behaviour proper to the detective genre. His response to Tony's remark about Sam Spade seems almost an instant reflex, characteristic of Lionel: 'When someone kills your partner you're supposed to do something about it' (185). Tony shows no recognition, but the sentiment is Spade's at the end of *The Maltese Falcon*, explaining to Brigid O'Shaughnessy why he must hand her over to the police by making reference to a tacit, minimal code of honour (Hammett 2005: 209). On the telephone to an angry Tony late in the novel, Lionel can nonetheless reflect sentimentally: 'We'd be two Bogarts to the end' (248). The primary meaning is that they will exchange hard-bitten dialogue, but Lionel also states that Tony has 'brought out the romantic in me': to be a Bogart in this context, at least for Lionel, also implies maintaining the code that Bogart's screen characters typically uphold despite their shabby circumstances.

If Lionel wants to be a hard-boiled detective, he has the good fortune to find himself in a story increasingly suited to such a figure. As Lethem would comment, 'The whole book, apart from the long flashback to beforehand, is one "guy walking through a door with a gun"' (Clarke 2011: 39). It was Chandler in his essay 'The Simple Art of Murder' who wryly advised: 'When in doubt, have a man come through a door with a gun in his hand'. *Motherless Brooklyn* cheerfully takes the advice, making the gun a piece of narrative punctuation which remains unexpected despite repetition, through the second half of the novel. Three pages into Tony's confrontation with Lionel in the Pontiac: 'Tony took a gun out from under his arm and pointed it at me' (181). A few pages further, a tap on the car window turns out to be a gun muzzle, pointed by the homicide detective (185): one gunpoint confrontation is interrupted by another, in a bold upping the ante of the gun as a device for shaking up narrative. In a subsequent confrontation on the street, the mysterious giant seems relatively cordial until 'He put the bag of fruit away, and when his hand reemerged it was holding a gun' (204). Lastly, on the Maine coast, Julia Minna asks Lionel to light her cigarette: 'By the time I had it lit she'd taken her gun from her purse' (299). Three of these four revelations conclude a section of narrative (followed by asterisks), and thus attain minor cliff-hanger status. They are joined in this by another moment that initially seems equally menacing, as Lionel stands in a reverie on the street: 'Two men took me by the elbows and hustled me into a car waiting at the curb' (145). All these incidents, which start to occur from around halfway through the novel, contribute to the atmosphere proper to the genre, in which physical danger is not only inherent to a case but is also liable to pop up almost at random, as a way of charging the narrative with energy.

Julia Minna adopts the role of *femme fatale* as surely as Celeste Stanhunt has previously done in *Gun*, but still tougher: 'the hardest-boiled of us all', Lionel realizes at the end (303), Julia also survives the story. She seems to the Minna boys 'a woman off a fading movie poster', altered by Frank 'with panty hose and peroxide and sarcasm' (294); 'tall, plush, blond by nurture, defiant around the jaw', she has been given the role of a mid-century Hollywood actress, and the 'crackle of electricity animating [the] insults' (97) between Julia and Frank, while part of a romance gone sour, also carries a trace of MGM dialogue. In her first proper appearance in the novel she is packing a suitcase to flee the city after her husband's murder, with a gun amid her luggage; she lights herself a cigarette, 'chopping at a matchbook angrily, throwing off a little curl of spark' (99); she asks the protagonist to zip up the back of her dress, and when confronted by the homicide detective over Frank's killer, defiantly tells him 'Let me know when you find out who killed him. […] Then I'll tell you if I care' (108). Playing her part in a *film noir* even as other characters fail to obey the genre's rules, she thus gives Lionel's aspiration to 'be a Bogart' circumstantial support. If the primary rationales for this are Frank's characteristically 'anachronistic' (231) makeover of Julia, and the bitterness instilled by their marriage, we also learn late on that Frank read her the works of 'Spillane and Chandler and Ross MacDonald' (288). Like Lionel, this moment suggests, she is not merely accidentally following a role but has in part chosen and rehearsed it.

Such generic support comes too from the enigmatic giant, who kills both Frank and Tony but is seen grazing healthily on kumquats and cherries. Most simply, the giant's size makes him fearsomely dangerous, adding to the menace of the novel; it also allows him to swat Lionel into unconsciousness, thus prompting his reflection on this state as a genre trope (205). More specifically, if the giant has any precursor it would appear to be Moose Malloy, the ambiguous criminal at the centre of *Farewell, My Lovely*. His act of lifting Lionel and effortlessly carrying him out of the Zendo (203) resembles Moose's with Marlowe at the start of the novel: 'A hand I could have sat in came out of the dimness and took hold of my shoulder and squashed it to a pulp. Then the hand moved me through the doors and casually lifted me up a step' (Chandler 2010: 3). The extremity of both giants' size enables a particular brand of sardonic commentary, in which their unusual scale is stressed through faux casualness and understatement. In Moose's case, in one of Chandler's most cited lines of description: 'He was a big man but not more than six feet five inches tall and not wider than a beer truck' (1). In *Motherless Brooklyn*: 'Maybe the giant would do me the favor of plummeting into the sea. Maybe he hadn't gotten around to noticing it – since it was only the Atlantic it might not have been big enough to make an impression' (282).

As he progresses through this world, Lionel's own language develops. It remains marked by Tourette's to the end, to be sure, but there is a change from his anxious speech in the immediate wake of Frank's death – like his entreaty to Lucius Seminole, 'could we consider this maybe another time? Because […] now I really urgently have to go home and […] eat this sandwich' (112) – to the way he addresses interlocutors by the end of the investigation. His latenight confrontation with Gerard Minna is instructive here, even though he is ultimately bamboozled by Gerard's mystical air: asking 'What's your role, Gerard? […] I mean, besides sending your brother out into the Polack's arms to die'; spontaneously finding the clipped, brutal idiom for 'So Fujisaki sicced the giant on Frank and the bookkeeper'; and consciously deploying one of Frank's old phrases: 'Don't try to hand me no two-ton feather' (232–3). In his own thought, just before the interview ends, Lionel considers inconvenient pieces of evidence 'three sour notes in a very pretty song' (236). Here he reaches Marlowe's tone: casually metaphorical, sardonic about the conveniently 'pretty' facade he is confronted with, inveterately alert to sourness. Clearer still is Lionel's attitude on the Maine coast. Discovering an older fisherman, he reports: 'I could see this called for the oldest investigatory technique of them all: I opened my wallet and took out a twenty', and suavely adds: '"I'd buy a guy a drink if he could tell me a few things about the Japanese"' (267). He is now sharp enough to tell Julia 'We're all coming up here for a Frank Minna convention', and that Tony, taken away by the giant, is 'on a boat ride' (272–3). Most significantly, he can interrupt the feared Client Alphonso Matricardi's sententious declaration, 'This is a terrible thing—': 'Yeah, yeah, terrible', and lay down his own terms for negotiation (284–5). All of this demonstrates what Lethem means in calling *Motherless Brooklyn* 'a coming-of-age story'. This particular coming of age, though, involves assuming the persona of the detective who would be equal to the world that the novel discloses. The paradox is that once he has attained it, he abjures it, returning to a newly legitimate car service. The novel increasingly envelops its characters in a genre, only finally to show them a way out of it.

Gun, with Occasional Music stages a direct collision between detective fiction and science fiction, making it the purest instance of the early Lethem's signature strategy of crossing genres. Four novels on, *Motherless Brooklyn* does something comparable, but more subtly. With no trace of science fiction, it belongs to the realm of the urban crime novel. It develops and resolves a complex murder plot. Yet as we have seen, it also complicates its own status as detective fiction. It compromises the status of the 'detective' himself, in what Julia Minna disdains as a 'corrupt and inept detective agency' (101), closer to the mob than to the police. It mixes his investigation with his personal development, such that it doubles as a kind of *Bildungsroman*. It crowds the canvas with extraneous cultural materials – Lionel's disquisitions on Prince records, Oreos or *Mad* magazine – which distract from the investigation and befit Lethem's speculative notion of the 'geek genre' (Clarke 2011: 107). And it is further crowded with the noise of Lionel's Tourette's, and his compulsive reflections on the condition. In this regard, on one hand, it installs a mechanism for constant self-interruption, the intrusion of a principle of sheer linguistic effervescence and recombination like that of James Joyce's *Finnegans Wake* (Brooker 2016: 114–7). On the other, it also joins a recent literary trend for the exploration of physical and mental conditions, which Marco Roth in a sceptical essay has dubbed the 'neuronovel' (Roth 2009). Though Lethem wrote the novel partly in response to reading the neurological studies of Oliver

Sacks (Clarke 2011: 82, 84), its participation in such an emergent trend was necessarily unwitting, of a different order from its highly conscious engagement with the history of detective fiction. But Roth's categorization demonstrates the multiplicity of projects and tendencies at work in the novel, and the extent to which its status as detective fiction is purposely surrounded with interference. To all this we can add the novel's tendency to make overt reference to the genre, and openly to quote Chandler himself. While it complicates and retards its performance of the hard-boiled formula, it also draws attention to it.

There is a kind of double-bluff in the novel's relation to detective fiction. All the above factors seem to distance it from the mode, or to render it so self-conscious that its actual execution of the protocols of the detective novel would be a secondary consideration. Yet its most remarkable achievement, in this context, is that it is also a successful instance of the genre. Literary awards are not usually particularly enlightening about the specific qualities of a text. But *Motherless Brooklyn*'s attainment of the 2000 Gold Dagger award for detective fiction is an exception. The novel was acclaimed not against a field of other metafictions or neuronovels, but in a field composed entirely of crime, by an awarding body rooted exclusively in that field since the mid-1950s. The five other novelists on the shortlist from which Lethem emerged are all accredited primarily as authors of crime and mystery fiction, sometimes having composed sequences of novels around the same fictional sleuth. The runner-up (Silver Dagger winner) Donna Leon, for instance, had published eight other novels about her Venetian hero Commisario Guido Brunetti prior to the title, *Friends in High Places*, that competed with *Motherless Brooklyn*, while James Lee Burke's entry, *Purple Cane Road*, was the eleventh in his series of novels starring the police detective and Vietnam veteran Dave Robichaux. In this context it is understandable that people expected Lionel Essrog to return. That is what a proper crime writer would do, and that is what Lethem credibly seemed to be.

We might see Lionel's insistence on being a detective as parallel with the book's own status. When Kimmery queries his reaction to Frank's death, he reiterates: 'I'm a detective, Kimmery'. She finds the notion difficult to accept – 'I guess I thought detectives were more, uh, subtle' – but he improvises the explanation: 'Maybe you're thinking of detectives in movies or on television. […] On TV they're all the same. Real detectives are as unalike as fingerprints, or snowflakes' (255). The novel's progress corroborates this. While the mode it inhabits is deeply, pleasurably, formulaic, it also allows for unique divergences. Someone as apparently 'unsubtle' as Lionel might still be a real detective; correspondingly, while his story performs many feats at once, it remains a real detective novel.

The Termite's Progress

A simple story could be told of Lethem's literary career. It would say that he has shifted from an engagement with genre to a position in the mainstream. Alternatively, with similar connotations, it would say that he has shifted from fantastic to realistic fiction. The two claims are not identical, as detective fiction – which we have just seen has been crucial to Lethem's career – is recognized as a genre yet is not innately fantastic. It is true that *Motherless Brooklyn*, for instance, offered Lethem possibilities that his science fiction writing did not, and vice versa. Yet in practice the two claims can be run closely together, as versions of a transition from margin to mainstream.

Indeed Lethem has provided a vocabulary for this. By 2011, he viewed his career through the binary of '"White Elephant Art" (big, ungainly, awards-season stuff)' and '"Termite Art" (prestige-immune routes of curiosity through the cultural woodwork)' (2011: xxi–xxii) that he had borrowed from the critic Manny Farber. The white elephant novelist would produce long, earnest books about the great questions of his time, earning mainstream cultural presence which was derided as much as revered, while the termite artist would scamper sideways through a range of subversive, debunking strategies. Genre was a way to be a termite. Both crime and science fiction could fit this bill, with their fond echoes of pulp. For the time being, though, the following analysis will highlight especially the fantastic element and its fate in Lethem's career.

Lethem had spent much time in science fiction circles (2011: 68–73), and until the mid-1990s published stories in science fiction magazines; a decade later, he was becoming more regularly a *New Yorker* writer. By 2007, the science fiction writer Nancy Kress, in a friendly blog post on Lethem, could say that he 'used to be an SF writer but has now levitated into the stratosphere of literary mainstream' (Kress 2007). The early work often takes place in environments qualitatively different from the real world as we know it: some time in the future (*Gun, with Occasional Music*, or the story 'Vanilla Dunk'), on another planet (*Girl in Landscape*), or in several of the stories, in a more indeterminate, shifting space (the short story 'Forever, Said the Duck' is set in a virtual reality projection). The later work often occupies environments analogous to the real world, crowded with real place names and references to historical events (say, the career of Richard Nixon), and furnished with often extensive verbal depictions of real objects and surroundings. An early flashback in *Dissident Gardens*, looking back to 1947, goes out of its way to exemplify the point, focusing on an ashtray ('obloid, smooth-polished black granite, weighing enough to use as a stop against a pressure-hinged door or indent a man's skull') as its way in to a whole historical interior setting, the home of a family of German Jewish emigrés: 'Broadway and Ninety-Second, the Knickerbocker Apartments. A one-bedroom on this island of Manhattan, furnished conspicuously with what could be saved apart from the ashtray, the half set of china, a crucial framed photograph or two (showing Alma among cousins, on Alpine vacations, they might as easily have been Nazi memorabilia to Rose's eye), Viennese-lace curtains' (2013a: 8). Here the object world is a way for Lethem to solidify the historical world, to a degree rare in his earlier fiction.

Indeed another aspect of the shift posited here is that Lethem's prose not only refers to different things, but itself becomes more capacious and detailed. Thus we progress from writing like this, in *Amnesia Moon* –

> The sky was bright but gray. Chaos squinted at what he could see of the town and didn't say anything. He thought about how he'd wandered into the green and taken on the Moon identity. He wondered if something like that would happen here, and whether he could be conscious of it, and struggle to resist, or whether it would overwhelm him. He envied Boyd, who'd boasted of immunity to the changes. (1995: 72)

– to this, in *Dissident Gardens*:

> An hour later they stood braving a cold wind at the gentle summit of the Brooklyn Bridge's rotting-plank walkway, the East River's boardwalk, and surveyed the transistor gleamings of the island they'd exited, contrasting it with the low-roofed smolder of Brooklyn Heights, the murk of their promised destination, *Mailer's Party*, down there somewhere, one of those faint flares amid a million darkened bedrooms, the sea of sleepers beyond. (2013a: 25)

The first passage is typical enough of *Amnesia Moon*, where the narrative appears to aspire first and foremost to the functional conveyance of information. This suits the story and environment, in which the state of world around the characters is profoundly unclear, and each day is a struggle with dystopian conditions. A functional verbal approach feels appropriate to convey the urgent, grim business of understanding and survival. The first sentence is blunt, taking little trouble to describe the sky. Three sentences in a row commence 'He', eschewing elegant variation. The second passage contains almost as many words as the first – 68 to 72 – but rolls these into one sentence, to the first passage's five. The effect is a sentence elaborately slung out across clauses, a little like the bridge itself in expanse, with subordinate clauses clarifying and defining ('the East River's boardwalk' a redefinition of the bridge's walkway), adjectives adding to the texture though not strictly necessary ('rotting-plank', 'low-roofed'), a striking metaphor (Manhattan's 'transistor gleamings', the city somehow lit like a radio), and the end of the sentence departing from mere syntactical logic (naming that with which Manhattan is being contrasted) to issue an associative series of items and locations, which loosely amass as the dark sight of Brooklyn.

The two passages evidently adopt different ways of writing. They may serve as opposite poles in Lethem's work, with much variation in between – *Girl in Landscape*, for instance, its style succinct yet evocative and reflective, might be a mid-point in the stylistic bridge. In the present context, the point is that this also represents something of a temporal change, from early simplicity to later complexity in literary style. Overall, then, we may posit a shift from genre to the literary; from the fantastic to the realistic; from imaginary, futuristic or abstract settings to concrete ones resembling the real world; and a verbal expansion into more elaborate syntax. The first phase would be the 1990s. A hinge point would be *The Fortress of Solitude*, which at once depicts an immensely detailed historical world, in a more elaborate prose than ever before, and introduces an element of the fantastic – a juxtaposition to be considered in more detail in Chapter Four. After this Lethem publishes a range of works – *Dissident Gardens* a significant example – typically more dedicated to fictional representations of the real world than his previous novels.

Lethem's own comments naturally bear attention here. In 2001, with *The Fortress of Solitude* in development, he described it as 'adamantly unlike any of the previous novels', and asserted that the models he was using for it, such as Ann Beattie and Richard Yates, were 'not supposed to be my strength!'; 'So I'm becoming a realist' (Clarke 2011: 44–5). In 2003, with *Fortress* under discussion, he talked of 'a greater and greater interest in some of the methods of literary naturalism' (76), and referred somewhat slightingly to the early novels, as though they were superseded by the richer aesthetic he had now achieved, which 'grows organically from character and voice, embodied in dramatic situations' (68).

The simple narrative indicated above thus has credibility. But it may also be questioned, in the name of a more nuanced view of Lethem's career. Asked in the same 2003 interview why he had started writing 'straight' novels, Lethem responded: 'I'm not writing straight novels. What's straight? I understand your assumptions, but you know that I have to point out how silly they are. There's no important sense in which I ever began or resumed or stopped writing straight novels' (Clarke 2011: 60). The terms of his reply insist on refusing even the idea of such a change, or contemplating the implied chronology: not only has he not started, but, confusing the framework, he has not resumed or stopped either. In keeping with this, we may also look for ways in which the story of 'going straight' can be complicated.

First, Lethem's own tendency to downplay the 'human' element in his early fiction can be misleading. In a 2005 interview he talks of the first three novels as 'puppet shows' compared with the 'method acting' that followed (Clarke 2011: 87), but the description neglects the stoical emotion gathered in Conrad Metcalf, or the insight into loss that underlies the offbeat comedy of *As She Climbed across the Table*. By the same token, we should not assume that the characters in later works necessarily have more richness than these earlier figures because they appear in a somewhat different mode of representation.

Second, the fantastic is not simply jettisoned. In *Fortress* it lingers in a magic item; in *A Gambler's Anatomy*, more ambiguously, it is repeatedly suggested that the protagonist has the power to read others' minds, which would be a greater departure from ordinary physical laws than most of what Lethem had published for the previous two decades. *Chronic City* is filled with lengthy accounts of characters' everyday interactions – on the face of it, the 'character-driven writing' that Lethem in 2005 said now interested him (Clarke 2011: 87) – yet also takes place in an alternate reality, containing details that do not belong to the world as we know it. This hybrid of the realistic and the fantastic suggests a more complex trajectory than the one sketched above.

It is true that several of Lethem's later works do without such devices and appear to operate in settings that are in principle directly analogous to the real world. Here a different distinction needs to be made. The story 'The King of Sentences', published in the *New Yorker* in late 2007, occupies such a mundane world, with two characters travelling from New York City to a small upstate town to find their literary hero. Yet the characters hardly behave in naturalistic fashion, especially the anonymous King of Sentences himself, who reacts to his admirers' arrival by tearing their clothes apart and leaving them stranded in a shabby hotel room (Lethem 2015: 38). Such a story is 'realist' by comparison with the post-apocalyptic landscape of *Amnesia Moon*, but not so much by comparison with the painstakingly rendered suburbia of Richard Ford or the hard-bitten scenarios of David Means. Something similar can be said even of *Dissident Gardens*, ostensibly the least fantastic of Lethem's novels. It comes to include scenes such as the elderly Rose Zimmer's protracted hallucination of the television character Archie Bunker, in which the distinction between reality and fantasy is not clearly maintained (Lethem 2013a: 269–78), and a Halloween episode in which her cousin Lenny Angrush careers across New York dressed as Abraham Lincoln before having a spontaneous sexual encounter with Rose who treats him as though he were the reincarnated President. In such a scene, mimetic motivation is secondary to symbolism; the characters' behaviour and appearance serve themes and ideas. If a primary model can be cited here, it is Thomas Pynchon, rarely referred to as a 'realist' writer. Indeed the notion of Lethem's trajectory toward a more conservative aesthetic would be modified if it were presented as a move toward Pynchon's orbit: a case supported by *A Gambler's Anatomy*, where the intimate relations between corporate power and counter-culture in Berkeley are strongly reminiscent of Pynchon's Californian territory, and by *The Feral Detective*, which recalls the late Pynchon's turn to detective fiction in *Inherent Vice* (2009) and *Bleeding Edge* (2013).

A third main point is that a case that holds for Lethem's longer works may need modification for his short fiction. The transition from 'Forever, Said the Duck' to 'Lucky Alan' certainly follows the general case: published in the *New Yorker* in 2007, the latter story tells an Upper East Side tale that could belong in a Woody Allen feature. And it is true that several of the stories in *Men and Cartoons* (2004) and *Lucky Alan* (2015) occupy such recognizable worlds, in the contemporary period on the East or West coasts of the United States, in a way less evident in *The Wall of the Sky, the Wall of the Eye* (1996). This distinction roughly corresponds to that drawn by Lethem in interview, between his early stories which were 'more like compressed novels, or like first chapters for novels that will never be written', and later ones with 'fewer elements and complications', more conventional in form because arising from a late-blooming 'love of the short story' (Clarke 2011: 86). Lethem makes the same distinction in his afterword to *How We Got Insipid* (2006), where he calls the latter kind 'true to the tradition' (Lethem 2006a: 104). He also notes here that 'How We Got In Town and Out Again' 'was my last appearance in both "Isaac Asimov's Science Fiction Magazine" and in *The Year's Best Science Fiction* series, and I think it's fair to say it was my last attempt to paint within those particular lines. It was a farewell not to the literature of the fantastic, but to the contemporary SF marketplace' (107). All of this suggests that the transition posited above is just as true for Lethem's short fiction as for his novels – even as he specifically resists the notion that he had yet bidden farewell to the literature of the fantastic.

Yet the collection *Lucky Alan* also contains two of Lethem's most experimental stories to date. 'Their Back Pages' is a twenty-page work about a gathering of surreal creatures – including 'Large Silly (a clown)', 'Peter Rabbit (a rabbit)' and 'C'Krrrarn (a monster)' – whose aeroplane crashes on a desert island. As if this cast of characters were not challenge enough, the narrative commences in the form of a verbal description of comic book panels – 'Page one, panel two, the plane. A bolted turnip with wings, now aflame' (2015: 71) – and is then broken up, in turn, by a series of different forms of discourse including extracts from a theatre critic's journal, an emphatically capitalized series of lines describing the monster's potential actions ('C'KRRRARN TEARS OFF A CHUNK OF THE OCEAN AND DEVOURS IT!!!' [76]), part of an Index (a form hardly encountered in fiction, with Virginia Woolf's *Orlando* [1928] and David Grossman's *See Under: Love* [1986] rare exceptions [77]), a poem which is in part a pastiche of Bob Dylan's 'Song to Woody' (85), and an extract from a dictionary (87–8). This story deliberately traverses and collages together a range of uses of language, all in the service of a story about implausible cartoon figures. Whatever the success of the project, it plainly does not abide by any polite canons of realism. If it has any evident precursor it might be the stories of Donald Barthelme in the 1960s and 1970s, which each invented their own terms of reference. That is true, in another way, of the other outlier in *Lucky Alan*: 'The Dreaming Jaw, The Salivating Ear', another fragmentary, multivocal piece which turns out to be arranged backwards, and whose concern is the fate of a 'blog' which seems to exist not online but as a building on the seashore. In sum, if Lethem has moved away from genre, it is not always towards a more respectable realism.

Several of Lethem's comments suggest a fourth, more fundamental way in which the fantastic/realistic binary can be challenged. In her 2001 interview with Lethem, Shelley Jackson disagrees with his description of *Motherless Brooklyn* as 'cartoonish', insisting: 'Reality is a literary construction. It's a cartoon too!' Lethem immediately concedes the point, and offers the tentative statement that 'I'm leaning away from certain kinds of reality-as-cartoon in my work, and towards others' (Clarke 2011: 44). This concession places the fantastic and the realistic on the same plane, as ways of constructing fiction through words: *The Fortress of Solitude* becomes one kind of construction alongside others. This way of seeing language is then quite recurrent in Lethem. In a 2005 interview he asserts: 'Language itself is a fantastic element. So you can't keep from becoming metaphorical or surrealistic. The moment you commit to storytelling in language, you've done it' (Clarke 2011: 111). In the introduction to *The Ecstasy of Influence*, Lethem writes the principle out more deliberately:

> All writing, no matter how avowedly naturalistic or pellucid, consists of artifice, of conjuration, of the manipulation of symbols rather than the 'opening of a window onto life'. [...] We writers aren't sculpting in DNA, or even clay or mud, but words, sentences, paragraphs, syntax, voice; materials issued by tongue or fingertips but which upon release dissolve into the atmosphere, into cloud,

confection, specter. Language, as a vehicle, is a lemon, a hot rod painted with thrilling flames but crazily erratic to drive, riddled with bugs like innate self-consciousness, embedded metaphors and symbols, helpless intertexuality, and so forth. Despite being regularly driven on prosaic errands (interoffice memos, supermarket receipts, etc.), it tends to veer on its misaligned chassis into the ditch of abstraction, of dream. (2011: xx–xxi)

The avowal is deliberately flamboyant (literally so, with the 'thrilling flames' of decoration at its centre), working up the notion of language as a 'vehicle' into an extended metaphor to prove its point about the medium's figurative tendency. The metaphor is enriched by containing other metaphors within it: a 'lemon' here means a faulty car, but its primary meaning is normally a citrus fruit, which thus gets juiced by association into the evolving image. The same can be said of 'hot rod' or 'bugs' (an odd term to use of a car, and thus effectively a mixed metaphor). The brief passage as a whole moves so rapidly between images that it becomes cheerfully disorienting: the 'window onto life' is a clear enough image, but is chased away in turn by 'sculpting' (as a description of what writing does *not* do), by the series of more ethereal images that Lethem presents as truer to the character of language ('cloud, confection, specter' – each of these with its own connotations, from the meteorological to the Gothic, but none of them allowed time to develop before the argument moves on), then by the metaphorical automobile that hogs the road for the rest of the peroration. The passage, therefore, aims at a bravura performance of what it states: that it is in the nature of language to get out of control.

This in turn bears upon the question of literary trajectory traced above. Christopher Boucher astutely links this passage to yet another, in a 2005 essay on Kafka, which asserts that 'language itself – even the very plainest and most direct – is innately metaphorical, fabulated, and grotesque', as ground for the claim that 'it is the quarantine between realist and anti-realist methods in fiction that [Kafka's] writing has made seem permanent nonsense' (Lethem 2017: 25). The logic is that what we typically label literary realism is formed of the same material as its fantastic other, and thus ultimately belongs to the same territory. The choice would not be between reality and fantasy but between different kinds of construct, fabricated largely from the same set of words.

Dissident Gardens is again pertinent here, as while some of its material is highly contemporary (around the Occupy movement of 2011), it also reaches back to the 1940s, with detailed scenes in the New York of the 1950s and 1960s. It thus qualifies as, in part, a historical novel, many of whose materials and settings are not made from direct experience or living memory but from research or speculation. In this sense, the novel involves a degree of world-making, fabrication through literary language, more obvious than is the case in a novel set in the present day. Indeed Fredric Jameson's declaration of a compact between the historical novel and science fiction (2015: 298) is suggestive here. For Jameson the connection ultimately involves complementary fictional ways of representing historical process, from Sir Walter Scott to Kim Stanley Robinson – but the more immediate and elementary point of comparison is in the use of words to build a temporarily coherent fictional world that evidently differs from the present-day environment of the author and reader. In relation to this shared task, Farah Mendlesohn offers the formulation: 'all literature builds worlds, but some genres are more honest about it than others' (2008: 59). This provocation would place *Dissident Gardens* or *The Fortress of Solitude* on the same plane as *Girl in Landscape*. What we have seen above is that Lethem, at least in some of his statements, agrees.

Another scene in *Dissident Gardens* subtly allegorizes the point. In 1969, the height of the hippy season, Miriam Zimmer and Cicero Lookins enter a Greenwich Village chess shop, which feels stranded in the past: 'Outside, the world had colors, and likely sounds other than the lung-rattle of opponents not yet informed of their deaths at some earlier date, possibly in the late 1950s. The interior of the chess shop […] was in black and white' (2013a: 60). The historical fiction thus contains a pocket of still older history within itself, a remnant of the uneven development of cultural time. When Miriam and Cicero exit, '1969 was permitted to reassert itself, resume its animation and flow. Though as much a confabulation, surely, as that thickened portion of time trapped behind the chess mezzanine's window, the present had the advantage of being still open to negotiation' (63). 'Confabulation' suggests discussion, as though the present is still a matter of debate, but the element of 'fabulation' in the word also offers its hint of imagination; the present is being collectively made up. The point is given an additional ironic edge by the fact that the fictional 'present' here is in fact over forty years past by the time of writing. In this light, the avowal that the present seems as much a confabulation as the past reacts, implicitly and perhaps only half-consciously, upon the process of the novel itself. It can be paraphrased to say that the present is as much a literary construction as the historical past – which would be a statement akin, in turn, to Lethem's 2001 concession to Jackson, that literary realism offers not the ultimate reality behind the cartoons but another way to do things with words.

Such a stance may be questioned. To claim that the realistic and the mimetic are 'quarantined' from one another rhetorically implies that the quarantine should end and the two should mingle, but it does not necessarily follow that no distinction exists between them. It remains the case, too, that there are objects in *Amnesia Moon* or 'Vanilla Dunk' that are off limits to *Dissident Gardens*; evidently Lethem, like other writers, allows himself to operate certain protocols of the mimetic, and the resulting division between a realist world and a fantastic one may, in practice, seem at least as significant as the fact that they are formed from the same linguistic substance. But Lethem's stance does offer us another way to speculate about where the fantastic has gone, when it does seem to have gone: into the texture of language itself, which can – as we saw in the quotation above about the Brooklyn Bridge – become more distended and adventurous even as the terms of what is permitted in the fictional world are, on this occasion, more conventionally bound to historical reality.

The factors listed above suggest reasons to complicate a simple narrative of Lethem's trajectory. A fifth and final reason can be given: the trajectory is unfinished, and pronouncement on it may be premature. Lethem has so far proved both more versatile and more prolific than many of his contemporaries. A quarter-century into his career as a novelist, he could plausibly announce a forthcoming work that would be space opera, soap opera or some combination of the two. In fact, in 2018 he returned with *The Feral Detective*. The novel is firmly set in the contemporary historical world of 2017, yet makes a return to genre: as such, it confounds some of the criteria discussed above, and demonstrates Lethem's continuing capacity to surprise. The novel may represent another attempt to combine white elephant status and termite tactics. Genre is a system of conventions that can also be constraints. But these constraints, we have seen, can also paradoxically be creatively liberating. An immersion in genre was always among Lethem's primary means of being a termite. It may continue to serve this purpose in the future.

3

Worlds

The characters of Lethem's novel *Chronic City* (2009) discover the existence of a virtual reality site called Yet Another World. Much of it, we are told, is 'pretty much like the world out here – homes, with belongings inside' (2010: 224). People manoeuvre around it with avatars of themselves, acquiring wealth and possessions. This virtual world does not merely mirror the real one, but contains an 'infinity of possible selves and possible neighbourhoods', in which people can take on fantastic identities and form obsessive communities. It also interacts with the real: a character makes 'real money' from his employment in the simulation, which he can cash in for actual commodities (226). Yet Another World is the latest of Lethem's engagements with the idea of virtual reality, a sequence running through his short stories: 'The Happy Man' (1991), in which the contents of a computer game make a Gothic allegory of real life; 'How We Got In Town and Out Again' (1996), where virtual reality provides entertainment in a grim landscape; 'Forever, Said the Duck' (1993), where an entire party happens in virtual space with everyone appearing as a transmutable avatar. As late as 'The Dreaming Jaw, the Salivating Ear' (2009), he reprises the theme in another form, by positing a 'blog' (which seems a purely virtual entity, only notionally a 'place' on the Internet) as a building on a seaside cliff.

This recurrent theme of virtual spaces is part of a still broader fascination with the idea of worlds. The present chapter will explore this theme by reading three of Lethem's early novels – *Girl in Landscape*, *As She Climbed across the Table*, and *Amnesia Moon* – in reverse chronological order to develop a thematic sequence. (As noted in the Introduction, the chronological sequence of the early novels is somewhat misleading – the third novel was being written five years before the second was published – which makes it reasonable to approach them out of the sequence of their publication.)

What, for practical purposes, is a world? The term is slippery, in seeming to demand paraphrase into cognates – 'the zone in which we operate', 'the universe of our perceptions' – which are themselves metonymically related to it. We can say that a world is a space in which subjects exist and things happen. Furthermore, it is not merely a particular, limited space (like a room) but the totality of available space in which action might be attempted: that which is bounded by a – figurative or indeed literal – horizon. Hence the force of the diminution when, for instance, for a character in Samuel Beckett a single room *is* equivalent to the world. Perkus Tooth in *Chronic City* enacts a version of this when, reduced to living in a canine apartment, he finds that the resident dog 'became a kind of new world to him' (2010: 315). For the effective world, the horizon of possibility, to be reduced to such a limited space, appears a severe reduction.

A further emphasis is useful: that a world is not merely an empty space but rather a sphere of experience innately connected with the being occupying it. To talk of someone's world would be to imply their relation to it and their capacity to undertake projects in it. Such a sense of world is implied by the young Samuel Beckett's remark that 'The creation of the world did not take place once and for all time, but takes place every day'. While Beckett's language feints to allude to the world's creation by a deity, he is actually referring to the continual reproduction of the world in subjective experience: 'the world being a projection of the individual's consciousness' (1970: 19). Switching registers, this view can find an echo in Ludwig Wittgenstein's statement that 'The world is *my* world: this is manifest in the fact that the limits of *language* (of that language which alone I understand) mean the limits of *my* world' (1974: 57). The emphasis is now on the enabling role of linguistic frameworks, but the implication remains that a world is something experienced, with limits that correspond to those of the subject in question. Such a perspective sits happily enough with the discussion of literary narratives in which, for instance, the forming of world seems closely bound to the verbal construction of a point of view.

If, in this sense, people have worlds, then do literary texts? An important reference point here is Brian McHale's *Postmodernist Fiction* (1987). The previous chapter noted Lethem's own view of 'postmodernism': at once wary of the term's invitation to generalization and the amount of contested discursive baggage it brings, and profoundly interested in many of the particular aesthetic strategies that have been associated with this label. McHale's emphasis on world-making as a feature of twentieth-century fiction is a notable case in point, and his analysis, by now classic, is a crucial one in this field. Part of its value is that it is not in fact restricted to 'postmodern' writing but offers far-reaching insights into the nature of fiction and worlds *tout court*. It can assist us as, in order to clarify the ground for the analyses ahead, we succinctly name a number of senses of 'world' that directly pertain to fiction.

First there is the real historical world occupied by the author: a world refracted in innumerable ways through fictional narrative, thus providing some of its content and inspiration. This sense of the term was often invoked by Edward Said; a phrase like 'the world, the text and the critic' implies the pressure of the world as a kind of outside to literature (Wood 2003: 3). Lethem is invoking something similar when he compares postmodernism as a mode of fiction with postmodernism as social reality: 'Postmodernism is the street. Postmodernism is the town. It's where we live' (2011: 83). Within this greater world, though, is the phenomenon of the fictional world, effectively located between the covers of a novel (or, to conceive it another way, configured in the mind of the reader from the materials provided on a novel's pages). Drawing on social theory, McHale points out that fictions offer 'subworlds', 'finite provinces of meaning' within a collectively shared experience of the real (1987: 37). The reader necessarily engages with the text to project its provisional world, which is typically larger than that which is actually referred to by a written text. McHale also draws attention to this aspect, drawing on Roman Ingarden's observation that fiction's light illuminates 'part of a region, the remainder of which disappears in an indeterminate cloud' (McHale 1987: 31). Thus, say, Lethem's *Motherless Brooklyn* is entirely set in New York and New England, but we do not doubt that Nebraska or Arizona exist in Lionel Essrog's world, even though he may never mention them. The readerly assumption is to project the world as we know it until given notice not to.

Fiction can deliberately fabricate a world that is clearly understood not to be an analogue of the actual planet Earth to date. This is the case with much fantasy writing, in which artists like J.R.R. Tolkien or Ursula K. Le Guin have produced elaborately codified alternative worlds. Even without such world-constructing labour, an author can still present a world that is in principle different from ours: a technique often essayed by Lethem's shorter works like *This Shape We're In* (2001). Critics of fantasy term these 'otherworlds' (Mendlesohn 2008: 30), which may sometimes be reached by portals from the primary world (classically the entry to Narnia in *The Lion, the Witch and the Wardrobe*) or may take up the whole of a narrative and thus be 'immersive' forms of fantasy (xx). In a comment partially cited in the previous chapter, Farah Mendlesohn remarks that 'The immersive fantasy is both the mirror of mimetic literature and its inner soul. It reveals what is frequently hidden: that all literature builds worlds, but some genres are more honest about it than others' (59). The suggestion is that non-fantastic fiction – which might include *Dissident Gardens* as well as, say, Richard Ford's *The Sportswriter* – engages in a project of rhetorical world-construction analogous to that of Tolkien, yet the project is occluded by the proximity of the 'mimetic' fiction's world to the real.

Fiction may often project a unitary world, self-sufficient in its own terms – whether this is a fictional San Francisco, Earthsea or unnamed space. Indeed one of the connotations of 'world' is such repleteness and self-sufficiency, that beyond which we cannot see. Yet some fiction also troubles this unitary sense, creating a sense of multiple worlds which coexist, collide or overlap. Indeed this tendency is prompted by the very existence of fictional worlds, by definition almost infinite in number, as a phenomenon in the real world: a fact that has stirred the imagination of such writers as Borges or Calvino to write of fictional worlds as internally proliferating and multiplicitous. For McHale, such fictions exemplify an ontological 'dominant': that is, they are less interested in the investigation of an uncertain world through multiple perspectives (what McHale terms 'epistemological' concerns and associates with modernism) than with the construction of worlds in the plural. In Lethem's own *oeuvre*, something of this emphasis will be explored below in *As She Climbed across the Table* and *Amnesia Moon*. Some writers have approached this idea in more openly textual terms. Thus Flann O'Brien's *At Swim-Two-Birds* (1939) depicts a series of narrative levels, one being scripted by another, which cross and interfere with one another, while in Italo Calvino's *If on a Winter's Night a Traveller ...* (1979), an inspiration for *Amnesia Moon*, a series of worlds are equivalent to different pieces of text. Such a coextensiveness between text and world characterizes the most exemplary cases of McHale's 'ontological' fictions. These fictions do not simply represent a plurality of worlds but enact them through a corresponding plurality of narratives. At their purest, as in some of Donald Barthelme's stories, they pit 'worlds of discourse' against each other: another world '*is*, in effect, this other mode of discourse', and 'the only worlds we are able to reconstruct are the worlds *of* discourses, and not any fictional world that might plausibly contain them' (McHale 1987: 164, 169).

Occasionally, Lethem's short fiction approaches such a mode. One short story commences with the startling sentences: 'The Dystopianist destroyed the world again that morning, before making any phone calls or checking his mail, before even breakfast. He destroyed it by cabbages' (2004: 105). These simple lines confound our understandings of the term under review. Part of the surprise of the opening line is in a sense that anyone could simply 'destroy the world' – especially without destroying himself in the act. In this sense our first understanding of the word refers to the primary sense given above: within the tale, the idiomatic phrase 'the world' appears to imply that it is the real world's fate that is at stake. Yet the developing context suggests that 'the world' is a fiction; that within Lethem's fictional world, the Dystopianist (an author) has produced a fiction in which the world is destroyed. His narrative is a kind of nihilistic, apocalyptic fantasy.

Yet the story does not allow these senses to remain clearly distinct. As the Dystopianist changes his fictional idea from apocalyptic cabbages to a flock of suicidal sheep, he answers a knock on the door, and finds a talking sheep on his doorstep. An item from the character's imagination has suddenly, inexplicably come to life, in effect crossing from one world to another. The emphasis of the story is on the curious reality of the sheep, which cuts athwart the Dystopianist's abstract project of fictional world-destruction. The sheep seems to belong in a different world – more detailed, cluttered, even more naturalistic, notwithstanding the presence of talking sheep – from the one the Dystopianist had intended. A story like this takes Lethem a little closer to the fictional practice of Barthelme or John Barth. But in truth, such a flagrant conflation of writing and world-formation is not the primary mode of Lethem's full-length novels. Indeed, he has gone out of his way to emphasize that his writing is not 'experimental' (2011: 136), as Barthelme was. Nonetheless, McHale's broader identification of an interest in world-making does offer a pertinent context for the novels that will be considered below.

'World' has one other concrete and relatively simple meaning. It can refer to a planet, a large sphere of matter travelling rapidly through outer space. Understandably, 'world' and 'Earth' – the only physical world that most humans have inhabited – are conveniently conflated in everyday speech. Yet the present inquiry needs to reach beyond this identification, as the spoken prologue to the television series *Star Trek* (1966–9) does in describing a five-year mission 'to explore strange new worlds'. Adam Roberts writes that it is 'axiomatic that science fiction depends on this notion of a plurality of worlds, and might even be defined as that genre that enters imaginatively into precisely that "otherness" (of worlds, of inhabitants and, by extension, of times)' (2006: 49). McHale, too, notes the importance of science fiction as a model for the creation of fictional worlds (1987: 59–72). As a writer rooted in science fiction, Lethem partakes of this sense of 'world' and its related acts of world-making, and the self-consciousness about worlds that results from this. His major work in this regard is *Girl in Landscape* (1998), to which we now turn.

The Final Frontier

'Space' has two major connotations. It can refer to the scene of human practices, as one might refer to a performance space or the space available on a sports field. This sense of space is in question in the work of Gaston Bachelard, Henri Lefebvre and other theorists of humans' occupation of the world. But the word also has the blunter meaning of outer space, so that 'theories of space' may concern urban planning or the distribution of asteroid fields. The ambiguity is strongly recalled by *Girl in Landscape*, which is at once the work in Lethem's *oeuvre* most concerned with space exploration and interplanetary discovery, and a work deeply engaged with space in the geographical or cartographical sense suggested by its title. When Lethem himself discusses the novel, he talks of its 'completely propositional space' (Clarke 2011: 127). The following discussion will explore the spaces proposed by this novel as it comes to envisage a new world.

The novel follows the Marsh family's emigration from a future Brooklyn to a distant planet, known only as the Planet of the Archbuilders after its native inhabitants. In the short first section, *Brooklyn Heights*, the mother, Caitlin Marsh, is suddenly stricken with illness, and dies in hospital, though not before introducing knowledge about the planet to her children. In the long middle section, *The Planet of the Archbuilders*, thirteen-year-old Pella Marsh explores the planet and encounters its inhabitants: the Kincaid family, local shopkeepers and workers, the forbidding outsider Efram Nugent and the indigenous life of the planet. The planet contains viruses that are thought to alter humans; human settlers take pills to avert these risks. Pella's father Clement, a former politician, has determined that his family will not take the pills but will encounter the planet in all its strangeness, even if this means being transformed by it. Pella accordingly finds herself in a fugue state in which her consciousness periodically enters the body of a tiny lifeform, 'household deer', as it travels the planet's surface and witnesses a range of encounters. Human settlers and the mild, absent-minded Archbuilders appear to exist in a truce, yet as the novel progresses these relations are strained and some settlers, with Efram as figurehead, turn on and scapegoat the natives for alleged sexual deviancy. This plot culminates in the death of Efram at the hands of another human teen, Doug Grant. The novel's brief coda, entitled *Caitlin*, shows the survivors starting again to construct a new town named after Pella's mother, while Archbuilders take over the empty home of their sometime persecutor Efram.

The novel is driven by location and mood as much as plot. Its typical action involves, say, Pella walking or running across the desert valley of her new planet from one homestead to another, in a traversal of space that is also, in this context, the mapping of a new world. The movement of a given character from one place on the map to the next constitutes much of the novel's action, which helps to make sense of Pella's thought that 'It was like the men were playing a board game' (Lethem 1998a: 104). Spatial terms and modes of perception proliferate. Diana Eastling, a long-term resident, informs Clement that 'I came here to make my own space [...] Most of us did' (168). The narrative plays upon variable perceptions of space and distance. Vast vistas are viewed: 'The sky was peach-hued, awesome and empty, no variation to give it more than two dimensions, or fewer than a billion' (127). Lethem here ingeniously plays on an arbitrary sense of the scale of perception, in which the huge desert sky might be seen either as simple or immensely complex, viewed telescopically or microscopically. Likewise a glass of lemonade holds 'a tiny galaxy of grains' (192), as though the interplanetary scale across which the characters have already moved to reach this planet is itself contained in microcosm within it. Lethem's gloss on his own novel confirms the emphasis on spatial perception and the formation of a world:

> *Girl in Landscape* and *Amnesia Moon*, the desert books, are very strongly connected for me to Mark Rothko's paintings, to the way certain abstract painters depict the horizon line (but then deny that they're painting landscapes). Just thinking about space, human space, the act of walking across a room or a desert floor, towards a horizon line that defines the human space. (Clarke 2011: 112)

This vision connects to another key element. It appears axiomatic that a novel set on a distant planet is science fiction; but *Girl in Landscape* also draws deeply on the genre of the Western, which in a variety of media – painting, dime novels, comic books, and most influentially the cinema – has told stories of the struggle for the American West in the nineteenth century. In connecting science fiction and the Western, Lethem is joining a tradition. As John Rieder observes, both genres have been closely concerned with the frontier: 'Much American SF reconstructs the nation's mythic pioneering past as a science fictional future, transferring both the symbolic and ideological values of the American frontier and the tropes of the American Western to outer space' (2015: 167). The single most pertinent precursor text is among the most celebrated of all Western films, John Ford's *The Searchers* (1956), in which John Wayne's character Ethan Edwards leads an obsessive quest to recover his niece Debbie (Natalie Wood) from the Comanche tribe. Lethem draws on the film partly to echo its questions of race and otherness, and the figure of Efram Nugent accordingly makes for a compellingly close shadow of Wayne's character, down to his patterns and emphases of speech. Yet a broader element of the genre is its own display of landscape – above all in the 'Monument Valley' of Arizona where Ford made a series of classic films showing equestrian characters against the mesas, mountains and desert horizons. Lethem's fictional desert planet, strewn with the broken monuments of the natives, deliberately recalls this.

On an interpersonal level, the distance between characters is intensely felt. In her first encounter, Pella feels exposed, 'out in the middle of the valley, without even a porch for context. It seemed mistakes of scale were possible in this alien landscape' (81). Walking to her house with Efram, Pella feels uneasy at the unwanted proximity, 'the sudden implicit alliance', and runs 'up the porch steps ahead of him' to re-establish her autonomy from his approach, then feels 'a strange panic that he might enter the house' (82). The disturbing significance of this new character is thus felt in highly spatial terms. Exploring the surrounding environment, the group of children make 'a survey of the outer valley […] the zone of the solitary adults, the ones on the edge of the town, outside the world of families' (95). Geographical space is thus dissected and imaginatively mapped out into its different 'zones' or indeed multiple 'worlds'. Yet these distinctions prove unstable and mutable: 'The houses out in this direction weren't any farther apart than those the three families lived in. It was as wrong to consider the place Efram and Diana Eastling and Hugh Merrow lived the outskirts as it was to call the houses to the east a town. They were each only clusters of crumbs on a vast plate' (96–7). This perception literally decentres Pella's known world, disconcertingly suggesting that everything is an 'outskirt'; the centre, with its thinly clustered homesteads, cannot hold. Pella's point of view also dismisses the settlement's claim to be much of a location at all: nameless, it is 'this place on the edge of nothing' (63). But dislocation can have its appeal: separating from the other children, Pella runs 'nowhere', 'to be in a place by herself' (102–3), while her brother Raymond also secretly mourns his mother at the base of a ruin, 'a nowhere on the human map of the valley' (160).

The 'ruined land' of the valley is described as an 'unhaunted, impersonal emptiness' (164–5). But in another uncanny process, human subjects seem to merge with this place. This happens above all to Efram, who is first seen on a ridge as 'almost like another of the broken arches on the horizon, somehow' – in another troubling shift of proximity – 'drawn suddenly close' (80). A page later his smile seems 'carved in rock' (81). Later, suddenly breaking up a meeting, he stands 'like a statue in the sunlit doorway' (140). Even his conversation is 'like the Archbuilder landscape, a series of things broken off' (153), and his words draw Pella into it:

> He handled her secrets so casually, like they and she were features of the landscape now.
>
> She *was* a feature of the landscape.
>
> She and Efram had that in common, she because she ran over it, hid in it, and he because he was like a chunk of it, broken off and ambulatory. The last intact tower. (173)

The image recurs at the novel's climax: he has become 'a faceless shape in front of her now, a part of the horizon, a craggy ruin. She could no more bring him down with her to the ground than topple the ragged monoliths in the distance' (255). And it is at last made literal when his body is subjected to an Archbuilder burial above ground: 'the figure turned the color of the valley floor, became another outcropping of the Planet' (277). *Girl in Landscape*, plainly, envisages this menacing man *as* landscape: partly due to his qualities of bulk and intimidation, partly as a way of conveying his deep ties to this alien land that he has inhabited longer than perhaps any other human character. All this unmistakably refracts what Lethem writes of John Wayne in 'Defending *The Searchers*': 'a sort of baked and broken monolith himself', he is filmed to 'loom like those distant towers of rock' (2005: 2, 10).

But place and space, above all that of the Planet, surround and inflect every figure in this story. When the children are brought indoors for an attempted school class, the spatial shift makes them 'feel they were creatures of the valley now, as much as the Archbuilders, maybe more' (135). In the same scene, an Archbuilder responds to the suggestion that the pupils are not all at the same educational 'level' by literalizing the spatial metaphor and ingenuously noting that 'We are all reading on the same planet'. The remark appears banal, but the teacher Joe Kincaid tries to make sense of it by concurring: 'I guess that's the point. One thing that's certain is we're on the same planet' (135). Space is a unifying factor for these beings of different age and species; in at least one literal sense, they share a world.

The novel's first world is Brooklyn. Though most of the book's action takes place far from Earth, it is emotionally rooted back in the events in the future New York that Lethem sketches here. In certain flourishes he fully establishes the tale's science-fictional credentials. A trip to Coney Island via subway turns out not to mean the clanking F train familiar to New Yorkers, but an alternative technology in which the family's domestic basement holds its own subway car, 'silent and ready in its port, its burnished shell radiant in the gloom' (5). The passenger keys in a destination, and the car is 'clipped' to a passing train (5–6). Caitlin Marsh talks of a time 'before the network, when it was just a few trains, real trains that everyone rode on together' (6). 'Network' now evidently signifies a system in which private subway cars are drawn in and out of the public mechanism, deposited in a 'vast parking garage under the station' on arrival. In effect, this future transport is a hybrid of private car and public railway. Lethem's future world estrangingly differs from the present, while retaining enough trace of it to support the emotional story: Pella on the subway 'was in a place where she belonged, under New York City, her family in their private car a discrete unit in a teeming hive' (7).

The larger novelty of this future New York is ecological. The first paragraph tells us that the family 'were going to the beach, so their bodies had to be sealed against the sun' (1). This statement's full meaning becomes clearer as we read of the characters' 'sun cones' (4), transparent shells that they don on reaching the outside world of the beach (8). Lethem renders the quotidian awkwardness of these items, strange to us yet taken for granted by his characters: little David complaining that his cone is too big, his mother replying 'That's good [...] You won't get burned. Better than too small'; Pella raising the side of her cone to feel a concrete wall (8). Climate change has made the outside world almost uninhabitable; solar radiation, without the mediation of Earth's atmosphere, is deadly. Caitlin casually remarks that the Planet of the Archbuilders is inhabitable because they 'didn't ruin their ozone' (13). Thus the domestic window Pella looks out of is 'darkened to blunt the sun' (4), and emergence from the subway brings 'SURFACE WARNING' signs (7–8). Pella feels 'climate-control devices' thrumming everywhere in the underground world, 'Everywhere except where they were going: outside' (8). Here at last the family, save for their protective cones, is exposed to the sky:

> the vaulting empty spaciousness of it. The blue or gray she'd seen framed through so many tinted windows, unbound now, explosive. Endlessly vaulting away from her eye.
> And the sun, the enemy: horrible, impossible, unseeable. (9)

The sky, rarely seen directly in this world, exerts power over Pella, as Lethem limns a Coney Island that has become a wasteland. The Atlantic Ocean is fended off by a barrier, but Pella gazes out to it:

> Even this distance exhausted Pella's gaze, from the sand where she stood to the place past the fence where the darker sand met the sulfurous, glistening ocean. Even before she grappled with the edge where the water met the sky. Even before she grappled with the sky.

> And now she was supposed to be able to look past that sky, into space. Caitlin wanted her to. But even the expanse of sand was space enough, too much. (10)

Here Lethem's own narrative puns on 'space', finding the outer space beyond the sky analogous to the terrestrial space of the beach. The passage begins to suggest that Brooklyn and the Planet of the Archbuilders, while vastly distant from each other, are connected. Most simply, the abandoned beach resembles an alien planet: a Coney Island ruined by climate change is a harbinger of life on another, inhospitable world. More specifically, the location is scattered with ruins: 'the blackened armatures of the abandoned amusement park', the Cyclone rollercoaster now 'a cat's cradle of ravaged iron that looked helpless and naked in the sun', its name echoed in 'the sprawling, pitched ribbon of cyclone fence' holding back the sea (9). This will find its echo in the ruined landscape of the Archbuilders, whose arches have crumbled: 'Eroded spires that rose a thousand feet into the air. Fallen bridges, incomplete towers, demolished pillars. The valley was a monumental roofless cathedral with only the buttresses intact' (48).

If the Brooklyn beach thus offers a premonition of life on an alien world, Pella perceives that this is part of Caitlin's intention in taking her and the two boys on the outing:

> The family was moving to a distant place, an impossible place. Distance itself haunted them, the distance they had yet to go. It had infected them, invaded the space of their family. So the trip to the beach was a blind, a small expedition to cover talk of the larger one. (1)

In just the second full paragraph of the novel, Lethem subtly sows its seeds: movement, place, the 'impossibility' of a place; distance; 'space', that primary category, which is also already 'invaded' (a phrase with science-fictional connotations), in parallel with a process of 'infection' (in a novel founded on the illness that overtakes Caitlin). The beach trip is 'a small expedition to cover talk of the larger one', but also preparation for it, a miniature model of that larger expedition to another, more distant desert. Likewise, at the beach, the boys ponder whether to construct a 'castle' or a 'fort', glossed as, on one hand, 'like a town. People live there […] It's permanent', and on the other 'a war thing […] just for being attacked' (10–11). The distinction only partially seems to map on to later events, in which no real 'fort' or 'war' features; but as the boys opt for the simpler and purely defensive 'fort', the unbuilt 'castle' will be echoed in the absent 'town' later: 'Isn't a town', insists little Morris Grant in the face of talk of a town, repeating 'Isn't any town' (196, 198). The castle, in the terms of the boys on the beach, is not successfully built.

In this Brooklyn that already resembles an alien planet, Caitlin builds an imaginative bridge across space to connect the two. Raymond's 'imagination', from the start, is 'straining to reach the place the family would go'; Caitlin seeks to encourage and ease this, as she 'spun the place into existence before their eager eyes' (2). Pella can 'hear her mother making the idea of the family moving to the Planet of the Archbuilders real, inflating it to fill the space' (7) left by the failure of Clement's political career. Again space is the primary element, here something that can be filled or improved with words; Caitlin's 'talk' is 'sweeping' the family away as the subway has swept them to the beach (13). Through the first chapter, she discloses much information about the Archbuilders and their Planet: partly a narrative convenience for Lethem, this also strongly seals Pella's association of her mother with the journey. After her collapse and illness, Caitlin continues relaying such facts, out of a book (31–3). The mother and the journey become more tightly wound together than ever: 'Pella's family was distorting, wrenching itself into a new shape in two realms: Caitlin's strange, rebelling body, her illness; and the impending move, the frontier that seemed to be rushing to swallow them like a horizon in motion' (32). Characteristically, the novel spatializes the issue, thinking in terms of a distorting 'shape' and twin 'realms' – another rough synonym for 'worlds' – then invoking two closely connected and telling words. 'Frontier' connotes the American West of the nineteenth century – a central influence on the imagination of this novel – but is here transposed into space, like James T. Kirk's 'final frontier'. The 'horizon', too, is an image with much potency in the Western genre – as John G. Cawelti remarks, the Western hero is often viewed in 'that scene of man against the sky' (1976: 200) – but also, as we have seen, a term closely entwined with the conception of a world.

The other suggestion of the passage above is an analogy between space, or world, and body. The novel has already thought this through explicitly, after Caitlin's first fall: 'Her naked body seemed terribly big, a kind of world itself, a thing with horizons, places where Pella's gaze could founder, be lost' (23). The image is reminiscent of J.G. Ballard's repeated conflation of body and landscape in his fragmented prose work *The Atrocity Exhibition* (1968), but rendered in another key: personal and melancholy, rather than Ballard's impersonal coolness. This image will be played out through the novel as Pella literally wanders or gets lost in 'a kind of world', 'a thing with horizons'. An equivalent image also closes the book's first section, highlighting the density of its language: in subtly, insidiously repeating and varying its images, the prose of the novel has some of the qualities of poetry. The surgical incision into Caitlin's head, attempting to remove her tumour, is inseparably analogous in Pella's mind from 'The tunneling devices that had hollowed out too much of the city's bedrock', hence causing 'the collapse of the subway' and in turn the end of Clement's political career (37). A compulsive, neurotic power of association guides the mind of character, and by extension reader, from one troubling image to the next, moving up and down the scale from subjective to objective, woman to landscape, micro (one human brain) to macro (the New York subway system). The journey through space, which might have made a whole novel in itself, is despatched in one sentence – 'a tiny ship where they were frozen alive for a trip that lasted twenty months, but seemed to them an eye blink, a dream' (38–9) – leaving Lethem to focus again on imaginative analogy: 'It was as though Clement had replaced Caitlin with the ship. As though they had tunneled inside her departing body for comfort and escape. They hurtled with it into the void' (39). The notion of the mother, or her body, as analogous with a space never quite leaves the novel, through to Pella's final renaming of the town (where once, it was insistently said, there wasn't any town) after Caitlin: 'Because Caitlin brought them here' (279).

We have seen that the Planet of the Archbuilders is compulsively linked back to the overheating world of Brooklyn. Yet it is also a new world, which confronts human arrivals with its strangeness. In this regard the novel resembles Farah Mendlesohn's category of the 'portal-quest fantasy': a journey into the unknown involving 'transition and exploration' (2008: 2), in which the reader closely follows the protagonist's own hesitant acquisition of knowledge. Indeed Mendlesohn openly says that such a narrative is close to 'the classic utopian or alien-planet story' (xix). In such a text, 'the need to describe and explain remains a driving force'; its narrative trajectory is to 'lead us gradually to the point where the protagonist knows his or her own world enough to change it and to enter into that world's destiny' (2008: xix). That is an accurate description of this novel.

Girl in Landscape also belongs to the sub-genre of the planetary romance: a tranche of science fiction concerned with the exploration of a new, extra-terrestrial world, whether in its geology, biology or social relations. The novel is unusual in Lethem's *oeuvre* in the length it goes to construct this new world, as reasonably internally coherent even if not conceived with the exhaustiveness of a Tolkien or Asimov. Lethem necessarily enters into the task of world construction, inventing alien flora ('The little vine led down into a moist crevice, where it turned into a yellow-green lace of veins covering a rubbery, translucent sac': the Archbuilders' so-called potatoes [49]) and fauna ('tiny figures [...] miniature quicksilver giraffe': the household deer [46]). He must also conjure the Archbuilders themselves, in a series of descriptions that may prove hard to gather into a coherent image: 'flesh and fur and shell and frond [...] the black leather of its ears and eyelids [...] the fur was everywhere, under the papery clothes, and it was black, too, smooth and tufted, perhaps faintly musky' (61). Lethem has remarked: 'People get angry at me because I can't confirm their impressions of what an Archbuilder looks like! I ought to say "if I knew I'd tell you", but a more honest response would be "if I knew I wouldn't have been interested in writing about them", or "if either you or I knew I would have failed"' (Clarke 2011: 33). By these lights, the aliens' elusiveness is better grasped not as an aesthetic failure but as an attempt to maintain strangeness rather than domesticate it and render it. Tellingly, when children and aliens gather in the schoolroom, 'Though no one admitted to fear of the Archbuilders, the children had given them plenty of room' (135). The fullest account of a human reaction to their strangeness is in Pella's first encounter, when 'the Archbuilder burned a hole in the world, changed it utterly' (62). Lethem's language here signals how world-construction can also involve a degree of estrangement that is world-breaking. The same applies when Pella, disoriented by waking in the planet's landscape, reflects on her mother's fate: 'Had Caitlin woken into a world as strange as this?' (78).

Pella can feel dismayed, at least initially, by the planet's mysteriousness: 'If the fish in the jar weren't important, something else would be, and she would have to learn that something else on her own. No one else could be counted on to tell her. She felt the burden of this lonely knowledge fall on her, instantly' (66). She later thinks of it with frustration as 'The Planet of Withheld Explanations' (94). The lines signal the author's awareness that 'knowledge' is at a premium in such an invented environment; that the measure of 'cognition' demanded by Darko Suvin needs a degree of 'explanation' to get off the ground. Much of the pertinent factual information about these inhabitants of the planet – from the Archbuilders' relation to language (32) to the tendency to 'witness' via household deer (16) – has in fact been provided by Caitlin in the first chapters: her surrogate planetary 'info-dump' is prompted by her enthusiasm for the family's new adventure, and in turn helps to seal the association that Pella makes between the planet and her mother. Other information is yielded by other narrative devices, such as the children's quite systematic spying tour of the different homesteads of the valley under the knowledgeable guidance of Bruce Kincaid (91–8). Lastly, the household deer themselves provide a means of narrative exploration, literally offering a way to 'witness' a range of geographical and social scenes: strikingly, for instance, when unknowingly occupying the body of the deer allows Pella's point of view to penetrate a dialogue between men at which she would not normally be present (103–7).

The novelist can thus be seen about the activity of world-building. In another sense, so can his characters. The human settlers on the Planet are, for the most part, not undertaking a radical reconstruction of the physical environment; their physical actions do not extend much further than building houses. (In keeping with the novel's strongly architectural imagination, we are shown a prefabricated house under construction and, conversely, the destruction of a ruined one [92, 224].) More figuratively, though, they are tentatively seeking to remake their new world, by forging a community. In a suggestively geological image, Efram calls the process 'breaking new ground' (106), while doubting that the new arrivals will see it through.

The project has numerous instances and signs. In E.G. Wa's general store, Pella notices the 'optimistically full pot of coffee' and trio of rocking chairs 'arrayed for the nonexistent coffee drinkers' (53). The rocking chairs are a nod to the longing for such a chair on the part of the character Old Mose in *The Searchers* – where the image thus primarily suggests ease and rest after life's struggle – but in the new context of the novel, the empty chairs image a community waiting to be born. Wa sets up a series of barter arrangements with fellow inhabitants, offering credit for Archbuilder potatoes or buying bread from Martha Kincaid: in short, trying to institute an economy, as the basis of a society (52, 230). The bid to start a school, teaching children along with Archbuilders, is the most ambitious sign of the attempt to forge a society in the valley (134). Here again the novel's iconography is happy to come close to the Western. In John Ford's film *The Man Who Shot Liberty Valance* (1962), the character of Ransom Stoddard (James Stewart) is a lawyer who stands for the civilizing influence of the East over a wild West occupied by, among others, another loner played by John Wayne. Among Stoddard's major projects is the establishment of a school where townspeople are encouraged to learn English and the importance of political organization. Mexican children are seen learning their alphabet, rather as the Archbuilders join the 'kindergarten' of Clement Marsh and Joe Kincaid (137). Ford's scene is a strong association in the background of Lethem's schoolroom scenario, which is disrupted by Efram just as much of Stoddard's work is challenged by Wayne's character Tom Doniphon.

Over a decade earlier, in striking black-and-white cinematography, Ford had staged a still more iconic scene of the forging of civilization in the American West: the walk to a half-completed church taken by Wyatt Earp (Henry Fonda) and the eponymous schoolteacher (Cathy Downs) in *My Darling Clementine* (1946). Clement Marsh surely draws his forename not only from his even-tempered liberalism, but from Ford's film, taken as one of the genre's great allegories of the cultivation of the Western wilderness. Diana Eastling tells Clement that she approves of his arrival: 'You people with children will make yourselves a town. Tame the wilderness' (72). Ben Barth, still more ambitiously, avers to an Archbuilder that Clement, with his political background, will 'scrape us up into some kind of society. Be the first real civilization on this planet since your great-great-grand-whatever and their pals built those arches'. Clement characteristically disavows the ambition – 'I'm just here to join the community' – but his modest statement cannot help but contain aspiration, as it is optimistic to think that there even is a community on the planet at this stage. The Archbuilder Hiding Kneel thus elevates Clement's potential for political organization with a signature play on words: 'I'm in a state of anticipation, anticipating statehood' (67). Again a link can be traced to Ford, for in *Liberty Valance* a central plank of Stoddard's civilizing project is to transform the mere district into a fully fledged state and connect it to the rest of the Union.

The issue is directly taken up in one of the rare moments when Lethem's novel turns its attention from the Planet back to Earth. In a confrontation with Efram over how far settlers should adapt to the local environment, Clement states that 'Emigration to the American sector of this planet is governed by a man named David Hardly out of an office in Washington D.C. I applied there, Efram, and I guess you did too. [...] Until someone explains otherwise I'll assume we're under Hardly's jurisdiction here' (119). This is the only moment that the Planet's 'American sector', sounding like a memory of Cold War Berlin, is mentioned. Clement's claim seems irrefutable under Earth law, but cuts little ice with Efram, for whom *de facto* trumps *de jure* order. '[G]rinning around his pipe', in telling mimicry of the intonation of John Wayne, he scornfully replies: '*Jurisdiction* [...] Now you're talking like a politician. Making sense like one, too. Dave Hardly's never even been up here. I've been living here seven years, mostly alone. You decide who you want to listen to' (119). The rough rule of the maverick outguns the earnest appeal to law, founded as it is in a state unimaginably far away. Lethem's names are often deliberately telling, and that of 'Hardly' appears to indicate the sway that his jurisdiction holds. The distinction between legalistic perception and brutal reality corresponds to the one that Efram draws – drawing on Lethem's own reading of Jorge Luis Borges – between 'The map and the territory', which only an innocent outsider would confuse (118).

Either way, Clement's or Efram's, implies the occupation of land. For all the sanctity of 'jurisdiction' and civilization, the taming of the West always held its own ambiguities. To forge a civilization in the 'wilderness' might be an advance on the chaotic gunslinging of the villainous Liberty Valance or Wyatt

Earp's nemeses the Clanton gang. Yet the supposed wilderness had already been inhabited for centuries before the arrival of settlers of European origin; a fact about which the Western genre has often been uneasy. John Rieder comments that some, typically more recent, narratives of the frontier have envisioned it 'not as an empty place waiting to be penetrated and settled by intrepid pioneers but as a meeting place between cultures and civilizations, a borderland or contact zone where there are always two sides to any story, and where exploring the radical differences between those two sides often becomes the heart of the adventure' (2015: 167). The observation is highly pertinent to *Girl in Landscape*, which is much occupied by questions of the right to occupy land. World-forming might mean remaking the world in one's own image, and erasing another's. Just arrived on the planet, Pella thinks of the surviving Archbuilders as 'like ghosts haunting the abandoned mansion of their own civilization'. The thought prompts another, more pointed: 'So what were the human families? Ghosts haunting someone else's mansion?' (49). It is telling in this context that the name of the planet wavers, in Pella's frustrated thought, from the primary Planet of the Archbuilders to the 'Planet of Efram' (258). Her final naming of the nascent town as Caitlin (279) is a more official blazon of ownership, if over a far smaller territory.

During the novel, the sense that human beings have claimed territory is sometimes highlighted, above all through the character of Efram. On her first encounter with his farm, encircled with its 'crooked wire fence', Pella reflects that 'Other homes clung to the floor of the valley like shells on a beach; this farm carved out a portion of the planet' (98). The farm is later seen as 'an enchanted circle, a zone of meaning' (175). Pella's perception is that other homesteads have merely, almost literally, scratched the surface, while Efram's dwelling has put down older roots and more authoritatively claimed its land. Thus 'She'd arrived on the Planet of the Archbuilders at last. The rest had been a facade' (175). Late in the novel she reflects more elaborately that Efram's buildings feel 'solid, planted': the farm is 'the place where human beings grew into the ground, knitted together with the Planet, and became permanent' (251).

Efram's power of ownership, though, extends even beyond his own home: temporarily occupying Diana Eastling's house, he 'moved through it as casually as if he owned it. They had entered his space. Possibly any space he had inhabited was his, the way he moved his shoulders to carve the air' (112). The character's occupation of space is thus double: implicit everywhere he goes, with its sense of the pioneer's right to the land he has discovered, along with the more explicit, physically visible plantation of his own home. To Pella, his very speech is 'a low ambient insinuation that wanted to surround her, take over the world' (114), but in the same conversation he is also talking more directly of the mechanisms of colonization: 'I think we ought to draw a line around this town we're starting here, Marsh', excluding Archbuilders and enforcing 'a *human* settlement' (114). Clement views this as a paranoid desire to 'become a little embattled preserve' (115), and is the only character to state the natives' own rights: 'This planet belongs to the Archbuilders' (115). Clement restates the principle to the Archbuilder Hiding Kneel himself, accused of misconduct: 'Don't let them do this to you. This is your place' (247). Clement's defence of Hiding Kneel's rights, as rooted in the 'place' of the Planet itself, is abruptly cut off by the vigilantes. Yet it finds a kind of vindication at the book's close when Efram's house is occupied by Archbuilders (279).

The new world of humans is founded on the evacuation of someone else's world. The novel thus stands with the revisionist Western as a postcolonial work, reflecting on the expropriation that often precedes or enables civilization. Yet there is something still more complex about Lethem's Planet, signalled by the strangely benign attitude of the Archbuilders themselves to their fate. It is not merely that they have been disciplined into a friendly resignation, as co-operative Native Americans may be in a Western narrative. It is also that they themselves are repeatedly said to be the remnant of a greater civilization which willingly departed the planet. Caitlin explains that 'There was a time before when the Archbuilders were very good at science' (5). With their 'strange science', they 'used viruses to build arches and a lot of other stuff, and then they changed the weather, so it was always warm and there was plenty of food around': at which point the Archbuilders' *'temperament'* changed. 'Some of them', Caitlin concludes, 'went into space. And the ones who stayed forgot a lot of stuff they knew before' (7). The precise truth of this back-story is uncertain. The broken ruins of the planet remain mysterious, a set of half-finished or half-baked tales. Clement confirms that 'The Archbuilders remade their world from the ground up' (116); Hiding Kneel alludes briefly to 'those who reshaped our world and then abandoned us to it' (137). The fullest vision comes from Efram, as the disdainful scourge of actual Archbuilders turns out to be an admirer of their predecessors: 'They remade their planet, built a civilization, and then they figured out a way to do the greatest thing anyone's ever done – explore the stars' (179).

The history of the world the settlers inhabit thus becomes more complex. For one thing, there is Efram's remarkable declaration that the original Archbuilders deliberately bequeathed the planet to humanity: 'Why else do you think we can breathe the air, drink the water? They invited us up to get a look around here, give us a taste of getting off Earth, to face us with a choice. We could try to follow them to the stars, to the real frontier, or we could bog down here with these idiots' (181). Chris Pak (2016) has outlined the importance of geoengineering in the history of science fiction, from H.G. Wells and Olaf Stapledon to Kim Stanley Robinson's Mars Trilogy. Broadly, geoengineering tends to imply colonization of space by humanity, remaking other worlds in the image of our own (even as Earth itself, as in *Girl in Landscape*, may become uninhabitable and necessitate the exile to other planets). The difference in Efram's account is that the geoengineering seems to have been done in advance, by the alien race. This version – 'They invited us up' – conveniently erases the ethical decisions and violence involved in colonizing another world. But the novel does not give us any particular reason to doubt Efram's tale, which seems corroborated, as he says, by the convenient inhabitability of the climate and atmosphere for humans. As the settling of the Planet goes from being a bold act of expropriation to the polite acceptance of an invitation, it also provides Efram with another historical narrative to cleave to: one in which there are good and bad Archbuilders, and the good ones are all conveniently absent. The pattern echoes the apocryphal Western phrase: 'The only good Injun is a dead Injun'. The only true Archbuilder is one that is long departed.

This pattern of thought recalls the complex relation that Wayne's screen characters, including Ethan Edwards, actually had with Native Americans, who are as apt to be respected as despised. The big white man is less simple than he looks. In a direct replication of this pattern, Efram turns out to be the only human settler fluent in the Archbuilders' tongue (151), and his home is decorated as a reconstruction of their historic architecture (175–6). Yet it remains crucial that his appreciation is entirely directed to the past, where it has no risk of involvement with the complexities of the present. Hiding Kneel, showing himself shrewder than Efram allows, observes this as a recurrent structure of thought. 'Efram Nugent's love of ancestors is quite poignant', he politely remarks, and Pella's feeling for Caitlin is an analogous case of 'the superiority of your lost ancestors' (239): 'you speak of her as legendary, like my departed fore-cousins', but 'perhaps those departed only seem greater to us because they are gone' (240). The alien's insight is one of the novel's most profound, placing in question not just Efram's account but, more radically, the point of view around which the book is primarily shaped. The planet of ruins is an apt location for people who venerate a lost past. A monument valley is not, it turns out, the easiest place to forge a new world.

Pella and her family might be not so much colonists as latecomers. Their belated inhabitation of this world suggests a term favoured by Lethem in a quite different context: what 'The Ecstasy of Influence' calls 'second use'. That term suggests poaching and recycling: the newspaper used to wrap fish, the narrative remade in fan fiction. Lethem's peroration for it talks of art's vocation 'to make the world larger' (2011: 105). By that token, human settlers' use of the Planet of the Archbuilders makes something – even the beginnings of a world – from what would otherwise go to waste. But the point must cut both ways. If humans are able to make a world of this semi-abandoned planet, so too the Archbuilders finally make their own use of the dwellings abandoned by humans. They are gracious enough hosts not to insist that they alone are entitled to such second use.

World-Spheres

As She Climbed across the Table is set around the campus of Beauchamp University in Northern California, where Philip Engstrand is an anthropologist of academic life, a scholar of 'departmental politics and territorial squabbles' (2001: 6). His partner Alice Coombs works in a particle physics lab, where her manager Professor Soft has generated a new universe. Failing to develop as planned, this phenomenon becomes known as 'Lack': a 'breach' or 'portal' in the fabric of reality. Soft seeks to examine this, along with an Italian physics team led by the effervescent Professor Braxia. Alice declares her love for Lack, detaching herself emotionally and physically from Philip. The lovelorn Philip spends the novel trying to invent ways to win her back. Meanwhile his progress is accompanied by two blind men, Evan and Garth, whom Alice had planned to use as experimental subjects. The pair provide an eccentric commentary on events, and Philip also almost becomes romantically involved with a 'couples therapist', Cynthia Jalter, who is working on the blind men's relationship. In the course of the novel, scientists try to insert various objects into Lack: some disappear into its maw, some are refused, with apparent arbitrariness. Braxia eventually explains Lack's logic to Philip: unknown to her, it has taken on Alice's own character and preferences. A number of characters also wish to enter Lack themselves; most fail. Philip finally succeeds in doing so, and discovers that Evan and Garth have gone before him. As the novel closes, Alice is about to join Philip inside this new dimension.

In various ways, this novel is concerned with worlds. First, the novel proffers its own fictional world, one that bears a loose resemblance to the real yet is also deliberately a zone of its own. Its stylistic debt to Don DeLillo's *White Noise* does much to shape its world. This passage is exemplary:

> Days passed. Classes were taught, seminars held. Papers were handed in, graded, and returned. The team won something, and the trees filled with garlands of toilet paper. It rained, and the toilet paper dripped to the pathways, and into the wiper blades of parked cars. A group of students seized the Frank J. Bellhope Memorial Aquarium to protest the treatment of Roberta, the manatee savant. The protest was a failure. I called a symposium on the history of student seizure of campus buildings. The symposium was a success. (23)

The sense of the passage of time, occupied by quotidian events and almost randomly unpredictable ones, recalls that experienced by DeLillo's narrator Jack Gladney, whose internal admonition 'Let's enjoy these aimless days while we can' (DeLillo 1985: 18) underlies his approach to the first part of *White Noise*. A pattern akin to Lethem's chronicle of events can be discerned in DeLillo's narration of the advent of Autumn: 'Soon the streets were covered with leaves. Leaves came tumbling and scraping down the pitched roofs. [...] Black bags were arrayed at the curbstone in lopsided rows. [...] A series of frightened children appeared at our door for their Halloween treats' (53). DeLillo's novel, like Lethem's after it, likewise revels in the campus environment: 'students on the Hill sat on lawns and in dorm windows, playing their tapes, sunbathing. The air was a reverie of wistful summer things, the last languorous day, a chance to go bare-limbed once more, smell the mown clover' (25).

In such occasional paragraphs as Lethem's above, narrative time speeds up, as notable events (the protest, the symposium) are despatched in one line, in contrast to the detail given to Philip's dealings with Alice. The economy of narration produces a degree of absurdity, with dissimilar events registered at the same speed and with the same level of commentary. Such absurdity is also built into the contents themselves – 'Roberta, the manatee savant' – while the contrast between the failed protest and successful symposium about protest renders with flat irony a perception of the university's ability to process anything into its own content, comparable to Lack's ability to swallow matter. Like DeLillo's, this novel's world is stylized, shaped by its deadpan prose. If it is populated by Professors with suggestive yet ambiguous names like Soft and De Tooth, its central characters also quietly share forenames with two relevant literary precursors: Philip K. Dick and Alice Liddell. That this fiction about world-construction is also a piece of world-construction itself is an additional irony never explicitly remarked on, but left to resonate gently.

Within this primary world, the novel imagines its fictional space in creative, proliferating terms, continually remaking and processing it into new zones and miniature worlds. Small details signal this. A goalkeeper in a soccer match is 'protecting the sanctity of the delineated space' (89–90). Circling Lack's table, Philip declares himself 'a question mark in orbit around an answer' (173). Philip feels that spending the night in the physics building has been like 'sleeping in the safe of a sunken ocean liner' (9), an imaginary interior within an interior. Entering the laboratory in a radiation suit (another nod to *White Noise*, where state officials in such garb proliferate to deal with real and simulated disasters), he becomes 'a clumsy earthbound astronaut' as he passes the airlock doors (31). Slumped in a corridor with Alice, 'the two of us bracketing the empty space of the hallway', he imagines 'that we were in the bowels of some vast interstellar vehicle, a futuristic ark that had fallen into disuse yet still drifted through the gulf of stars, and that we had lost our way [...] in our search for the control room' (85). In such moments the novel reaches for metaphors to depict the experience of space, of being inside or located; often what is imagined, as with the 'interstellar vehicle', is a world within a world, a bounded space amid the larger universe. A miniaturized version is 'My heart and the elevator, a plummet inside a plummet' (30).

A more complex version of this figure appears when Philip descends again into the physics building and discovers its 'extra depths, layers the elevator skipped': 'I wondered if the building contained its own opposite, an anti-building where anti-physicists collided anti-particles' (114). This is only a passing fancy, but it exemplifies the novel's quiet obsession with the multiplication of spaces; the physics faculty which has already generated a portal to alternative worlds is imagined as enfolding an alternative version of itself. At a party late in the novel, Philip still reaches for recursiveness: 'I was a storm at the eye of the storm' (172). From the outset, he has signalled his relation to conceptual space in informing us that 'My nickname around the department was the Dean of Interdiscipline. Interdean, for short' (6). Studying physical sciences from a starting point in the social sciences, he is a transitional figure, his work dedicated to framing one activity in the language of another. The 'Interdean' might govern a disciplinary 'interzone'.

The novel's physical spaces include the campus itself – a world within a world, which Philip has sometimes been able to inhabit as a self-sufficient universe (7); individual sections of it, like the physics faculty or 'Lack's chamber' within it; or Philip's apartment which is in turn repeatedly broken down to different sleeping zones (63, 181). But spaces here can also be defined by emotion. The blind men 'stood outside of Alice's narrowing circle of favor' (35), while Philip finds that he has made his own move from 'inside' to 'utterly outside' another imagined space: 'the circle of Alice's silence' (49). Seeing Alice as 'living on the brink of the void', he considers that 'the same void yawned out underneath me, too. Unrequited love' (68). He tells Alice that the two of them, exiled to apartment and laboratory respectively, inhabit 'islands of misery' (85), and in the momentary reconciliation that follows, 'Our bodies made one perfect thing, a topological whole [...] hollows turned to each other, hollows in alliance. We made a system, a universe' (86). Alice later returns 'to the margins, the zone of silence' (136).

The notion of a 'system' operating between people is persistent. Evan and Garth, far more enduringly than Philip and Alice, form 'a closed system as perfect and impervious as a perpetual-motion device' (28). Even while in the same physical dimension as Philip, they already seem 'alone together, in another world' (122). Cynthia Jalter, as an analyst of human relations, is handily explicit about such ideas as 'the delusory or subjective worlds that exist in the space between the two halves of any dual cognitive system' (79). Philip and Alice, she avers, 'formed a vulnerable mutual world-sphere' which ruptured under pressure (131–2). 'World' here is extended into its near-synonym 'sphere', as the novel playfully proliferates terms. One of its most provocative suggestions is that a 'private world', in Philip's phrase (79), may not merely be a solipsistic one of the individual mind, but a shared understanding or intersubjective 'system'. Within the novel, Philip seeks to be part of such a shared world with Alice – and is even offered a version of such 'coupling' by the persistent Cynthia – but is primarily confronted with the melancholy evidence of the 'dual cognitive system' of Evan and Garth, who are cordial to him yet whose sensory predicament encloses them and excludes him.

The blind men bring a significant element to the novel's meditation on the formation of worlds. They are first encountered as 'voices, odd voices', and much of their presence in the novel is vocal. Philip hears them navigating together through space: 'This is the place'; 'We're three blocks from the pay phone'; 'Correction [...] Four blocks from the bus stop'; 'The pay phone and the bus stop are two blocks apart' (13). From such talk it emerges that the pair apprehend space relationally: not by viewing a particular spot or sight and recognizing it but rather by measuring time and sensation between one phenomenon and another. Theirs is a world in which the distance between two bus stops or pay phones is the most significant thing about them as landmarks. The possibility that 'we're speaking of two different pay phones' would undermine the whole developing spatial sense; when one of the two replies 'There's only one pay phone', Lethem adds a fine comedy of pedantry with the addendum: 'I mean, we only speak of one pay phone' (13). The rest of the world, containing many other pay phones, is presumably out there and not to be verbally denied; what can be managed is the local frame of reference, in which the pair have agreed to let 'pay phone' mean one in particular.

Admitted to Philip's apartment, Evan and Garth proceed by rebounding off walls, running their 'hands everywhere: mapping frantically, too frantically' (15). Touch is important in their cognition of the world. On a rainy day, 'Weather seemed to lull the blind men to silence. It provided proof of an environment, so they no longer had to conjure one up by inventory. Turning their wet faces upward, losing shoes in the sucking mud of campus paths, they were finally convinced that their verbal weather was redundant, that a world loomed out around them' (99). The senses of touch, taste, sound and smell allow a sensory world of weather to take shape in the absence of vision. At a meal, they can be seen 'browsing the collage of smells and sounds, the gentle clinking of silverware and ice' (17). Philip echoes this practice when the pair go missing and he drives around town seeking them: 'I exhausted the routes, but I kept on driving, repeating my path. I was mapping' (142).

Yet speech normally remains crucial: as Alice says, 'They map their environment verbally' (16). So it is that Evan and Garth form the 'dual cognitive system' announced by Cynthia Jalter, with their own idiosyncratic speech patterns bouncing back and forth to generate an ongoing apprehension of immediate environment. This obsessively includes time as well as place. Part of the joke of the blind men's obsession with synchronizing watches is that mere agreement between the two of them does not prove that either is correct – 'We could all be wrong', as Garth gravely says (16) – and the same could in principle be true of any other aspect of reality. Thus Garth suddenly asks Evan: 'What if I'd been lying about the precise location of certain objects?', proposing: 'You'd be living in a world of my imagination' (49). Garth later admits that there is no danger of this – 'I don't know where they are either' (122) – but this hardly detracts from the thought that speech, in Evan's condition, could form a world of its own – a *'Delusive conditioning'* (49) – distorting or displacing what others take to be the actual one.

The blind men draw attention to the way a human experience of the world is contingent upon particular bodily functions and organs. Without vision, spatial apprehension operates in other ways. Their distinctive experience of the world also serves as a special case of a general theme: the role of the observer in relation to physical reality. Alice declares that 'In physics we have an observer problem', meaning that the spin of an electron 'lies along whatever direction we choose to observe from' (18). The observing subject, it seems, is difficult to dissociate from the physical reality under experimental observation. It may even be that 'the observer's consciousness determines [...] the existence of the electron' (18). The novel spins out a number of variants on this theme. Evan interests Alice because his neurological condition, involving eyesight without corresponding brain function, offers the possibility of 'Observation without subjective judgment' (20). Garth insists on a thought experiment in which the world is destroyed and leaves two people with their watches showing different times: 'there's no other reference point, no other *observer*, and for me it's five-thirty and for you it's five, isn't that a form of time travel?' (78). Shorn of external reference, time is in the eye of the watch-bearer. Philip makes a rhetorical speech complaining that physics assumes that reality will speak its own language: a case of 'leading the witness', when a different kind of observer or query could constitute reality differently (41). Lack, he observes, is 'an explosion of metaphor into a literal world', prompting human beings to reach for ready terms: 'Breach, gap, gulf, hub' (26). Scientists proliferate words to name this emergent reality, as the blind men do with theirs.

The theme is more fully explored in a later scene with Professor Braxia. 'Consciousness creates reality', Braxia avows: 'Only when there is a mind to consider the world is there a world' (153). He even dips into a textual idiom more familiar to Philip, or to his author: 'Consciousness writes reality, in any direction it looks' (153). Braxia's rationale for this is 'a principle of conservation of reality': in effect, reality only bothers to exist when being looked at, otherwise saving its energy (154). Given its author, Braxia's disquisition carries an echo of Philip K. Dick's *Ubik* (1969), whose protagonist Joe Chip ultimately occupies a world that seems to unfold around him as he moves through it, and disappear again in his absence. The same model is directly reprised by Perkus Tooth in *Chronic City*, who hypothesizes a simulated world that would save processing power by only activating those locations visited by human subjects (2010: 266). Braxia's meditation allows the inference that Lethem's novel itself comprises a world that only exists for as long as one looks at it, or indeed operates it with certain modes of narrative understanding. As Philip, a fictional character, tells Braxia when informed that reality is 'unwilling to fully exist without an observer': 'I can relate to that' (2001: 154).

Lack itself provides the ultimate instance of world-formation in this novel. A 'gaping rent in the texture of the universe' (51), it represents a mysterious aperture in which the given world appears to open on to another. Professor Soft, after all, has been attempting to 'create a new universe' (3): one that has, contrary to intention, become tied to the present universe and produced interference between the two. Hence the phrases exchanged by Alice and Philip: 'the edge of the territory'; 'the horizon of the real' (11, 37). Soft also believes that his 'creation event' is 'being infinitely reproduced', 'spinning out universes, one after the other' (25): a theory which multiplies Lack's disruption of the universe, and appears to be borne out at the end of the novel (182). The edge of one territory would then be only one of an infinite series. In accordance with Philip's humanistic judgment, numerous descriptions of Lack are essayed. It is 'a pothole malformed by subjectivity' (156); it is, Georges De Tooth hazards, 'editing the world for us, sorting it into those things that truly exist and those that do not', and thus presenting a 'threshold into reality' (112). Braxia speculates that Lack may contain 'a tiny little universe', so that 'every time I drop a strawberry [into Lack] I crush three or four suns' (95). The existence of Lack also variously changes attitudes to the given world: perceiving the fresh morning outside the lab, Philip initially reflects 'Maybe this was the new universe' (12), while a student protesting against Lack points out that the Earth is already 'a small oasis in an endless desert of nothingness', and does not need the additional dose of nothingness forged by Soft's experiment (52). Lack also encourages a perception of a 'human world' counterposed to it, in Philip's desire to 'draw [Alice] back to the human realm' (64), and his visit to the academic party as 'a parting taste of the human world' before directly confronting Lack (159).

Lack thus forces the idea of alternate worlds, and the very condition of worldliness, on to the novel's agenda. It is only in the final chapters that we at last find out what kind of world it really offers. Tumbling through Lack, Philip enters 'a new world' (175). Mendlesohn's taxonomy of the 'portal-quest fantasy' envisages a protagonist travelling through a portal and then embarking on a journey through an unknown land. In her examples, transit through the portal typically happens *early* in the story, leaving space for the adventure that follows. In this light, the oddity of *Table* is that it announces the existence of its portal from the start, yet then withholds entry to it until the end. The fantastic 'otherworld' beyond the portal is thus only briefly visited, in comparison to the relatively extensive campus narrative building up to it. The other world provides a climax to the narrative, rather than its substance. In a sense the novel consists of the delay of this climax, as various characters try and fail to enter the portal: the alternate world exists, but is withheld by the novel.

The primary world behind the breach consists of an ersatz version of the campus, constructed from materials that the alternate universe has so far been fed by its scientific interlocutors. The portal from Philip's own universe 'led out of the base of a gigantic onyx replica of the Statue of Liberty' (175): suggestive of *Planet of the Apes* (1968), but evidently, in this fictional context, magnified from a model offered to Lack twenty-three chapters earlier (50). The campus has been reproduced in terracotta clay, inspired by an ashtray (50); a cat passed through Lack has been 'photocopied into many cats by Lack' (177), and a copy of Lewis Carroll's *The Hunting of the Snark* has likewise been multiplied and used for kindling (176). Philip summarizes: 'The new universe was clinging to its parent reality. The results were poor. Lack was trying to make a world, but he couldn't get the parts' (177). The world beyond Lack is parasitical upon the primary universe, unwittingly generating 'a beautiful ruin, a haunted Zen garden' (178): a kind of psychedelic dreamworld like, say, Pepperland in The Beatles' film *Yellow Submarine* (1968), itself partly inspired by Carroll's Wonderland.

Again Dick's *Ubik*, whose characters occupy a fragile world that proves to be a mental projection, is a model for the notion that another world might be not radically other but instead desperately derivative. Dick's 1978 essay 'How to Construct a Universe That Doesn't Fall Apart Two Days Later' conceives of the novelist's role as 'creating whole universes, universes of the mind', and admits: 'I like to build universes which do fall apart. I like to see them come unglued, and I like to see how the characters in the novels cope with this problem. I have a secret love of chaos. There should be more of it.' There is something of this struggling, 'unglued' universe in Lack's alternate campus, a poor copy of the real trying to hold its own. Likewise, the protagonist here echoes Dick's, struggling to 'cope' while strung out between worlds. For something of Soft's prediction of the 'creation event [...] infinitely reproduced' appears to have occurred. Seeking to return through Lack, Philip enters another version of the campus, swathed in infinite darkness and occupied only by Evan and Garth. The explanation given is that following Evan and Garth's penetration to the first alternate universe, Lack has 'taken' their blindness 'and made another whole world': 'Along with making a facsimile of our world, Lack had reproduced himself. [...] [E]very world Lack made would have a flaw, a Lack of its own. And every Lack would want to make a world' (182).

The novel thus seems, in its final stretch, to postulate an infinity of worlds, each of which would test the author's capacities of world-construction anew. Philip has also casually offered a parenthesis about the original campus '(if mine was the original)' (176), which hints at a Dickian prospect of undecidable realities where the first world turns out only to be another copy. The remark is not pressed within the novel, but again it holds its measure of metafictional truth, in the literal sense that Philip's campus is actually a written copy of some of Lethem's own experience and his reading of other writers' campus novels. Within this novel, though, that thought remains unformulated. What remains pressing is that the seemingly infinite series of universes finds an abrupt end, as Philip climbs once more through the portal and enters a state of sheer nothingness. After a novel preoccupied with the proliferation and inhabitation of multiple worlds, Lethem offers a brief, virtuoso treatment of their absence: a kind of anti-world void of time, space, bodies, so 'wealthy with nothing' that the memory of actual things or people becomes residual (187). The novel never spells out the precise reason for Philip's arrival here. But we know that Evan and Garth have found their blind universe – 'They were happy here. They were home' (183) – after previously speculating about a world that might be more receptive to their state (119). Although Philip hardly gains sufficient consciousness to realize it, we can deduce that this nothing-verse is his own true goal, as it means that he has become identical with Lack, the object of Alice's love. So it is that she prepares to enter his world at the last, and we can guess that she is about to become continuous with Philip as the consciousness of this void: another form of Cynthia Jalter's 'dual cognitive system' (79), a 'mutual world-sphere' (131) too hard-wired into the fabric of the universe to be vulnerable. Lack has turned out to be what the social scientist Philip had always suggested: a site of wish fulfilment in which individual subjects can find themselves mirrored by their own worlds.

Finite Subjective Realities

The theme of world-making is also crucial to Lethem's second novel *Amnesia Moon* – which in its provenance contains some of his earliest writing. Here the sense of world formation is different once more, encompassing neither the physical exploration of a planet nor the controlled scientific generation of alternate universes. In *Amnesia Moon*, the proliferation of worlds is more explosive and less controlled, in keeping with the initial name of its protagonist: Chaos.

The novel takes place after a disaster – sometimes referred to as the break or the rift – which has profoundly affected the United States. The character and date of this disaster are discussed throughout, yet no consensus is reached.

The story commences in Hatfork, Wyoming, a post-apocalyptic territory where Chaos lives in an abandoned cinema. The territory is run by the corpulent Kellogg, who, based in nearby Little America, dominates the dreams of local people. Chaos flees Kellogg's jurisdiction, taking with him a local girl, Melinda, who is covered in fur. Driving across Western states, they traverse other strange local communities before arriving in Vacaville, in California. In this town every inhabitant is compelled to move house twice a week, and is monitored by a record of their Luck, closely akin to the Karma points in *Gun, with Occasional Music* – save for the 'government stars' who also serve as heroes of the town's media entertainment. Chaos is drawn further into California, to San Francisco where he has led a former life as Everett. (This is very much an alternate future San Francisco, with locations renamed as the Submission District, Ate-Hashbury and the Golden Gape Bridge [133, 167, 149].) The local area of No Alley is under the mysterious governance of Ilford Hotchkiss, father of Everett's old friend Cale – who is found to be still alive in an alternate dimension only accessible through drugs. Cale has in turn seemingly fabricated a version of Everett's former partner, Gwen, and both try to persuade him to turn the hallucinatory dimension into reality using his own psychic powers. Everett mentally transports with Gwen back to Hatfork, then back to San Francisco where he finds himself inside Ilford's clock. In a confrontation with Ilford, he destroys the house, then returns to Vacaville, which has changed: all inhabitants save the government stars now display physical deformities. Everett drives Melinda, Edie and her family away from the town towards an uncertain future.

Such a summary already makes plain that this is Lethem's wildest novel. Its plot developments add up to an extraordinary breviary of fantastic events, as though a compendium of multiple science fiction stories has been concertinaed into one narrative. This results in part from the novel's gradual composition as a reworking of Lethem's earliest fictional materials: its bold creativity is youthful, and the book's multiplicitous events reflect a patching together of different fictional projects. The result is one of Lethem's most challenging treatments of the theme of worlds and world-making.

Late in the novel, Chaos's weight has ballooned under the influence of Vacaville's conditions. Struck by his own size, he reflects: 'He was like a world' (Lethem 1995: 234). The identification of individual and world seems here just to be a matter of physical description, yet it is suggestive of a larger theme. A keynote of the novel is struck by Kellogg's declaration that Chaos will 'always be living in an FSR'. What sounds like an agreed technical abbreviation is one of Kellogg's own making: 'Finite Subjective Reality. That's what I call it. I ought to copyright that, in fact. You go creating a little area of control around you, until you bump into the next guy with his. A little sphere of reality and unreality, sanity and insanity, whatever you pull together' (200). Kellogg's term might be a gloss on the whole novel, with its landscape of social spheres living adjacently to each other, yet seemingly not much impeding on each other's peculiar character and laws. The people of San Francisco and Vacaville have heard of each other's customs, yet remain relatively autonomous – as they do from Hatfork or Little America, or the mysterious mountain covered in green fog which induces amnesia. The American West of this novel is suggestive of what Brian McHale dubs a 'zone', a 'heterotopian space' in which real geography has been overlaid with 'hallucinations and fantasies' (1987: 44–5). To return to the terms that McHale draws from social theory, these miniature worlds have seceded from a collectively agreed reality into separate 'subuniverses' that no longer share an understanding (McHale 1987: 37). They can also be designated by the critical term *polders*, developed by John Clute. In the *Encyclopedia of Fantasy* (1997) Clute explains that 'polders are defined as enclaves of toughened Reality, demarcated by boundaries [...] from the surrounding world. [...] A polder [...] is an *active* Microcosm, armed against the potential Wrongness of that which surrounds it'. Clute's term corresponds suggestively to the relative autonomy of the social worlds crossed in *Amnesia Moon*, and especially to the defensiveness of a given world – notably the mountain of green mist – faced by challenge from outside.

Lethem's polders bleed across to each other mainly through the transitory presence of Chaos himself, or through tantalizing rumour. Thus Boyd, a stray character met on the road, can talk of the mountain as 'the Emerald City [...] the Green Meanies, the Country of the Blind', as a 'scenario' he 'couldn't relate to' (58–9), and advise Chaos to steer clear of Utah and of Nevada which has 'got some military stuff going on' (67). A later character is amazed to hear of Everett's time in 'the one where everything is green', and has also heard of a place 'where they're having that war with the aliens' (158) – the most outlandish notion of all, but apparently corroborated when Everett visits a version of the alien battle zone inside Cale's alternate dimension (178–82). To a large extent, though, one world here is barely able to imagine another. Chaos remarks with bemusement that the people trapped in the green mist imagine that their situation is universal, failing to appreciate that 'The green isn't a problem. You only have to go a few miles away'. A psychiatrist briskly and, we can see, inaccurately retorts: 'The green is everywhere' (54). In the phrase that Boyd uses of another group, the 'little pocket of weirdness' is unable to realize how local it is (65). The coexistence of all these spheres corresponds to the novel's picaresque quality: a bewildering new world can be left behind with bewildering swiftness. It is eventually suggested that this extreme atomization has been a defensive strategy in response to alien invasion: 'Reality shattered to isolate the [alien] hives. [...] The more the world coheres, the more they can grab. It's a countermove' (181). This is the most dramatic explanation of the situation of the novel, but it is not given any ultimate proof of veracity.

An important emphasis is that the United States has fragmented. Boyd says that after the rift, 'Things got all broken up, *localized*' (60). Chaos's old associate Billy Fault explains that 'a lot of the old connections between things fell away, which gave people a chance to make up new ones' (117). Ilford remarks: 'I'm sure you've noticed how local things can get nowadays' (139). The naming of an area of Wyoming as 'Little America' (a phrase that was also the title of a pop song by R.E.M. in 1984, early in the protracted composition of this novel) highlights both the theme of nation and its actual absence. When Boyd urges him to eat a burger on the grounds that 'This is the U.S.A.', it is a quietly comical touch that 'Chaos didn't ask what the U.S.A. was' (63). But later he is brought to reflect more fully on this question. A casual reference to 'America' jolts him: 'Chaos remembered that name, too. It was the name for everything, all of this: Wyoming, California, Utah, and lots more. It wasn't just the second word in Little America. There was a Big America, only it was so big, they didn't have to call it that' (114). That the dystopia corresponds to the break-up of the United States is unusual, in that the paranoid tradition that Lethem admires – Pynchon, DeLillo, Dick – has been apt to see the centralization, bureaucracy and growing complexity of the American state as sinister. Here it is the shattering of that edifice that has brought the trouble.

Among these localized worlds, a scale could be plotted between those closest to ordinary reality and those elements that most stretch its logic. Thus Vacaville on Chaos's first visit is, by normal standards, a bizarre social scenario, its features – Moving Day, Luck, Government Stars – clearly extrapolated for satirical effect. In its conflation of government and entertainment, it may prompt reflection on the entwining of these two spheres (a phenomenon which would reach new levels over two decades after the novel's publication, with the election of the reality television personality Donald J. Trump as President of the United States). The motifs of Moving Day and Luck are both stimulating dramatizations of the challenges of class, social status and precarity. Yet all this remains at a secular level, conceivable within reality as we know it. The same is true of the near-abandoned commercial Strip occupied by Boyd, where the only survivors of disaster are a group of fast-food employees whom Boyd dubs the McDonaldonians: 'rail-thin white ghosts in their late teens or early twenties, wearing grease-stained food service uniforms in the company colors' (62). The employees feel compelled to continue working for McDonalds, despite the collapse of infrastructure or evidence of the corporation's survival: 'The company rulebook is their Bible', says Boyd (64). This scene is as close as Lethem comes to the excitable social satire of Britain's *2000AD* comic, itself deeply influenced by the legacy of science fiction writing; indeed the scenario is close to a Judge Dredd story from 1981 (and banned, for legal reasons, for the next quarter-century) in which a devotee of McDonald's rules a small town in a post-nuclear wasteland. These situations are fanciful and satirical, but again remain hypothetically plausible.

A different matter is the motif of dreaming, in which a given character effectively dreams for a whole community, broadcasting unconscious narratives as though they were mental television programmes. At first this seems the special preserve of Kellogg, his 'obsessions radiating outward, invading Chaos's dreams' (8) and those of everyone else around. Kellogg has also renamed things – including Chaos himself – and redefined the local world according to his own whim (9). Yet he repeatedly insists that Chaos himself is just as important to the local hegemony; that his subjectivity is also crucial to the Finite Subjective Reality (23, 200, 243). Thus when Chaos arrives in San Francisco, Ilford's associates are keen to enlist what they see as his world-creating powers, of which he is barely aware: 'With your help we'd like to create a broader coherence, a sort of viral coherence that would roll outward from here, reclaiming other territories, other realities' (161–2).

Chaos, then, is one of a number of mysteriously gifted figures whose mental capacities can reshape the worlds of others around them. Another is Elaine, the old woman who dominates the mountain of green mist – 'Mostly we dream of her, her voice speaking to us, reassuring us' (54). A different kind of alternative space is occupied by Cale, who can only be witnessed by taking drugs. Chaos sees him 'on an invisible chair in a featureless expanse of blank space' (143); uncertain where this encounter is taking place, he reflects: 'Anyway I'm *somewhere* [...] And you're in it, this somewhere I'm at', before viewing it as 'this null-zone that had replaced the world' (144). Walking into a church later reminds Chaos of this experience, 'entering a hidden space' (171). Yet Cale proves able to decorate the 'null-zone' with detail: on a subsequent visit, Chaos finds himself amid 'a scene, horizon, hills, trees, a nestled lake'. What seems a mere image – 'depthless, flat, a brilliant mural inches away' – turns out to feel more substantial: 'as he moved his head, it bloomed into three dimensions, a world' (173). The world in question is a simulation of Chaos's former home, one that has much occupied his dreams. Cale explains that his primary activity now is 'Making worlds. I've made a lot of them' (174). We later, briefly, learn that Cale when alive had been 'working on virtual reality stuff on his computer [...] That's where all the world-building stuff comes from' (210). When he hands the remnants of Cale's drug to a robot televangelist late on, Chaos tells the robot that this is a kind of god: 'The world-making kind' (218). Yet Cale's world-creating capacity seems strained – the effort to maintain it makes his hallucinogenic presence wear off faster, and at a moment of anger 'The world around them flickered and flattened, briefly short-circuited' (174–5), seemingly showing its electronic origins. Cale is the occupant of a pocket universe who multiplies further worlds within it, and also keeps a 'record' of the world in which humans are fighting aliens: he can take Chaos to this alternate experience, flying in a helicopter over Los Angeles, at a moment's notice (178). Yet Cale also wishes to invert the relation between primary and pocket universes, imploring Chaos to use his mental powers to turn this world into the real: 'Make a world here. [...] You could dream it into reality' (174). Rather than needing someone in the primary world to inject drugs to bring him into being, Cale proposes: 'Turn it inside out. [...] Ilford and Kellogg and everything, all the broken-up, tired American reality – make it small. Make it into a drug we can take if we want, the contents of a test tube. And make this the real world, the one that persists' (176). The scale of what is requested here – for reality as we have known it thus far to be folded into a kind of secondary world – is bewildering. Whatever Chaos's powers, he does not accede to Cale's requests; a sense abides that the pocket universe of the drug lacks the substance truly to take over from the rest of reality.

Yet that external reality is also rendered equally strange by Ilford Hotchkiss, whose power has the capacity to turn people into objects (210). With Ilford's metamorphic world, we reach the opposite pole from the relatively coherent scenario of Vacaville: a Finite Subjective Reality in which the controlling subject is able deliberately to manipulate matter and minds together. Chaos, installed in Ilford's clock, in turn interferes with his world by stopping time long enough for Billy Fault, occupying a nearby bonsai tree, to explain the situation to him. Ilford, meanwhile, is paused in mid-action, 'the scotch in his glass tilted against gravity' (208). The novel reaches a chaotic crescendo here: the collapse of Ilford's floor as the characters tumble into the basement (212) is suggestive of the implosion of ontological coherence in the narrative that Lethem has been keeping afloat till now.

It could be said that the novel has traversed the spectrum from one aspect of Dick's example to another. Vacaville and McDonaldland are pieces of speculative satire, commensurate with ordinary physical laws: they show autonomous 'worlds' of a kind, but only enforced as such by legal convention or hegemonic consent. As Chaos himself reflects, 'the effect was milder here. The Vacaville equivalents to Kellogg and Elaine – the government stars – lived in the media instead of invading dreams. And you could always turn the television off' (99). In Dick's terms these scenes are broadly comparable to, say, the stories 'The Defenders' (1953) or 'Foster, You're Dead!' (1955), satirical commentaries on Cold War attitudes, paranoia and human beings' readiness to accept social control. The dreams of Kellogg or Elaine take us to another level, in which the operations of the mind itself are subject to hegemonic broadcasting. As Boyd puts it in countercultural idiom, 'The Man got into everybody's head' (60). The vision of world-creation here is political – Kellogg and Elaine stand as instances of rulers dominating local populations through manipulation – but the means of its achievement are more metaphysical, or belong to an unexplained, post-apocalyptic science in which ordinary notions of the autonomy of the individual human mind no longer apply. In Dick's oeuvre this appears closer to *Do Androids Dream of Electric Sheep?* (1968), where a relatively coherent post-apocalyptic world is augmented by media-driven cults and new technology that can alter an individual's mood on demand. Ilford's world, with Chaos turned into the consciousness of a golden clock and a house liable to collapse due to the conflicting mental operations of two of its inhabitants, is finally a different kind of reality again: closer to, say, the later stages of *Ubik*, in which the whole world occupied by the protagonist is a facade that can change shape at any moment. The unpredictable logic of this last world then seems partially carried over, even as Chaos escapes it, to Vacaville, where the world is stable yet individual bodies are radically mutable. Chaos, exasperated, 'wanted reality to sit still for him for once' (226).

Amnesia Moon, we can see, is a novel about unreliable, partial and multiple worlds, which is itself internally unpredictable and multiple. It refuses to maintain a single logic of world-construction, instead radically shifting its sense of what a world could be, and how it might be created or operate, as it goes along. In this sense it is Lethem's most radically challenging novel, even if, like Dick's, Lethem's radicalism here implies a gamble with textual coherence. We can finally compare it with the two other novels considered in this chapter. The planetary romance *Girl in Landscape* takes on world-construction in the most literal sense, imagining an alternative planet. In Brian McHale's terms it remains 'epistemological': dramatizing the gradual discovery of a coherent world via the different subjective perspectives of Pella's fugue state. *As She Climbed across the Table* embeds its alternate world differently, beyond a portal that is only crossed late in the book but that yields some of the most creative images of Lethem's novelistic career. Multiple dimensions are disclosed, though from a stable starting point: a satirically tweaked version of contemporary California with a strong undertow of emotional attachment. *Amnesia Moon* ostensibly stays on Earth, but multiplies worlds, first across its numerous localized polders, then into the virtual reality of Cale and the mysterious powers of Ilford. *Amnesia Moon* comes closer than any of Lethem's other novels to McHale's radically ontological fiction, in which the sense of any stable grounding is at risk amid the pluralization and disintegration of spheres of experience. Simultaneously, more than the other two novels discussed here, *Amnesia Moon* emphasizes the politics of the making and maintenance of worlds. Through the hegemonic figures of Kellogg, Elaine and Vacaville's President Kentman it draws a direct connection between world-construction and social control, whether implicitly or explicitly through media and ideology. In this the novel is very true to the dissident and sceptical example of its primary precursor, Dick. This theme is more muted in the other two novels, but they share a fascination with space as a social construct (as in the 'circles' of Alice or 'systems' of Evan and Garth) or as contested, even colonized territory (as in the differing occupations of the Planet of the Archbuilders made by Efram and others). In different yet parallel ways, all three novels dramatize processes of world-making and the challenges they bring, while also undertaking such processes themselves as works of fiction. A few books later, after encountering Yet Another World, Perkus Tooth fears that he may be living in a simulation (2010: 227–9). As a character in a novel, he has a point.

4

Heroes

During *Motherless Brooklyn*, the Minna Men Lionel Essrog and Tony Vermonte are confronted by the homicide detective Lucius Seminole. When the detective asks about the 'Clients' who pull the strings of local organized crime, Tony sarcastically replies: 'They had to get back to their hideout, since they've got James Bond – or Batman, I can't remember which – roasting over a slow fire'. Despite the initial hesitation over two action heroes, James Bond falls away as Tony goes on: 'Don't worry, though. Batman always gets away. These supervillains never learn'. Provoked by his Tourette's, Lionel yells: 'Uncle Batman!'; 'Unclebailey Blackman! *Barnamum Bat-a-potamous!*' (Lethem 1999: 191). Two years earlier, during *As She Climbed across the Table*, Professor Philip Engstrand finds himself in a sexual encounter with the therapist Cynthia Jalter. As she stimulates his penis, he thinks of it as 'my hot line, my Batphone' (2001: 134). Later, at a party, he suggests to a feminist academic that for a woman to use male-dominated language is 'Like Superman trying to build his house out of kryptonite' (164).

These moments demonstrate how Lethem's 1990s fiction is occasionally apt to turn to the world of superheroes as reference points. For Philip, the Batphone is an instance of a privileged line of communication, and the thought of Superman working with the mineral that drains his powers offers an elementary image of someone compromised by the material in which they are condemned to work. For Tony Vermonte, Batman is a corny adventure narrative that he can sardonically contrast with real life. Batman and Superman are part of the mental furniture, established names, references that the reader is expected to grasp immediately. Such moments could stand as hints that Lethem had more to say about superheroes. How much more would only become apparent over the following decade.

Locating the Superhero

The genres crucial to Lethem's career have crossed media. Science fiction, detective fiction and the Western have inhabited magazines, novels and films.

The superhero genre has also appeared in multiple media, but is strongly rooted in comic books: graphic narrative forms in which the action takes place across a sequence of drawn panels with written captions and dialogue. Like any genre, the superhero story is in part formed from precursors in other modes, but it also represents the single most influential intervention made by the comic-book form into the gallery of genres. The American comic book has always contained a plurality of content: Westerns, Greek myth, adaptations of hit films like *Star Wars*, or the teen romantic comedy of Betty and Veronica. Nonetheless, the medium remained strongly, even sentimentally identified with one kind of narrative and visual content – the superhero – to a degree perhaps without parallel in other media. Even those who wished to challenge and rethink comics, such as Frank Miller, remained tellingly fixated on the world of superheroes. The connection between graphic narratives and superheroes would only be loosened, around the late twentieth century, with the rise of numerous adult-oriented comics of everyday life along the lines suggested by such artists as Jaime Hernandez (*Love & Rockets*, 1982–) or Daniel Clowes (*Ghost World*, 1993–7).

The superhero's precursors can be traced to such earlier sources as ancient Greek heroes (Heracles), folk heroes (Robin Hood), and powerful protagonists in other genres like the Western. The critic Marco Arnaudo (2013) emphasizes the genre's roots in ancient mythology, Norse as well as Greek, and in a range of religious and shamanic narratives. In the early twentieth century, key avatars included the science-fiction adventurers Edgar Rice Burroughs's John Carter of Mars (in prose fiction from 1912) and Buck Rogers and Flash Gordon, in comic strip form from 1929 and 1934, respectively (Roberts 2006: 185). Significant too was Doc Savage, 'The Man of Bronze', who first occupied his own pulp fiction magazine then appeared in comic-book form from 1940. As Adam Roberts comments, the character is the prototype for 'those superheroes who were never anything more than human' (2006: 225). Yet the first figure who would take the emblematic form of the superhero in the twentieth century – the costumed, indeed caped comic-book crimefighter – was Superman, conceived by Jerry Siegel and Joe Shuster and appearing in *Action Comics* from April 1938 (Wright 2001: 7–15). This figure derives his immense power from his status as an alien from the planet Krypton. Despite his omnipotence he hides behind the persona of the mild-mannered Metropolis reporter Clark Kent. A persona like Kent would become known as the hero's 'secret identity': despite being known to other people (like his colleagues at the *Daily Planet*), its relation to the powerful, publicly celebrated hero remains hidden. Beyond Superman, masked heroes would further emphasize this element of secrecy. This is true of the second paradigmatic superhero: Batman, who premiered in 1939 with Detective Comics (DC). These pioneering characters inaugurated what would become known as the 'Golden Age' of comics from the end of the 1930s to the mid-1950s. The arrival of a new version of The Flash, with the secret identity Barry Allen, in 1956 is taken to commence the 'Silver Age': a period, lasting until the early 1970s, in which DC would join battle with its great rival Marvel Comics, the two stables developing somewhat different identities and styles (Wright 2001: 204–24).

Superheroes can be considered a subset of science fiction. Their powers typically have pseudo-scientific explanations (as in the radioactive spider and Gamma rays that energize Spider-Man and the Hulk respectively); they sometimes (Superman, Fantastic Four, Silver Surfer) venture into the classical science-fiction environment of outer space. Yet as their typical vocation is 'crime-fighter', superheroes also relate to the crime genre. Batman and Spider-Man are paradigmatic of this aspect of the superhero's role, their daily bread and butter consisting of foiled muggings and interrupted bank heists. Despite the importance of the Detective Comics label to the genre's history, with Batman even assuming the title 'The Darknight Detective' in the 1970s – Lethem himself has imagined the character as a transfigured Philip Marlowe (2017: 52) – the cerebral element of detection associated with Sherlock Holmes is generally downplayed. Gothic also has its place in the composition of the genre, from Batman's brooding inhabitation of Gotham City to the Fantastic Four's menacing nemesis Doctor Doom. Despite the genre's evident overlap with these modes, the superhero story remains clearly recognizable in its own right, with its own typical iconography, idioms, character names and dialogue: all demonstrated by the fact that the genre is easy to parody or pastiche.

Superhero comics have had two key periods in Jonathan Lethem's life. One was the 1970s, when Lethem was a child and teen, joining other fans to conceive and draw their own heroes as well as to debate the strengths and weaknesses of extant characters. During the 1990s, as well as the fleeting references cited at the head of this chapter, he also signalled an interest in the genre in the brief and fragmentary prose piece 'The Notebooks of Bob K', first published in 1995: this outlier will be considered below. But Lethem's second major period of engagement with the superhero was the 2000s. Now he published *The Fortress of Solitude* (2003), an autobiographical novel drawing on that earlier period of fandom and imaginatively extending it. He undertook similar operations at smaller scale in the story collection *Men and Cartoons* (2004), notably in the stories 'The Vision' and 'Super Goat Man' which respectively allude to actual comic-book figures and invent a new one. Lethem openly recalled his passion for the genre in a number of occasional pieces of criticism or memoir (several would be grouped together in *The Ecstasy of Influence*); and he brought this whole period to a culmination in authoring a revival of a superhero comic, *Omega the Unknown*, for Marvel in 2007–8.

It seems accurate to say that this wave of superhero writing satisfied an urge in Lethem, and allowed him to leave the field behind in subsequent work. Yet as this period was one in which Lethem came to public prominence, he also became associated with the genre and with its deployment in literature, a strategy hitherto unexpected among respected writers. At the same time, other writers were exploring related territory. Michael Chabon's *The Amazing Adventures of Kavalier & Clay* (2000) achieved critical and popular acclaim with a story of two young boys inventing new superhero comics in the New York of the early 1940s: in effect a bold, affectionate re-imagining of the creation of Superman and the beginnings of Captain America, which also traces the consequences for the rest of the characters' lives. Junot Diaz's *The Brief Wondrous Life of Oscar Wao* (2007) told the story of Puerto Rican immigrants to the United States and the political history of their home country, with extensive reference to popular–cultural references including science fiction and comic books as well as Tolkien's Middle Earth. Both novels won the Pulitzer Prize for Fiction, in 2001 and 2008 respectively. These prominent examples suggest that Lethem's project at this time was not wholly idiosyncratic but part of a somewhat wider opening of literary culture to such resources. Indeed the apparent parallel between Lethem and Chabon was made curiously closer by the fact that both of them moved from writing novels about superheroes to producing actual comic books: Lethem's *Omega* was preceded by a graphic version of Chabon's own superhero *The Escapist* in 2004.

This chapter will first look at Lethem's non-fictional essays and short pieces about superheroes to reconstruct his relation to them. Next it will turn to *The Fortress of Solitude* and at length explore the role of superheroes in this work. Finally it will consider Lethem's *Omega the Unknown* itself.

A Fan's Notes

Most of Lethem's non-fictional works about superheroes date from the 2000s. The relevant essays include 'Identifying with Your Parents, or the Return of the King' (already analysed in Chapter One above), in 2004; a substantial review of the film *Spider-Man* for the *London Review of Books* in 2002; and three other pieces later collected in *The Ecstasy of Influence*: the introduction to a 2009 collection of early (1936–41) comics; the eccentric 2002 piece 'Top Five Depressed Superheroes'; and Lethem's imagination of 'The Epiphany', an invented hero based on a painting, published in *Playboy* in 2009. Lethem's review of the Batman film *The Dark Knight* (2008) expressed disgust with the moral quagmire he found the film to express, but a more positive, highly insightful discussion of Batman would also appear in a later *Rolling Stone* essay, 'The Only Human Superhero' (2012), eventually reproduced in *More Alive and Less Lonely*.

Lethem had evidently been carrying this preoccupation with him from childhood, yet only now did he discuss it extensively in the literary press, as he was offered space to share his tastes and opinions. In the early 2000s he became a 'go-to' figure on superheroes, on whom an editor could rely for an authoritative and informed view of comic books. His reputation was becoming entwined with memories of the form. At the same time, he will have known that his fictional engagements with comics (above all *The Fortress of Solitude*) would be read in the light of his non-fictional statements. Life and art were becoming visibly related.

What main tendencies can be taken from this set of publications? One we have already emphasized in Chapter One: the personal character of Lethem's engagement with comics, and the tendency of this to permeate his writing on the form. If in 'Identifying with Your Parents' a story of comics was inseparable from Lethem's friendship with Karl and Luke, so too *The Ecstasy of Influence* states that his preferred approach to superheroes is as 'private cargo cult' (2011: 141). So his introduction to *Supermen!* commences rhetorically with the question '*Who was your first?*' He means not merely the first superhero comic that one might have read, but the first trace of the genre in one's life, 'the first human outline in a cape flashing through your dawning gaze', which might include Adam West's TV Batman or a child on a beach pretending to fly (141). Lethem proceeds to offer a brisk history of his own superhero fandom (141–2), which is also reprised at greater length in his *Spider-Man* review (153–6). The turn to memoir as criticism that we have already observed has a particular rationale at this point in Lethem's career: it corresponds to his fiction's turn towards more strongly autobiographical material. Critic and novelist are closely aligned.

A second observation is that reading comics involves expertise. The invocation of Lethem's friends posits the analysis of comics as a collective matter with its own protocols and shared understandings. As Lethem's discussion of Jack Kirby, in particular, demonstrates, the child or teen reader enters into an ongoing aesthetic debate about styles of pencilling or quality of dialogue, extending over a historical spread of shifting evidence and a range of titles. Such knowledge might easily be classed as 'geek' culture. But Lethem's work coincides with a transition in which it is revalued and the term 'geek' itself ultimately reclaimed and used as a boast. In these essays, the teen's detailed knowledge of a mass-cultural form is asserted, without apology – though with a measure of irony – as a form of cultural capital worthy of reconsideration.

Third, comics are generational, with specific historical phases. The earliest of all these is what Lethem discovers in his *Supermen!* piece: its emphasis is on challenging the misremembered notion of a simpler past and rediscovering its strange reality. Tracking curious awkward or extreme moments from early comic books, Lethem discovers that this 'primitive stuff, when you turn your eyes to it, is so rich and singular, so jam-packed with curdled or mangled sophistications borrowed from other mediums and forms, that it verges on precognitive sight in its total blindness' (143). Beyond this belated discovery of an unruly past, though, his own childhood experience of comics has a steady structure. Superman and Batman, the 'anchor DC characters', are 'stolid', racially identified with 'deep whiteness', perhaps 'heartening to have around', but 'increasingly, dull and taken for granted' (141, 152). They 'were pretty much like my parents' – notwithstanding Lethem's other emphasis on 'identifying with your parents' – making other DC veterans like Wonder Woman or Flash, in an ingenious logical step, 'your aunts and uncles, familiar without being vivid' (141–2). It may seem incongruous that the male Superman and Batman should simultaneously be 'parent' figures, without a corresponding female presence; while this is probably an unwitting consequence of the general conceit developed here, one could choose to press it further into Lethem's sense of the family unit – fractured during the 1970s, and bereft of a mother after 1978 – and his insistent fascination with surrogate father figures, from Kellogg in *Amnesia Moon* to Frank Minna in *Motherless Brooklyn* (and including his reading of the relationship between Jack Kirby and Stan Lee). More obviously, given Lethem's insistence on the stolid status of these Golden Age heroes, it is noticeable that they are nonetheless the names to which his characters turn in the earlier novels. However unfashionable Superman and Batman may have been to teen readers of the mid-1970s, they still presented instinctive archetypes for Lethem as a writer in his thirties, and of all superheroes, they were the ones most likely to register as meaningful with a wide fiction-reading public.

The generation beyond them is Marvel's Silver Age gallery of the 1960s: Thor, the Fantastic Four or Hulk 'were something like cool kids who'd lived on your block in the decade before you started playing on the street, and now were off at college or in the army, but their legend persisted' (142). The image responds in part to Marvel itself, in that these characters typically were seen operating in New York unlike the 'fantasy cities, Gotham and Metropolis' (153). It also corresponds closely to *The Fortress of Solitude*, with its emphasis on the residential block and its lore: writing this in 2009, it is as though Lethem can now lean on this reference point from his own fiction as a signal for the reader. Among Marvel's New Yorkers, Spider-Man has a special place: in familial terms, 'your older brother, of course – a great guy, an idol, but he didn't belong to you' (142). The essay on this character discloses more ambivalence: 'disliked and distrusted' by Lethem and Karl in 1976 for 'resting on his laurels', coasting through the 1970s an uninteresting figure compared to the exploits of the 1960s that the boys could only rediscover in retrospect (153–4). A structure familiar from 'Identifying with Your Parents' is outlined again here: 'Karl and I resented Spider-Man like we resented the Beatles, for being such lavish evidence we'd been born too late' (154). Nevertheless, by 2002 such earlier nuances can be placed in perspective, to the extent of celebrating Spider-Man as something of a local hero: 'a bridge-and-tunnel person, from Queens, in the real New York'; 'the first superhero whose civilian identity would be a likely reader of comic books' (153), such that, with the advent of the film, 'my old resentment of Spider-Man was sublimated beneath a surge of proprietary feeling when I first heard […] that "my Spidey" was getting his fifteen minutes' (156).

This still leaves Lethem's own generation of comic fandom, tied neither to pre-war 'anchor characters' nor to Stan Lee's Silver Age but to Marvel's new output of the 1970s:

> What was wholly yours were your contemporaries, the oddities launching themselves before your eyes: Ghost Rider and Warlock and Luke Cage and Deadman and Ragman and Omega the Unknown, or nutty gangs like the Guardians of the Galaxy and the Defenders. These were as thrilling and unreliable as new friends in the schoolyard, and they lived in a world your parents, or Superman, would never even begin to understand. (142)

The same array – whose era comics fans would eventually agree to call the Bronze Age – is reassembled in other essays; in the *Spider-Man* review it is joined by the Vision, Black Bolt and Son of Satan (154). Now Lethem describes this era of heroes more fully: 'brooding, tormented antiheroes', dosed more strongly than ever in 'the outsiderish, sulky Marvel scent'; recapitulating Spider-Man's own 'rejection of icons in favor of darker, more amorphous figures' and leaving fans 'on a quest for Ever-More-Spidery-Man' (154). The emphasis on marginality and darkness combines with a fact Lethem does not especially advertise here – the failure of these characters to break through and gain wider, longer-term recognition – to make them fit his 2011 description of his favoured 'popular' culture: 'I usually preferred Unpop: comics canceled for lack of readers, bands sans career, paperback-original novelists who'd filled word counts behind interchangeable covers' (135).

A fourth and final emphasis remains, specifically in Lethem's *Spider-Man* review: the connection of superheroes to the idea of race. He reports the 2002 film being applauded by an audience comprising 'eighty percent inner-city blacks', and explores this sense that such an audience 'knew that Spider-Man was *for them*' (152). Against the 'deep whiteness' already observed in the original DC heroes, Lethem sees Spider-Man as encoding an urban experience keyed to the 1960s and 1970s and closer to a black audience. Spider-Man, Lethem ventures, is an underdog figure, 'misrepresented in the media' and 'always short of a buck': a point of identification different from the omnipotent Superman or billionaire Bruce Wayne. That Spider-Man has a precursor in the trickster figure of African legend (153) only assists this case. The connection and tension between urban, racial identity and the figure of the superhero will be crucial in *The Fortress of Solitude*: it is plain that Spider-Man was one of Lethem's routes to this crux.

The comparatively 'Unpopular' Bronze Age receives another treatment in Lethem's 'Top-Five Depressed Superheroes', who all belong to the 'brooding, tormented' 1970s. Lethem's formative affection for that era of Marvel is here reprised in a different key, as non-fiction blends into fancy and facts become humorous. 'Top-Five Depressed Superheroes' stakes Lethem's claim as an authority on this newly prominent field, simply because the material is so obscure. Eschewing such cases as an introspective Superman or Batman, the list – Black Bolt, The Vision, Deadman, Ragman, Omega the Unknown – comprises not merely depressed superheroes but comparatively forgotten ones. If The Vision retains slight currency among a reading public, then Ragman's claim on popular memory is assuredly less steady.

Other than its obscurity, this list of heroes raises three other points. At a first level is the 'brooding' element: this is a version of superheroes darker than their precursors, afflicted with melancholy rather than intoxicated by their powers. Superheroes have been becoming 'dark' at least since Dennis O'Neill and Neal Adams's reworking of Batman in the 1970s (Levitz 2015: 17–18); indeed some fans insist that the Batman of the very first issues was already a dark and brooding figure, whose seriousness would be lost during the colourful exploits of the 1950s and 1960s. Yet the framing of Lethem's top five at once asserts and diminishes this quality. The word 'depressed' does its own work: the article's title looks like a wilful confusion of categories. Part of the incongruity is that such heroes can hardly afford the enduring drawback of depression, as their role is to be active in fighting crime.

Second, therefore, this is a piece of comic writing. Humour derives from actual details: of Black Bolt, 'His wings resemble accordions, the most harmless and charming of instruments (apart from the kazoo), mocking the cataclysmic potential of his speaking voice' (144), while 'Deadman rarely bothers to dress as a civilian, since his secret identity is a corpse' (145). Lethem's deadpan treatment of these characters helps to draw out some of their real strangeness, in the way that he ascribes to early comics. But he also adds fancies of his own. 'During the Giuliani mayoralty Ragman was discreetly paid off to move to Baltimore, where he remains' (145): not merely a joke on gentrification and zero-tolerance policing, but also one at the expense of run-down Baltimore. A comedy of incongruity inheres in bringing the superheroes up to date into a real milieu where they should not belong.

This is then the third effect of Lethem's piece: reimagining the heroes as though they were real people. 'In restaurants it takes Black Bolt hours to decide on the simplest order', and 'it can be infuriating waiting for him to scribble a note'; Deadman is embarrassed about his treatment by the Spectre, 'so he never calls him anymore' (144, 145). In this respect Lethem's depressed superheroes become comparable to a new generation of narrative, in which such figures are imagined coping with the indignities of mundane reality. This had been a major turn in the genre during the 1980s, through Alan Moore's reworking of such titles as *Swamp Thing* and *Miracleman*; but the paradigmatic case is Moore's *Watchmen* (1986–7), where the sagging crimefighter Nite Owl squabbles in the kitchen with his grubby friend Rorschach or sighs at his own middle-aged existence. Lethem cites this comic as a case of 'even more antiheroic antiheroes' than his favoured 1970s pantheon, 'needed to gratify our recomplicating appetites' (142). In his brief top five list of 2002 he implicitly combines these two generations. The fictionalizing move he makes – imagining superheroes as real, troubled citizens – will be emblematic for his major novel on this theme.

On a smaller scale, it is also taken up in his story of the same period, 'Super Goat Man', which we observed in Chapter One to overlap significantly with *The Fortress of Solitude*. Here Lethem fabricates a brand new hero, notable for his lack of distinction: his adventures, in his five back issues from Electric Comics, involve 'rescuing old ladies from swerving trucks and kittens from lightning-struck trees' (2004: 121). The calm, neighbourly Super Goat Man is not so much a 'depressed superhero' as one unembarrassed by his own limited scope. The peculiarity of the scenario is the way that Super Goat Man has been both a character in comics and a real person in the historical world, to which he has now returned: the same figure can be seen on the page and on the porch down the street. The categories of superheroic existence and real life are confounded: Ralph Gersten became Super Goat Man to take on a new political life, 'Sometime around when they shot Kennedy', but stopped being a superhero (and thus appearing in comics) because he was 'being too outspoken about the war', and as a 1960s radical 'wanted to accomplish things on a more local level' (125). The categories are troubled from the opposite direction in the contemporaneous story 'The Vision', which centres not only on a boy who dresses as the eponymous figure – one of Lethem's depressed five – but on his adult life, in which it is revealed that his partner has fabricated her own Scarlet Witch costume to strengthen their relationship (Lethem 2004: 19). Here, in an inversion of the motif, the characters are not superheroes with the rough edges of real adults, but real adults with a fantasy life as superheroes. Once again, the figure of the costumed hero is relocated in an unexpected environment: a refurbished apartment in a gentrifying Brooklyn brownstone, like the one that Super Goat Man occupied two decades earlier.

The attempt to imagine the superhero as a living citizen, and the associated bathos, also resurfaces in Lethem's vignette 'The Epiphany' (2011: 147–50). First published in 2009, this comparatively late entry in Lethem's superhero career is based on a painting by Scott Alden, which takes the form of a comic-book cover for an imaginary title. Lethem extrapolates the superhero who would correspond to such a name. An epiphany is generally understood to be a flash of mental insight, by nature as fragile as it is illuminating. Accordingly, Lethem's character 'may perish at any instant', aware that 'every waking second is a matter of life and death', 'mortality his middle name' (147). The Epiphany's origin involves no external scientific force: rather, lying awake one night as a teen, 'he'd with a sensation of ineffable unquantifiable yet unmistakable intensity *discovered himself* [...] with a thrill of self-understanding as complete and all-encompassing as it was quick to shudder from him and vanish' (149). The Epiphany, we learn, only has brief 'Interludes of Power' punctuating his mundane existence.

The sense, perhaps, is that the character barely exists, subsisting only as a margin of difference from somebody's everyday life. Yet the text derives effects at once from closely following the genre's conventions and from giving them a crucial twist. A whole new superhero world is imagined, but its names and locations follow the example of The Epiphany, in referring to concepts, mental states or behavioural phenomena. Villains include *Stockholm Syndrome*, *Freudian Slip* and *Wandering Eye*; fellow heroes include *Eureka!*, *Tour de Force* and *Non Sequitur*. Most of these names undercut the superhero idiom – *Eureka!* might be a real title, *Freudian Slip* surely not – and complicate the tone: the child-oriented lexicon of comics is rewritten as a set of more adult psychological concerns, to disorienting effect. This is true also of *Le Petit Mort*, which as well as being another phrase from outside English ('the snide, jaded, and callous French Supervillain' [147]) also suggests orgasm: the character provides Lethem with a running joke about masturbation, his powers producing 'staggering sensations of emptiness, self-loathing and doubt' (148). The overall effect is plainly comic – never more so than in The Epiphany's battle with '*Déja Vu*, in *The Forest of Trees Falling*, which no one ever actually ever heard about' (148) – but in an elusive, unsettling tone, as the brash framework of Marvel is filled with material normally foreign to it.

To the Batcave

Such a disorienting combination of idioms is also at stake in one other superhero piece by Lethem, issued over a decade earlier. 'The Notebooks of Bob K.' appeared in *Gas* magazine in 1995, then was revised and republished in *Kafka Americana* (1999). The title alludes to Bob Kane (1915–98), who with writer Bill Finger co-created the character of Batman in the late 1930s. The first section, 'The Batcave', consists of two paragraphs adapted from Kafka's considerably longer late story 'The Burrow' (1923–4). 'The Superhero' adapts Kafka's 1917 vignette 'A Crossbreed'. 'The Penguin', a single long paragraph, reuses Kafka's 'The Vulture' (1920). Lastly, two pages of 'Selected Reflections' derive directly from fifteen of Kafka's aphorisms from the early 1920s; they include occasional reference to figures of the DC pantheon besides Batman, namely Superman and The Flash.

'I have completed the construction of my Batcave and it seems to be successful. All that can be seen from Gotham City is Wayne Manor; there is no sign of the Cave below' (Lethem and Scholz 1999: 16). A reader might assume that the sentences are Lethem's own, and that he has personally created this strange new discourse for Batman. It is unusually formal, even stilted: 'I make no boast of having contrived this ruse intentionally; the Manor is simply the remains of my previous existence as a millionaire. I cannot any longer imagine living in that way, but the carapace stands' (16). This Batman is afflicted by dread – 'At any moment it may be shattered and then all will be over' – even as he insists: 'you do not know me if you think I am afraid, or that I build my Batcave simply out of fear' (16–17). He is also surprisingly whimsical: 'Sometimes I lie down and roll about in the passages or slide down the Batpole with pure joy' (17). This Batman is rather puzzlingly divided between different moods.

Yet as we have noted, these two paragraphs rewrite two passages from the start of Kafka's text, whose narrator discloses how he has constructed an underground lair in a spirit of great paranoia. The textual correspondence is close. 'I have completed the construction of my burrow and it seems to be successful', begins Kafka's narrator. To Batman's retention of Wayne Manor corresponds, less impressively, 'a big hole' resulting from an abortive burrowing attempt (Kafka 1960: 176). The relative proximity of the two scenarios in fact allows Lethem to repeat Kafka with almost no variation for a line or two at a time. In Batman's declaration, 'But the most beautiful thing about my Batcave is the stillness', only one word is different. Lethem sometimes changes details in a mixture of registers: Kafka's narrator disconcertingly reports catching little creatures in his teeth, Lethem's 'with a non-lethal tranquilizer dart'. In sum, he replicates (while editing and foreshortening) Kafka's translated text, while inserting Bat-details wherever they appear pertinent. The resulting combination has Kafka's (translated) voice, yet contains pieces of content that do not belong to Kafka, making for a synthesis alternately urbane and disconcerting.

A like method drives the other pieces of 'The Notebooks'. Kafka's 'A Crossbreed' is narrated by the owner of 'a curious animal, half kitten, half lamb', which is displayed on Sundays for 'the children of the whole neighbourhood' (1991: 75). The founding idea here is that Batman himself is a crossbreed – 'half bat, half man' (Lethem and Scholz 1999: 17). The story uses Kafka's image to reimagine Batman as not merely a man wearing some bat paraphernalia but a unique hybrid animal. Kafka's kitten and lamb seem a strange pairing – 'From the cat it takes its head and claws, from the lamb its size and shape; from both its eyes, which are gentle and flickering' (75) – but Lethem's organic Batman is stranger still: 'From the bat it takes its head and wings, from the man its size and shape; from both its eyes which are wild and flickering' (17). Lethem's piece has two other elements. One is the obtrusiveness of the Bat-details, which here take on a childish quality. So Kafka's crossbreed 'runs away from cats and has a tendency to attack lambs' (75) (both, of course, its own biological cousins), but Lethem's superhero 'flees from policemen and makes to attack the Riddler' (17). Yet there is serendipity in Kafka's creature – 'by the hen-coop it can lie in ambush for hours, but it has never yet seized an opportunity for murder' (76) – matching Batman's refusal to shed blood: 'Beside the mugger's alleyway it can lie for hours in ambush, but it has never yet seized an opportunity for murder' (18). (The character's refusal to fire a gun is sufficiently part of his legend to be remarked on by a journalist in *The Fortress of Solitude* [2003: 423].)

The other aspect that Kafka bequeaths to this bestialized superhero is pathos. His crossbreed looks 'unhappy in its own skin', and its owner wonders whether 'the butcher's knife would be a release for the animal' (1991: 76). The superhero's owner likewise admits that 'the rotating knives of the Riddler's trap' might be 'a release for this superhero', and that the Batman 'sometimes gazes at me with a look of human understanding, challenging me to do the thing of which both of us are thinking' (Lethem and Scholz 1999: 18–19). The notion that Batman yearns for the release of death is unfamiliar, though not wholly incongruous with his tortured origins as an avenging orphan. Pathos and death are also keynotes of 'The Penguin', where 'A Vulture' becomes 'The Penguin', a passing gentleman with his gun is Green Arrow with his bow, the narrating Batman has been trapped in 'unbreakable titanium bonds', and the Penguin's final thrust is not 'through my mouth' but 'through my cowl' (19). Otherwise the action of the text is identical, as abruptly troubling as Kafka's.

What is the overall effect of Lethem's processing of Kafka through this Bat-recycler? First, Batman is rendered more serious. The wistful tones of 'The Batcave', in which he appears a solitary eccentric who welcomes his new home as 'great good fortune for anyone getting on years' (17); the sadly unique animal ('Why is there only one such superhero', wonder the children) in 'The Superhero'; the figure seemingly condemned to his violent death at the beak of the Penguin despite, in a characteristic Kafka motif, the supposed adjacency of the means of rescue – these all comprise a 'dark' Batman, but in their strangeness and vulnerability they are darker, or sadder, than many of the newly darkened versions of the character that have periodically appeared since the 1970s. Of course, most of the labour here is performed by Kafka and his original translators. His epic melancholy is applied to a comic-book character, who emerges fragile and fated.

At the same time, Lethem's experiment affects Kafka too. Most simply, his work gains new moments of comedy here: the inhabitant of the Burrow 'slid[ing] down the Batpole with pure joy', the crossbreed 'Climbing on a parapet' and speaking 'into a radio on its belt' (17) are incongruous additions to the original tone, and their specificity adds to the incongruity. The transformation of Kafka's figures into Batman also concretizes them anew. The inhabitant of the Burrow, for instance, has always been shadowy; Batman allows us to put a face, or a cowl, to him. In a surprising effect, the fantastic figure of Batman brings a certain solidity to Kafka's vignettes, because of his familiarity. Their pathos is not diminished (Batman merely rendering Kafka ironic) but heightened (Batman rendering the scenarios newly visual, more real than before).

The 'Notebooks' are a comedy of disparity – Czech high modernism and American comic book – yet the wager of the piece is that, as the Joker is apt to tell Batman, they are not so different. The Batcave, bristling with defences and electronic sensors, *is* like the paranoiac Burrow; Batman *is* a kind of unnerving crossbreed; and his world *is*, like Kafka's, an alienating, perilous, urban one, modern yet Gothic. In a later essay, as though spelling out the logic of this early piece, Lethem explicitly calls Batman 'a creature worthy of Kafka – emerging from his burrow wearing his traumatic identity humiliatingly on the outside of his body, like a bug's shell' (2017: 54). In fact this resemblance is the deepest implication of the fact that two of Lethem's fifteen 'Selected Reflections' are simply repeats of Kafka, not adapted or enhanced. 'From a real antagonist boundless courage flows into you'; 'Knowledge of the diabolical there can be, but not belief in it, for anything more diabolical than that could not exist' (Lethem and Scholz 1999: 21) – the implication is that in working through Kafka's aphorisms for phrases to be turned in Gotham's direction, Lethem has identified these as already Bat-ready, statements that, admittedly enigmatically, function in both Kafka's and Batman's worlds. Lethem's title, 'The Notebooks of Bob K.', turns on a coincidence: that the man who took credit for creating Batman happened to have a surname that could be shortened like those of the protagonists of Kafka's novels. Yet the implication is that this coincidence points to a genuine resemblance. Perhaps 'Bob K.' should be understood not exactly as Bob Kane, but as a halfway, crossbreed figure himself, an imagined author who writes like Kafka but writes about Batman.

As a work of literary creation, 'The Notebooks of Bob K.' is close to nugatory: six pages of prose almost entirely drawn from someone else's oeuvre. Yet by the same token it stands as exemplary of one strand of Lethem's aesthetic. To make a work about Batman by repurposing pieces of Kafka is a kind of procedural art, reliant on concept and combination rather than individual style. The text is highly distinctive, yet also, paradoxically, bears few of Lethem's own stylistic fingerprints. In tune with his description of *Gun, with Occasional Music* as 'a piece of carpentry' (Clarke 2011: 51), 'The Notebooks' resembles that debut in being a deliberate conjunction of two contrasting resources. Lethem might have said of this text, echoing his remarks about *Gun*, that it tried to locate the exact mid-point between Kafka and Batman – or perhaps more accurately that it is four parts Kafka to one part Gotham. In accordance with 'The Ecstasy of Influence', literature here is 'in a plundered, fragmentary state'; 'appropriation, mimicry, quotation, allusion, and sublimated collaboration consist of a sine qua non of the creative act' (2011: 95, 97). This affectionate 'second use' of both Kafka and Batman exemplifies, ahead of time, that essay's declaration that 'Any text that has infiltrated the common mind […] inexorably joins the language of culture' and 'has moved to a place beyond enclosure or control' (2011: 110).

Arrowman

The Fortress of Solitude's concern with superheroes develops along two parallel tracks. One is young Dylan Ebdus's growing interest in comics. The other is the presence of an actual superpowered figure and the source of his power. These two converge in the creation of a new hero, Aeroman. Let us trace these two paths in turn, to discern how this novel reveals and treats its superhero theme.

The first hint of the theme comes before comic books have been mentioned. Dylan Ebdus accompanies his mother down the street to tell the elderly Isabel Vendle that he will no longer work for her on Saturdays. Other children are playing outside with a baseball. One of them, Earl, waves: 'but he could have been pointing out a bird or a cloud in the sky. Instead of returning the wave Dylan looked up at the sky himself, pretended he'd seen something move there, a body dart across the cornices, or leap from one side of Dean Street to the other' (2003: 38–9). Dylan is mainly avoiding his friend's attention, on the basis that a child with his parents does not get mixed up in the children's autonomous games. The second sentence clearly states that he has only 'pretended' to see something above, and the next clauses describe what he pretends to see: 'a body dart across the cornices, or leap from one side of Dean Street to the other'. Yet a figure leaping across the street sounds too fanciful to be something that Dylan spontaneously pretends to be looking at. Something that begins as a feint, a gaze away at nothing, has turned into a gaze at something, too quickly for the feint to be unravelled by the sentence describing it.

A few pages later, the figure of a 'flying man' is suddenly much more fully drawn. The figure is imagined looking down on 'The elongated rectangular grid of these streets' (46), and thus being the only witness to a white woman beating a black boy. This is Rachel Ebdus's revenge on Dylan's tormentor Robert Woolfolk, an event that will resonate through the book in the nervous spell it casts on the bully. Lethem uses the device of the overhead view to highlight this moment, as a kind of spotlit scene on a cleared stage ('These streets always make room for two three figures alone in struggle, as in a forest, unheard'), and also as a way of showing an event at which his main protagonist is absent. The flying man here thus starts as a conceit of point of view. 'Imagine the perspective of a flying man' places him in a different, more provisional realm than the characters we have already more concretely encountered. Yet the narrative cannot help fleshing out this figure, turning him from a perspective into a character with features and feelings. The narrative voice asks:

> Is this a *mugging*? Should he *swoop down, intervene*?
> Who does this flying man think he is anyway – Batman? *Black*man? (46)

The first lines pick up a stylistic tendency in the novel to italicize certain words and phrases that come loaded with understanding: Dylan's neighbour Henry's claim to '*captaincy*' (58) is an example, Mingus Rude's 'in principle *showing off*' (54) another. Here the sense is that the flying man is conceiving of his own options in the terms of superhero narratives. Having introduced this notion, the narrative appears to turn on him: its rhetorical questions mock his claim to the superhero's role. Yet in doing so they etch him into existence. 'Blackman' has gained a new degree of specificity. When the last line of the passage announces that he 'flies on, needing a drink more than anything', it ascribes to him a corporeal quality that would be difficult to erase back into a mere conceit.

Thus an image introduced through disavowal – first as an imagined distraction, then as no more than a narrative convenience – inexorably gathers substance. A few pages on, Dylan runs ahead of his mother and looks up: 'In that instant Dylan was sure he'd seen it again: the ragged figure arching from the roof of Public School 38 to the tops of the ramshackle storefronts on Nevins, to disappear then under the sky. The impossible leaper. He looked like a bum' (54). The narrative works retroactively on the glimpse in the previous chapter: 'sure he'd seen it again', now, means that he does think he saw it then. We later learn that the flying man was 'something Dylan did and didn't wish to have noticed' (112).

This gradual mode of revelation is apt enough to the subject. The flying man is fugitive, a secret: something to be faintly suspected rather than flatly announced. His next appearance is another fifty pages on, inadvertently interrupting Dylan's bid for a first bout of graffiti in an empty lot: 'First a shadow flashing at the corner of the boy's eyes as he crouches under the slide, an immense bird- or bat-like stretch of black against the brick wall. Flight, reversed. Then a collapsing thud, someone thrown, and the wheezing sigh, the exhale thrown from a body by force of impact' (101). Visceral terms depict the flying man's topple to the ground. Though the 'bat-like stretch of black' carries a clear superheroic reference, the figure's fall is not an elegant recovery like one of Batman's: his 'wheezing sigh' lacks the dignity of his muscular comic-book colleagues. The figure is indeed, as Dylan has suspected, 'a bum': urine-scented, 'dressed in jeans oiled gray with filth and a formerly white shirt, cuffs shredded, a button dangling by a thread' (101). He is also, as the narrative has provocatively hinted before, an African American, evidently of disadvantaged background. His first words identify Dylan as a racial other: 'Little white boy' (101). His speech is rough, idiomatic: 'Scrawling up some nassyshit on the walls, I seen you'; 'Tangle me up, hurt my leg, dang'; 'I axed if you got a dollar', 'I used to fly good' (101–2). He thus inverts several norms for a costumed hero: typically (as Lethem's essays suggest) white, physically fit and powerful, verbally precise if not elevated. This flying man is a failed, or failing, hero: 'Can't land right no more'; 'Got to be fallin' all the time'; 'Muthafucking [...] *air waves* always got to be knocking me down' (101–2). Dylan has come upon the figure at the end of his career, and whatever may have preceded it remains untold. Yet he just about retains the trappings of the superhero – his 'bedsheet cape, knotted at the neck', and his true secret, 'a silver ring on his pinky finger' (102) – and perhaps its vocation too. It is unclear whether his last muttered utterance to Dylan is '*Fight evil!*' (150).

This vocation makes sense because superheroes have become so integral to the novel's texture. They enter, in fact, in the same incident as Dylan's first glimpse of the flying man. Isabel Vendle's nephew Croft has purchased 'a scattering of violently colorful comic books', which claim Rachel Ebdus's enthusiastic attention. They are unknown to Dylan, though, and thus appear as mere vivid impressions: 'A man of stone, a man of fire, a man of rubber, a man of iron, a brown dog the size of a hippopotamus, wearing a mask' (40). Comics, in this first instance, are counter-intuitively an *adult* pursuit: Dylan learns their lore from Rachel and Croft, rendered in a single run-on sentence (41), and the sense is that Rachel and Croft begin their affair, which will transform the whole novel, by bonding over them, flirtatiously trading aesthetic passions. The scene can be placed in the context offered by Lethem's essays, in which his own generation felt itself to suffer from belatedness: the 'psychedelic' Silver Age in which, as Rachel announces, 'Jack Kirby's a God' (40) belongs to those who were youthful a decade before. Marvel comics are now, in around 1974, a kind of counter-cultural hangover, a 'violently colorful' memory of the decade of Pop Art.

Dylan thus enters the realm of comics as a bluffing latecomer. When Mingus Rude asks him 'You like comics?' – one of the most fateful, emblematic questions asked in all Lethem's fiction – Lethem registers the ambivalence of the reply with precision:

> 'Sure', said Dylan unsure. *My mother likes them*, he almost said. (55)

Mingus's comics form part of a series of displays that he makes in his first encounter with Dylan, along with his father's gold discs and the uniforms that he solemnly dons and removes in sequence: Boy Scout, hockey player, American footballer whose shoulder pads suggestively give him 'the outline of a superhero' (55). Comics appear as an option, one of the aspects of identity that Mingus has brought from Philadelphia. Yet Mingus is in fact committed to his small collection. After Rachel and Croft, he shows us a different way of relating to them: 'They'd been tenderly handled to death, corners rounded, paper browned by hot attentive breath, pages chewed by eyes'. Mingus has already signed his name on each comic, a fact that will bemuse him, in a different persona, years later ('Dang, I even wrote my *name* in all these, check it out' [281]). Comics at this stage are still a focus of passion, communicated from Mingus to Dylan: Mingus treats comic books as 'a presence delicately alive, some piece of still-beating flesh he and Dylan might be capable of healing by their absolute fixity of attention, by their reverence' (65). The repeated act of reading is vividly staged, registering the setting of this bodily experience, and indicating the thoroughness of the reading process by listing the paratextual minutiae that surround the superhero story itself:

> Two afternoons a week, in the dimming light on Dylan's stoop [...] shoulders hunched to protect the flimsy covers from the wind, puzzling out the last dram, the last square inch of information, the credits, the letters page, the copyright, the Sea-Monkeys ads, *the insult that made a man out of Mac*. (66)

These lines bookend a protracted passage that is crucial in establishing the theme (65–6), and which is mainly dedicated to reciting facts about the heroes: 'Spider-Man's girlfriend, Gwen, had been killed by the Goblin'; 'Captain Marvel wasn't Shazam, it was confusing'. Methods exist for acquiring knowledge: 'In *Origins* you learned how superheroes got started, the answer generally being: radiation'. This theme is congruent with the novel's general status as a *Bildungsroman*, its capacious interest in how Dylan gains understanding of the numerous codes of the streets where he lives. Yet as the case of Captain Marvel demonstrates, facts about a long-standing narrative form can become ambiguous, and much of the burden of the passage is to emphasize the difficulty of acquiring clear knowledge. In this, too, comic books are typical of the uncertain process of personal growth, in which even knowledge of what has happened on one's own sidewalk is unstable (29). If superhero stories are 'a field of expertise […] all fine print and ritual' (65), this can be forbidding. Thus the Silver Surfer 'was a situation you couldn't really understand if you came in too late' (65): a statement that, in reprising Lethem's recurrent motif of cultural belatedness, emphasizes in fictional context the genre's multi-generational complexity. Comics are a lesson in the multiplicity of aesthetics, applied to the same material: 'Different artists drew the same characters different ways – you could hurt your eyes trying to account for it, to grant continuity to these hobbled stories' (66). The multifarious details cited fly at the reader, even as the voice listing them retains a measure of irony in its relentlessness. 'Dylan was really horrified to learn he'd let so much time slip past, so much essential cultural history' (65): Lethem's tone is delicate, ironically playing off a sense that this is a childish pursuit, barely deserving the term 'essential cultural history' for an adult reader, against the equally strong instinct of the children that this material is indeed of the essence.

In the novel's first section 'Underberg', then, comics become shared and developing lore, ever ramifying into more specialized tracks. Arthur Lomb, with his garrulous spill of facts, disdainfully informs Dylan of the history of Charlton Comics (whose characters, including the Blue Beetle mentioned here, would become the prototypes for Moore's *Watchmen*) (115). Both Dylan and Arthur, buying multiple copies of a first issue (278), show the impulse of the collector (which also happens to be Rachel's nickname for her husband [34]). Dylan and Mingus experience Jack Kirby's return from DC to Marvel as Lethem and Karl Rusnak did in the real Gowanus (77). But as an integral part of imaginative life, where Halloween egg throwers wear Spider-Man masks (47), comics also become a way of imagining life, a source of metaphor. So in Mingus's absence, 'for all [Dylan] knew Mingus might be off fighting the Mole Men at the I.S. 293 annex, where sixth graders went, while Dylan, in fifth grade, was still trapped in the Negative Zone' (69–70). A silent, distracted Mingus on a graffiti mission is also 'in some other quadrant, the Negative Zone maybe': '*Just another revoltin' development*, to quote Ben Grimm, more commonly known as the Thing' (96). During another disappearance Mingus is 'like the flying man, a rumor with himself Dylan couldn't confirm' (118). In a piece of narrative that speeds through passing time the two boys are seen in parallel: 'White kid, black kid, Captain America and Falcon, Iron Fist and Luke Cage' (79), though the comparison of Dylan to the super-soldier is fanciful. If DC comics lack appeal it may in part be due to another unspoken parallel: 'Superman in his Fortress of Solitude reminded you all too much of Abraham in his high studio, brooding over nothing' (66) – a phrasing that also evokes Dick's *Man in the High Castle*.

Yet the DC imagery is ready to hand for Robert Woolfolk's use of an apprentice bully – 'Call it the Batman-and-Robin' (195) – and a pair of would-be bullies are 'a couple of mugging Robins lacking a Batman to back them up' (240), while Dylan's bedroom is also casually a 'Batcave' (204) in the narrator's idiom. A larger dose of irony is present in the teenage band name Stately Wayne Manor (259), but the reference to Batman's home still demonstrates how far comics' idiom has permeated the life of one or more generations, as does a reference to Superman in the novelty record 'Rapper's Delight' (245). When Dylan and Mingus approach a sexual encounter, the language of superheroes conveys the sense of estrangement from normal life that allows Dylan to venture into such unprecedented behaviour: 'The world was unnamed, you wore disguises, were Inhumans. Mingus's room was another Negative Zone, under water, under the house, detached from Dean Street and whirling away to another place' (208). Retreating to Mingus's basement, 'on their own deep exploration' the pair settle into the recurrent imagery of 'Mole-Men', drawn from a sworn foe of the Fantastic Four (209, 224). More generally, 'Teenagerdom was a secret identity in the first place' (191): the superhero's penchant for secrecy suggests an allegory for the furtive adolescent, working through multiple options of self. Likewise, 'Marvel Comics had it right, the world was all secret names, you only needed to uncover your own' (93).

Yet Dylan is not fully able to make use of comics as a redemptive model for his own life. *Omega the Unknown*, the one comic that we closely observe Dylan buying, is implied to parallel his situation, devoting attention as it does to 'a twelve-year-old kid with an unexplained psychic connection to Omega, a bullied, orphaned kid who's going to a public junior high in Hell's Kitchen'. The parallel is highlighted – 'Hey, maybe even the geniuses up at Marvel Comics knew you were in hell' – then instantly disallowed: 'didn't help, because you weren't allowed to know it yourself, not really. There wasn't any connection between you and the poor, helpless kid in *Omega the Unknown*, not that you could permit yourself to see' (83–4). The comic-book reader, these examples show, might fancifully identify with a superhero, but not with a mere human boy, who offers no transcendence of real life. A more successful imaginative connection between comics and life comes in Barrett Rude Jr's recording of '(Did You Press Your) Bump Suit' with Doofus Funkstrong, aka the Funk Mob. At the studio in Manhattan he assesses 'these men dressed as cartoon pimps and superheroes' (133); when they visit him in Brooklyn they look like, among other things, 'Batman villains' (155); the neighbour Lonnie tells Mingus 'They looked like superheroes, man' (161). The repeated analogy hints at a connection that we have noted before, in Lethem's thoughts on Spider-Man: the closest thing to real-life superheroes in the mid-1970s might be extravagant black musicians.

It is in this world in which comics are integral to daily life, a continuous source of narrative that furnishes the terms of imagination, that Dylan and Mingus come to use the flying man's ring. Dylan builds up to Aeroman in halting steps. He tries and fails to persuade himself to leap off his own roof – 'smacked by a vast hand from the sky' into fear (154) – then discovers his power at last unwittingly, in leaping through the air to catch the ball repeatedly in the street game of stoopball: 'He nestled easily in the air, under the branches, above the cars' (164). It is now that Dylan explicitly connects the ring to the genre that he has learned from comic books. His reflection takes off from the suggestion that the visiting Funk Mob are superheroes: 'Dean Street possessed superheroes: not musicians in a limousine but Dylan, the flying kid. He'd sew a costume and take to the rooftops, begin *bounding down on crime* and they'd know then what they couldn't be allowed to know yet' (165).

Aeroman's costume is first sighted during Dylan's trip to Vermont. It is decidedly home-made: a cape 'cut out of a worn Dr. Seuss bedsheet featuring *A Lion Licking a Lemon Lollipop*', with the lion centred as 'a suitably enigmatic logo'. The front of the childish costume is decorated with the Spirograph that we have seen Dylan using since the book's earliest chapters: its 'oscillated circle' suggesting '*bands of power*' also looks, from a distance, like 'a fat zero' (180). The sight of the first Aeroman does not impress Heather Windle in Vermont, but this serves to reinforce the character's association with the city (181–2). Dylan's first attempts to act as Aeroman in Brooklyn are again halting: 'It was somewhat unclear how to begin' (191). From deep immersion in comics he understands how a superhero should operate, but cannot see how to apply it to his local environment: 'He needed an isolated nightscape, an alley, a woman yelling for return of her stolen pocketbook, the classical Spider-Man mugging scenario: exactly what he'd never seen in his life' (192). A discrepancy emerges between the conventions of the comic book and the awkward reality at street level. Gowanus seems too 'mixed up' for the binary division of the superhero; the subway, the most likely location for a mugging, is not hospitable to Aeroman's power of flight (192–3). In a telling encounter, Aeroman's first attempt to avert crime, following a woman down an empty street, scares the woman into flight: 'Aeroman had met the enemy, and it was Aeroman' (193). The moment draws on Lethem's experience of mischievously stalking a girlfriend home from the same station, to which he would confess two decades later in 'Speak, Hoyt-Schermerhorn' (2005: 56–7). Aeroman's intentions here are better than Lethem's on that occasion, but his experience of realizing that he appears the potential criminal rather than the saviour introduces a paradox about the character that will linger into his revival in California.

What takes Aeroman to another level is the participation of Mingus, a direct consequence of the sexual experience of mutual masturbation that he and Dylan share: the sharing of this secret makes another possible (211). It is noticeable that such physical intimacy inaugurates the collaborative exercise of Aeroman, in which the two boys notionally become two halves of one fictional self. The narrative describes a series of incidents in which the newly dual Aeroman project ventures out to fight crime: no more than 'eight or nine', with 'maybe three bona fide rescues, legible crimes authentically flown down on and busted up' (225). Dylan serves as bait for muggers, taking his experience as the repeated victim of 'yoking' and making his vulnerability into a deliberate performance: victimhood is replayed as a covert strategy of aggression. Mingus, having rehearsed 'for weeks, on backyards and on roofs', wears the new Aeroman costume – white cape, 'sewn white mask [...] open at the top to vent his Afro to the air, like Marvel's *Black Goliath*' (213) – as he flies down from on high to attack Dylan's assailants. Aeroman is also seen combating more substantial crimes – one knife mugging, one holdup of a Chinese takeaway – before the mishap of being blown from the top of the Brooklyn Bridge (226–7). After this sole season of crimefighting, the character's trajectory shifts. The *New York Times* reports Mingus's arrest for attacking a plain-clothes policeman working on a drug bust: the sense is that Mingus is involved in the drug deal itself (240, 285), thus shifting Aeroman from crimefighter to criminal. After this, Aeroman is 'dead or at least on hiatus'; the costume 'lost or destroyed' (243); the ring stowed away until Dylan buys it from Mingus at the end of 'Underberg'. Aeroman winks out of existence until his brief revival in mid-1980s Berkeley.

Plainly, Aeroman is among the more remarkable adventures of Dylan Ebdus's life – even if he is spurned as irrelevant by Mingus Rude (462), who comically coins his enduring misnomer Arrowman (213). But what is the significance of Aeroman to the novel? Five related points can be made.

First, in Aeroman the world of comic books is animated. What is otherwise a matter of arcane childhood lore and plastic-bagged first issues takes on a corporeal form. The superhero goes from being background – part of the cultural furniture amid which Dylan and Mingus experience childhood and youth – to foreground: a character on the same plane as Dylan and Mingus (who are effectively his secret identities). Aeroman focuses the personal and cultural memory of comic books in an unexpected and dramatic fashion.

It follows that Aeroman is also a case of the motif alluded to earlier: the thought experiment 'what if superheroes were real?'. In this context it is significant that Aeroman remains a halting experiment. With his costume shelved, he 'might as well have been the lead in a quickly canceled Marvel title like *Omega* or *Warlock*, or a murdered sidekick, quickly avenged then forgotten [...] in other words, no superhero at all, not really, not one anyone remembered' (225). As Aeroman brings the promise of the superhero into Gowanus, he is also compromised by it. As we have seen, Dylan's first attempt to enact the character at night is frustrated by the lack of 'isolated nightscape' in which a hero can simply '[splice] criminals from victims' (192); the subway is an unpropitious environment for his powers; and even Mingus, 'a natural' at flying with the requisite 'organ for sensing *air waves*' (212), is blown into the East River at the moment he should be swooping on muggers (227). The childish improvisation of Aeroman's costume, from Dr Seuss and Spirograph, also shows the ideal of the superhero being snagged on the contingency of the available material world. Lethem records that for a decade he had thought of 'writing a big book about growing up in Brooklyn, and conflating that with a story about a real but pathetic superhero' (Clarke 2011: 109). Even as it is rooted in the Bronze Age and memories of the Silver Age, then, *The Fortress of Solitude* joins a post-*Watchmen* era of dramatizing the superhero, not as an ideal but in his awkward interactions with limiting circumstances. The novelty here is that the figure, unlike Alan Moore's grizzled and disappointed veterans, is barely an adolescent. The exception is Aaron X. Doily, the original flying man, who comes even closer than Aeroman to being pathetic.

Third, Aeroman allows a different engagement with the city, in action and point of view. The development of Aeroman takes the narrative to the rooftops, yielding a different perspective on the borough. As we have observed, almost the first introduction of Aaron X. Doily in flight is as a point of view on 'The elongated rectangular grid of these streets' (46). Aeroman in turn encourages an overview of the urban landscape; we shall look more closely at the resultant panoramic quality in the next chapter. Dylan perceives the neighbourhood differently with Aeroman in mind, 'ear cocked to the damp howl of the late-summer wind as it bore voices through the night' (192), and as bait for muggers he turns another block into 'a human stage', seen through its coordinates ('This block's bounded on the Court side by Atlantic's Arabic shops, at Boerum by St. Vincent's Home for Boys') and overshadowed by 'a parking garage, a concrete embankment of ramps four levels high' (211): a location specifically singled out as a perch for the costumed Mingus. The sense of an alternative view of the city being opened up by Aeroman is connected to the other distinctively urban activity that Dylan and Mingus share: graffiti. Mingus's ventures out to spray graffiti in fact foreshadow the adventures of Aeroman, such that the two seem parallel options, which might be converted into one another. Aged just twelve, Mingus in 1975 leads his friend out 'on a solemn mission Dylan didn't understand' (77), its goal two 'lavish word-paintings' on the Brooklyn Bridge which are perceived to have 'conquered the bridge, pinned it to the secret street, claimed it for Brooklyn' (78). The moment is presented as a milestone in the development of their career in graffiti, and the same scene is recalled when Aeroman ventures to the bridge: 'Dylan standing as bait by the massive shoring tower still bearing Mono's and Lee's fabulously weathered autographs, Mingus flown to a perch on the high, swaying cable' (226). Both graffiti and Aeroman are illicit activities, involving movement into inhospitable urban spaces that would otherwise not seem of interest: among them the parking garage on which Mingus perches, and the 'hidden patch of land' at the edge of the Brooklyn–Queens Expressway whose stone wall is covered with 'patient graffiti masterpieces to be viewed by the passing drivers' (94).

The most direct connection between graffiti and Aeroman is drawn when Mingus, obscurely estranged from Dylan, paints his own tag, 'DOSE', on the wall of the Brooklyn House of Detention. The sight is introduced in Golden Age superheroic terms, as a passer-by points up at it, 'his mouth hung open in some kind of *look, up in the sky, it's a bird, it's a plane* posture of astonishment' (271). The narrative's first reaction, which may be relaying Dylan's own, looks dismissive: 'Doesn't he know there *ain't no such thing as a Superman*?' (274). The dismissal is double-edged, though, for the novel and its protagonist know that there *is* an Aeroman. When Dylan looks up:

> There on the vast glass-brick and concrete face, maybe ten stories above the street and three stories tall, was a brazen impossibility, the biggest tag in the history of tagging. [...] however ragged, the thing was a masterpiece, dwarfing Mono's and Lee's bridge stunt, and meant to shock the viewer's brain with the obvious question: *How the fuck DID it get up there?* (274)

Once more the original sighting of the Brooklyn Bridge is recalled for comparison; now Mingus has outdone it, by combining his passion for graffiti with the power of the superhero. The coexistence of the two aspects gives the scene its force. For Mingus simply to spray his tag somewhere would be commonplace, and he could choose to fly without telling Dylan. Here he has flown and left a trace of it, with graffiti that only a flying man could produce. The tag can thus be taken as a personal message to Dylan: 'a cry, a claim', suggesting that 'Someone's betrayed someone but you can't say who' (274). The tag also has a still broader social significance, in uniting two unspoken realities: 'The looming jail which no one mentioned or looked at and the trail of dripping paint that covered the city's every public surface and which no one mentioned or looked at: two invisible things had rendered one another visible' (274). Both are connected to crime (according to graffiti's status as a petty crime, which is noted later in the novel [455–6]); both, at the historical moment described, are predominantly the territory of black men. Mingus's daring unification of paint and prison is noticeably in tune with what Lethem has persistently said was a project of this novel: 'I had to name things that weren't ordinarily named' (Clarke 2011: 92).

Those things, like graffiti and the prison, especially involve race, and this is the fourth aspect of Aeroman's significance. The magic ring is bequeathed from a black man to a white boy, who tests it in the predominantly white environment of Vermont – where the idea of Aeroman is rejected. The ring only gains practical power in the collaboration between white and black (or mixed-race) boys. It is a significant detail that 'They'd meant to swap [the ring] back and forth, the changing from black to white one of Aeroman's mystifying aspects, another level of secret identity' (239), even though in practice this never happens: the Aeroman concept is a collaboration in which, in principle, white and black might swap places in an alternation that would confuse local observers.

Yet it also appears that a large proportion of the street crime in their neighbourhood is committed by black males – a fact seen as continuous with Dylan's lengthy experience of being 'yoked' and robbed of dollars on the way to or from school. When Dylan first ventures out seeking action, he is highly aware of his status as 'A white boy on the corner of Bond and Schermerhorn at eleven at night' – potential victim, not perpetrator – and that of the 'white woman' whom he imagines 'regretting she'd ever heard the word *Brooklyn*' (193). The same night, the secret of Aeroman emboldens Dylan, for once, to defy the African American bully Robert Woolfolk: Dylan's rare courage is 'a crack of daylight in the night' (197). Aeroman's first successful swoop is upon 'two black teenagers […] their whiteboy's radar's operative' (211–2): youths used to treating a white contemporary as a target, now battered by a masked black boy. So too the two boys Aeroman intends (but fails) to combat on the Brooklyn Bridge are 'two homeboys', whose opening gambit is 'Hey, whiteboy, lemme borrow a dollar off you, man' (226). The other most visible local ethnicity is Hispanic, and two of

Aeroman's other victims are specified as tall Puerto Ricans (225, 228). All this means that Mingus, in his occasional mission to 'fight crime' (225), is primarily attacking non-white citizens, some of whom have deliberately been goaded into the scene. The novel does not dwell on this, and Mingus himself is untroubled by it, reflecting only that 'Half the yoke artists they clocked were chumps Dose knew from around the projects anyway' (462). 'Crime', for him, is in this sense close to home.

The idea of Aeroman as actively hostile to black people, never openly suggested in 'Underberg', is voiced directly in the novel's third part, 'Prisonaires'. Here in Berkeley a black bus traveller revives Dylan's memories of humiliation on the Brooklyn streets, and this directly leads him to use the ring's new powers against local criminals. The petty gangsters he encounters are again African Americans, who call him a 'ghost-face' (419) before he becomes invisible and disrupts their affairs. The *Oakland Tribune* thus develops a highly racialized account of Aeroman's latest action: 'the mystery white boy had come in with gun blazing'; the victim, OJJJ, explains that Dylan was *'another crazy white motherf****r gaming to cap some n****rs'* (421). For local journalist Vance Christmas, Dylan is 'Oakland's Bernhard Goetz', the name of a white New Yorker who had fired upon four black muggers in 1984. On the telephone, Christmas asks Dylan 'You don't hate black people, then?' Though his reply is a simple 'No', Dylan's reflection before answering is curiously ambiguous: 'For a moment, it nearly poured out of me: the yearning to compensate for "Play That Funky Music", the desolation which had once birthed Aeroman and now brought him back to life' (423). 'Play That Funky Music' is a single by the white rock band Wild Cherry which Dylan has experienced as an oppressive item of mockery on the Gowanus streets (111). What he now means by 'compensation' for this is left unclarified: perhaps most simply he suggests that Aeroman has been an attempt by someone ritually humiliated to regain a measure of power – a function it retains in the wake of his Berkeley yoking. In this respect Aeroman, and especially his second life in California, takes part in a context of racial difference, violence, resentment and guilt, even if the character's most successful spell is as a rare moment of black–white cooperation. This complexity, as well as the fear of actual arrest, is surely one reason that Dylan retires the ring once more (425).

The complexity is also replayed in the ring's last mission. Dylan enters the prison specifically to offer it to Mingus a means of escape. Mingus, content to wait for his own release, bids him take it instead to Robert Woolfolk. Robert, unaware that the ring has changed its power, perishes in attempting to fly. The ring, here, is offered as salvation to one black prisoner, then prompts the death of another. In a sense the sequence re-enacts the logic of Aeroman. One black male, Dylan's friend and at one time the visible avatar of Aeroman, is encouraged to use the ring's power for emancipation. (Despite his rejection of Aeroman, Mingus has not quite forgotten superheroes: in a tiny, poignant detail, his record of infractions in prison includes the entry 'Inmate climbs on bunk, states he is Superman' [458]). The other, who has tormented Dylan in a series of meetings so recurrent as almost to go beyond naturalism and into the realm of legend, is effectively killed by the ring: as though Aeroman's violence upon the 'yoking' muggers were taken to a lethal extreme. Dylan himself sees Robert's death this way: 'I'd wakened Aeroman to kill Robert Woolfolk.' Just as Aeroman's original missions were a collaboration of white and black, so this fatal event is described as 'a collaboration that had taken Mingus and the ring and my half-conscious hatred years to devise, though the seed of inspiration had been unmistakable, in Aaron X. Doily's plunge into the Pacific Street vest-pocket park, twenty-three years ago – what goes up comes down. Aeroman was nothing if not a black body on the ground' (501). That Doily and Robert are substantially linked in this way is the fancy of Dylan's guilty mind. After all, Doily falls to the ground for different reasons from Robert. But Dylan's last line might hint not just at the parallel between the deceased Robert and the collapsed Doily, but at Aeroman's other victims, including OJJJ in Berkeley. A measure of guilty ambivalence runs through Dylan's reflections, as he both acknowledges the damage that Aeroman has done (at least, specifically, in bringing about Robert's demise) and seems to confess a kind of desire for it, in his long-brewed 'half-conscious hatred'. Once more, the ring and Aeroman cannot be extricated from a context of racial difference, which Lethem deliberately refuses to efface.

Aeroman has one more layer of significance, which is formal. He affects the texture of the novel. Lethem's sixth novel was by a long way his most richly rooted thus far in real places and times. The magic ring is the major exception to this. It punctures a seemingly mimetic fictional world with a narrative element that is even more fantastic than many of the features of *Gun, with Occasional Music* or *Girl in Landscape*. Where those novels carried a notional assumption that their content had a scientific explanation ('evolution therapy', 'viruses') somehow continuous with the world as we know it, Lethem does not provide any such context for the ring. It remains completely discontinuous from any real-world assumptions or known physical laws. It also remains entirely isolated: at no point in the novel is there any suggestion that another such item exists.

In Farah Mendlesohn's terms (2008: xxi–xxii), the ring may be characterized as an element of 'intrusion fantasy': something out of this world that appears amid the quotidian and offers unprecedented challenges and experiences within it, without (like the fantasy 'portal', to Lewis's Narnia or Lethem's Lack) opening on to another imaginary world. The irruption of the fantastic that the ring represents could be viewed as an aesthetic insurance policy from a writer who had come from the precincts of the fantastic. The attempt at a realistic novel of the modern United States is not to be assessed on the same terms as others (Franzen's *The Corrections* would be a pertinent contemporary comparison), because it contains this qualitatively different material. Lethem's anger at James Wood's failure to mention the ring in his 2003 review suggests this: Wood had judged the novel on terms (semi-autobiographical realism) within which Lethem did not wish to be delimited. By the same token, the ring is also a discreet badge of honour that Bat-signals the author's continued affiliation to the constituency of writers and readers committed to science fiction and the fantastic (a constituency suggested in the novel itself by the ForbiddenCon audience, 'converting feelings of inferiority and self-loathing into their opposites' [347]). It serves as evidence that he has not truly abandoned such aesthetic projects, despite his new immersion in a mimetic New York.

But these descriptions are too defensive to do the device full justice. Lethem has given his own accounts of the aesthetic significance of the ring. In his riposte to Wood, he describes it as a 'brute component of audacity', the one 'distinguishing feature that put the book aside from those you'd otherwise compare it to (Henry Roth, say)' (2011: 386). The ring presents a 'formal discontinuity': 'that of a book which wrenches its own "realism" – *mimeticism* is the word I prefer – into crisis by insisting on uncanny events' (2011: 387). In interview he talks of the novel's formal radicalism by comparison with *Motherless Brooklyn*, in 'smashing together in a far more intense way my commitment to the fantastic and the commitment to realism. The two poles are each developed to a greater extent, so the attempt at their reconciliation is more violent. That juxtaposition, which is so uncomfortable for many readers, has been made unavoidable, unmistakable' (Clarke 2011: 110). In a further interview, Lethem emphasizes that Aeroman is the latest instance of a compulsion running through his work: 'to push together realistic character, and emotion, and naturalistic or mimetic textures, with the stuff of dream, fantasy, symbol – and to make the fit between these different areas very prominent' (Clarke 2011: 122–3). His own emphases, then, are on a project of confrontation and collision. Aeroman and the ring trouble 'mimeticism', making 'uncomfortable' some of its readers, even as such mimeticism is so deeply pursued. They do not achieve a synthesis of the realistic and fantastic so much as an explosive encounter between the two, like The Thing and The Incredible Hulk crashing shudderingly into an office block.

The magical item is thus an estrangement effect, a *novum* in the idiom of Darko Suvin. It is a lifeline back to the narrative possibilities that Lethem had previously assumed, in which the writer could invent new physical laws or states of being almost at will. It thus allows Lethem a particular kind of creative freedom that the novel's subject matter otherwise would not. And in doing so it coincides with the less flagrant remaking of material, in which what seems like autobiography is processed and redirected in various ways, to the point that the protagonist ends up breaking into a prison, something that the author has never done, through magical means. The magic of the ring, spectacularly distracting the reader's attention, might give fiction licence to fly in patterns not simply dictated by life.

Familiar Forms

Omega the Unknown is mentioned numerous times in *The Fortress of Solitude*, as though it is the lost comic whose cachet of obscurity that novel is keenest to claim. As we have glimpsed, the insistence of the title in the novel also relates to the sense that *Omega*'s alternation between New York schoolyard and superheroics is a model for the situation of Dylan Ebdus himself. It thus made sense that when Marvel Comics, altered to Lethem's credibility as an interpreter of comics in the literary world, asked him to author a comic-book series, he should opt to revive the title. The result is his major work in a medium in which he was unknown as a professional writer, even if he had dreamed up various superheroes in the 1970s. He did that in dialogue with his friend Karl Rusnak, who was now brought on board as co-author, while art came from Farel Dalrymple and Paul Hornschemeier (and additional art from Gary Panter for one interjected sequence). The final major creative statement from Lethem's superhero period, *Omega* relishes the opportunity to deploy the superhero's primary medium.

Lethem's *Omega* centres on a fourteen-year-old boy, Titus Alexander Island (who comes to be known primarily as Alex), who has been reclusively raised by his parents but is about to move to school at New York City. On the way to the city, a car crash kills both parents and it is revealed that they are robots. Alex is taken under the wing of a nurse, Edie Fallinger, in Washington Heights at the north of Manhattan. At school he experiences the daily grind of bullying and sees another victim shoot himself; but he befriends a girl, Amandla, who becomes his effective sidekick through the adventure. Meanwhile a more epic sequence of events is taking place. A horde of robots colonize distant planets, and are only deterred by a series of superheroes with the power to shoot flame from their wrists. A range of different alien races take on the superhero costume, with its Omega symbol logo; on Earth, one has already perished and Alex has been conceived to replace him, by parents mysteriously 'touched by cosmic power'. But another Omega has also just arrived on Earth, and is seen mutely battling his way through hordes of robots in each episode as he tries to foil their invasion. The alien horde proceed by infecting humans' bloodstream with nano-robotic components: a race of zombies is accordingly created, and is only vanquished by a combination of chemicals produced by Omega and distributed in the form of salt on citizens' food. In parallel with all this, Washington Heights is also dominated by its own superhero, The Mink: a worldly figure whose power is based on scientific expertise and financial resource, and extends to an industry of minions, game shows and comic books. The Mink seeks to capture the warring protagonists for his own interests, but is finally killed by his own severed hand which the robots' technology has turned against him. Omega destroys the invaders' lair by smashing the bust of a figure who has observed and occasionally narrated the story, an extra-terrestrial being known as The Overthinker who appears to take a range of inanimate forms while on Earth.

The ten-episode *Omega* differs from the original ten-issue run in 1976, though it also deliberately echoes particular scenes. Much of the plot of the first episode parallels that of the original first issue, with the car crash revealing the protagonist's parents as robots, the alien robots' pursuit of him to his hospital bed, and the closing scene where the boy (originally called James-Michael Starling) is found to have the Omega symbols on his fire-shooting wrists. Lethem likewise revives a further dramatic moment when the boy discovers versions of his robot parents in a closet. Lethem and Rusnak were profound enthusiasts for the original, yet they note that due to uncertain sales and editorial control it veered a strange course, temporarily losing its metaphysical thread and 'flirt[ing] with the totally generic' while hosting guest stars such as The Incredible Hulk. The new version can be seen as a homage to the original; a parallel version of the narrative that coexists alongside it; or even an attempt to compensate for the halting fate of the original, a kind of making amends. Lethem avers that it neither continues not 'repairs' the original but 'paraphrases' it. Plainly, this is yet another case of the artistic principles examined in Chapter One, above, in a work that emerged almost concurrently with 'The Ecstasy of Influence'. A source is reactivated into a new narrative, with a combination of repetition and difference. This *Omega* could not exist without its precursor, yet is also a quite distinct artefact, not least in the way that Farel Dalrymple's drawing and Paul Hornschemeier's colouring differ from the generic Marvel house-style pencilling of Jim Mooney.

The revived *Omega* deploys a range of narrative methods. Unsurprisingly, given its veteran comic-reader creators, it is seasoned with reference to comic-book history: an onlooker in the street warns that a supervillain 'must be headed to the Baxter Building', the headquarters of the Fantastic Four (Lethem 2008: VII: 14); police officers say that it is probably a job for the Marvel team The Avengers (VII: 16); sarcastic capital is made from Omega's inability to fly (IX: 3, 16). More ambitiously, The Overthinker periodically acts as narrator, reframing and summarizing the story, while at the close of Episode Six he also figures as a kind of audience, a 'narrative junkie' addicted to what happens in this story, who 'flips channels' between panels to catch up with particular characters. In a still more baroque narrative device, early in Episode Eight he takes up the story of the abortive progress of the previous Omega, Silliman Renfrew, with a lyre in his hands, making him an explicitly Bardic narrator. When he tires of his lack of metrical prowess he conjures, for one large panel only, a punk rock band in which he sings a brief version of the events he has just narrated, while the protagonists provide backing. In such an instance the primary world of the story is suspended and its characters momentarily, fancifully allowed to occupy different roles. A more sustained narrative experiment sees the final episode take place with almost no words spoken in twenty-two pages: we witness the range of characters interacting mutely, with only a minimal exchange between a married couple breaking the silence. The narrative gambit mirrors the condition of Omega himself, thus, in effect, allowing him to have the last word by muting everyone else's.

The Mink stars in his own series of fictional comic books: during Episode Six, Omega reads these while imprisoned in the Mink's headquarters. We see a number of panels from the Mink's comic, drawn in a different style (by Paul Hornschemeier, confined to the role of colourist for the rest of the series): clearer, simpler, their clean lines and bright colours closer to earlier versions of Captain Marvel (or indeed, as the Mink's domestic scenes develop, to modern independent artists like Adrian Tomine). This already breaks up the comic page and places the dominant visual aesthetic of *Omega* on a spectrum of styles, but the effect is reinforced considerably when Omega, inspired by the Mink comics, draws his own graphic narrative showing the galactic history of his own kind. This commences Episode Seven with a five-page burst of crude, schematic art, which also inflects the front cover and makes it look more like a vintage science-fiction comic from several decades earlier. The Mink and his associates read Omega's output; showing himself a reader of Bronze Age Batman, the Mink grants 'He's no Neal Adams, but he does get his concept across' (VII: 7). The sequence again makes the new *Omega* into something of a compendium of styles, placing its own mode into dynamic contrast with others, while providing internal narrative motivation for each of these other visual approaches. The superhero becomes a reader of superhero comic books, then a writer of them: a sequence that emphasizes the close historic compact between the genre and the physical medium.

The most subtly persistent theme of the revived *Omega* is its own condition, as a revival of something already existing: a repetition with a difference. If the comic is an instance of this condition, it also consistently alludes to it. Thus, if the Omega who comes to Earth in this story repeats the Omega who did so in 1976, he is also repeated by Alex (who dons his own identical version of the costume, so that at one stage there are two Omegas battling robots and zombies in the same building). But he also repeats, or is repeated by, a host of other Omegas – as we see on the cover of Episode Ten, where more than twenty other beings of diverse humanoid species are seen in their Omega suits, watching Earth's version on live transmission to their distant planet. This image has also been forecast by the final page of Omega's own crude graphic narrative, where thirteen different alien Omegas are seen blasting their rays at a bolus of robots (VII: 7). The Mink's typically sardonic remark on his encounter with Omega that 'Where there's robots, there's blue guys' (II: 15) acknowledges this sense of a repeated scenario, possibly because of his awareness of the earlier Omega stored in his vault.

The theme is reflected in the comic's first words, a series of captions that seem to represent Omega's unspoken soliloquy: 'Yes./You've been here before, however much you might like to pretend otherwise./These forms are so dreadfully familiar' (I: 3). Lethem is using a standard feature of Omega's caption soliloquies, as developed by Steve Gerber: they offer a general, sometimes worldly or melancholy reflection on life, which doubles as a commentary on the fight Omega is currently involved in (or vice versa). Omega's thoughts here refer most immediately to the robots swooping to attack him: these are the 'forms' that are 'so dreadfully familiar', and which (in shooting him) 'have their own sense of priorities' (I: 4). But given its placing at the very start of the series, this commentary also asks to be taken as a meditation on the comic book itself and its work of reprisal. As it begins, the story admits – 'You've been here before' – to a sense of déja vu. A similar logic is at work in Omega's captioned reflection, late in the same first issue, that 'some tasks need doing twice' (I: 20). The sense might be that this Omega is the same one witnessed in the original comic: but that can hardly be the case, as they do not occupy the same narrative timeline (this is not a sequel). It would be more suggestive to say that the comic book is registering suppressed memories of its precursor.

The theme of replication and difference is signalled again in the film that several characters go to see (VII: 15): *Photocopy Shop 2*. Even The Mink's ticket order – 'Four, please. We're having a double date' – joins in the theme of doubling. The whole film would seem to be set around technology for copying, but also to double this in its number, two. Alex asks: 'I'm not sure I understand. Is this a sequel, or a remake?' Like Omega's melancholy reflections in his opening battle, Alex's query about the film plainly also gestures at the work in which he is appearing, where 'remake' is closer to the correct answer. The implication that the film is bad (Amandla answers Alex, 'I'm not sure which would be worse') is a self-deprecatory gesture, a remake admitting to the perils of remakes.

Another term becomes especially important in this developing sense of repetition. This is *franchise*. When Alex tells his graduate assistant mentor Frances Fenton that the malicious robots are 'being built on *behalf* of someone, or *something* else', by brainwashed Columbia students of robotics, Frances provides her analysis: 'It's called "Franchise Theory". [...] Franchising means you get other people to build your outlets for you. They do the work, they take the risk – while you expand your brand all over the place' (VII: 12). The killer robots are a franchise – like Butterdog's, she adds: the fictional fast-food franchise which in this comic has secretly become a centre of alien invasion.

In literary–critical discussion of notions of repetition and borrowing, 'franchise' is a relatively little-used term, compared to, say, intertextuality or collage. Yet in a wider media economy, as in business, the notion of a franchise has much currency. Frances's first examples are burger franchises, including McDonald's and White Castle (a New York company that neglected to use a franchise model and suffered as a result), but one can also talk of, say, the Batman franchise. Here the hero is in effect a brand who can be remade by others (Frank Miller, Alan Moore, Tim Burton, Christopher Nolan, and designers and makers of extensive ranges of merchandise) in a deal that benefits both the owners of the rights and the artist or entrepreneur who takes on the franchise. Within *Omega the Unknown* this is quite directly shown in the form of The Mink's industry. He has created a brand that is portable and reusable, such that when he is preparing for his TV game show *Mink of the People* and has to leave to confront Omega, another of his associates can readily step in to replace him (II: 6–7). The Mink's comic books show a version of him different from the real thing, stylized and dramatized, again pursuing its own profit. Thus Frances, the voice of analysis on these matters, watching The Mink's aeroplane pass, understatedly comments that 'It's interesting to consider The Mink from the point of view of corporate branding, actually' (VII: 20). If The Mink's brand is something to be cautious of, then the invaders' organization via the Butterdog's franchise and the 2U Quik truck delivery firm make corporate replication positively dangerous.

In this context it is striking that The Mink also casually applies the term to Alex himself, as the latest avatar of Omega: 'Your fellow *Omegas*. Your team. Your brand. Your franchise' (IX: 2). The implication is that he sees the superhero Omega tacitly functioning on the same terms as himself. There is, in the abstract, a real resemblance between the franchise model explored by the comic and the way that Omega works: a form of resistance in which an individual can step up and wear the same outfit as others. The Mink has identified a structural analogy, though he omits to add that the Omega 'team' acts obsessively for virtue alone and would consider financial reward meaningless. It may also be said that the virtuous distribution of the magic salt in Episode Ten is by a kind of franchise structure – each individual food cart collecting salt from the central source then fanning out to distribute it around the city, battling the influence of the homogeneous 2U Quik distribution – though these food carts take on no one else's branding in undertaking their dispersed mission. David Coughlan, in a reading sensitive to the issue of repetition in *Omega*, ventures that this method of distribution also suggests 'countering the globalised food industry by supporting local providers and traders' (2011: 210).

The story ends with a further enactment of the franchise principle. The Mink's game show, seen on TV, is now replicated by homeless people in the city's subway. One of The Mink's former employees, perhaps the one who took his place in the game show shoot, lives in an underground hovel but now takes his place at the centre of the refashioned game show. Omega himself, in a wheelchair, is invited on to the platform. The Mink brand turns out to have a 'second use' for the homeless. No money is being made here: this franchise has found its way out of the cash economy and into the potlatch world that Lethem in 'The Ecstasy of Influence' posits existing alongside it. The suggestion here is that once established, a successful idea or image – like The Mink's outfit and logo, and his game show format itself – may take on an unofficial life among consumers, just as superheroes have long done for their fans.

At the same time, this entire theme of the franchise evidently rounds on *Omega the Unknown* itself, as a revival, in effect, of a franchise that has been untapped for thirty years. Frances's original discussion of the idea again makes sidelong comment on the work in which it appears: 'See, the downside of franchising is *quality control*. You can't know what people are going to do with your brand, once you hand it over to them' (VII: 13). The comment reflects on the doubts of comic fans, even diehard readers of the original *Omega*, about the right of Lethem and his collaborators to take over the title. The doubters included *Omega*'s creator Steve Gerber himself, who fiercely clung to his own right as original author and reacted to news of the revival by declaring that 'the writer of the book has [made] an enemy for life by taking the job' (Coughlan 2011: 200), before Lethem reassured him of his esteem for the original. Taking on these considerations in the text itself is a discreet comic device and a strategy of disarmament, forestalling the criticism of fans by anticipating it. It also offers an opportunity for real reflection on the issues of repetition and remaking, which gains potency from taking place in a work that is a remake.

Lastly, it can be added that the *Omega* revival also repeats and varies motifs from Lethem's own earlier work. Most evidently, in taking up the importance of a superhero to an intelligent schoolboy at an intimidating public school in New York (III: 1–8), the comic reprises the scenario of *The Fortress of Solitude* – a scenario which was in good part inspired by the Hell's Kitchen street bullies of *Omega* in the first place. We have already observed Dylan Ebdus's own recognition and denial of his resemblance to James-Michael Starling (Lethem 2003: 83–4); for Lethem to author a comic replaying this scenario plainly brings the wheel full circle. The small detail of The Mink's observation that in Omega's weakened state, the robots would have 'taken his lunch money' (V: 9) is also reminiscent of the daily bullying described in Lethem's novel. The association of superhero with graffiti in Mingus's 'DOSE' persona is echoed here by the sight of youths spray-painting a subway train with an image of Omega (II: 1). Less obvious details may also sound familiar to Lethem's readers. The 'Mink-Man' who wonders what he becomes in the absence of The Mink (IX: 18) might recall the Minna Men asking themselves a similar question in *Motherless Brooklyn*. The verbal associations uttered by the deformed Councilman Edgardo – 'Small plane. Deep shame. Champagne. Real friend. Real pain. Sham friend. Shampoo. Realpoo' (VIII: 1–2) – recall the compulsive, distorting associations of Lionel Essrog in the same novel. On a larger scale, The Mink's labyrinth reprises an image from *Amnesia Moon*, and the Nowhere Man who dwells within it, carrying a jar that is a portal to a blank space featuring '[someone] you couldn't [talk to] otherwise. Someone dead, say, or imaginary' (VIII: 11), recalls the way, in that novel, that Cale and Gwen occupy virtual worlds that Chaos/Everett can visit through the portal of drugs.

Omega the Unknown, recycling *Omega the Unknown*, also discreetly recycles some of Lethem's own motifs and concerns. 'These forms', thinks Omega, 'are so dreadfully familiar'. We have seen in this chapter that the superhero comic book is indeed a deeply familiar form to Lethem, but that he has also turned that familiarity to the production of new work, which has encouraged many people to look again at superheroes themselves.

5

Streets

When *Motherless Brooklyn* begins, its protagonist Lionel Essrog has never left New York City (1999: 105). He implies a profound allegiance to the place in the throwaway remark that 'New York is a Tourettic city', obsessive and frantic like him (113). On his first trip out of the city, he drives through Maine, and finds: 'I had trouble believing any of it was real [...] I felt as if I were driving through the pages of a calendar, or a collection of pictorial stamps' (263). When he reaches the coast on foot, he experiences not the region's kitsch unreality but its overpowering reality: 'I was off the page now, away from the grammar of skyscrapers and pavement. I experienced it precisely as a loss of language, a great sucking away of the word-laden walls that I needed around me' (264). For the first time, he perceives that New York has cocooned him in a protective shell of Tourettic language and habit: only on leaving the city behind and encountering the vertigo of the open sea has he realized his reliance on his home town, as he becomes 'shrunk to a shred of Brooklyn stumbling on the coastal void' (264). His adherence to his own city makes him likely to sympathise with Frank O'Hara's more self-possessed declaration that 'One need never leave the confines of New York to get all the greenery one wishes – I can't even enjoy a blade of grass unless I know there's a subway handy, or a record store or some other sign that people do not totally *regret* life' (O'Hara 1994: 87).

Lionel here offers a suggestive comparison with Jonathan Lethem. The author, too, is a native New Yorker, who to many readers has seemed almost equally tied to the city. The *Brooklyn Paper* referred to him as 'the Bard of Boerum Hill'; when in 2010 he left for California for a second time, the paper reported on a farewell reading at which fans were 'appalled, offended, betrayed', and quoted one as saying 'I can't believe he'll actually be gone' (Campbell 2010). The offence was likely limited, but the association of Lethem with Brooklyn was real. That Lionel presents the city's protection and familiarity in the form of 'walls of language', which tumble when outside it, suggests a link between the tongue-tied character and the artist who necessarily makes his worlds through words. Yet we can also observe that Lionel learns more about his relation to the city by leaving it. Lethem has said the same about his own writing: 'It's the long estrangement of being away from New York City and rejecting it for a decade, that enabled me to get to this material' (Clarke 2011: 92).

This chapter is about New York in Lethem's fiction. It proposes that Lethem's relation to the city is one of the major recent instances of those profound relations between writer and place that have marked modern literary history: Joyce's Dublin, Woolf's London, Pessoa's Lisbon. It looks closely at his rendition of that city's urban space and experience in three major novels. The caveat can be entered that Lethem has been as much a California writer as one of the East coast. If *Gun, with Occasional Music* projected a dystopian San Francisco at the start of his career, then *The Feral Detective* demonstrates a much later interest with the 'Inland Empire' of Californian mountain and desert, and the unorthodox social forms that might populate it. A study could be made of him on those terms, as has been done for Thomas Pynchon (McClintock and Miller 2014). Nonetheless, for the time being, it is the city where he grew up that Lethem has most profoundly and memorably explored in writing, and the streets traversed in this chapter will be those of New York.

This chapter will first read *Motherless Brooklyn*, as Lethem's first sustained rendition of New York in fiction. Second, we shall return to *The Fortress of Solitude*, by far Lethem's fullest direct artistic confrontation with the Brooklyn of his childhood. Finally we turn to *Chronic City*. What happens when Lethem turns to Manhattan, and how is his depiction of the borough affected by the strategies of speculative fiction?

Crosstown Traffic

In 1996, Lethem returned to New York after a dozen years in California. He intended to write about Brooklyn, directly, after three novels set in the West and one which commenced in a future version of the borough. The notion of *The Fortress of Solitude* fermented over time; meanwhile *Motherless Brooklyn* was intended as a short bridge towards that more ambitious work. The earlier book, Lethem recalls, thus proved to be 'imbued with energy from the project I was holding at bay. [...] I was delaying writing an emotional journey back to Brooklyn, and in fact I was *unable* to delay it. So those feelings saturated *Motherless Brooklyn*. And I wrote a longer and more serious book' (Clarke

2011: 63). In this sense, the two Brooklyn novels are part of the same creative movement, an idea corroborated by the fact that *Motherless Brooklyn* would have served well as a title for its successor. Both represent the New York of the present (the late 1990s) and the recent past (the 1970s and 1980s), in a way unprecedented in Lethem's novels.

Both are also part of an aesthetic turn towards denser description. Writing the first novel, Lethem explains:

> I took a much greater interest in the texture of my real surroundings than I had before. The earlier books are all set either in California or a sort of cartoon desert, a Nowheresville [...] Suddenly I got interested in talking about real stuff – sandwiches, sidewalks, the subway – because the project dictated it, and because I'd moved back to New York and was falling in love with Brooklyn again. (Clarke 2011: 109)

To another interviewer he explains that 'I wanted to describe the streets of Brooklyn. [...] I began to be a writer who slowed scenes down more and offered more visual information of various kinds. Needless to say, the corner I turned in *Motherless Brooklyn* became a whole new world in *Fortress of Solitude*'. The new emphasis evidently involves a fuller depiction of setting: where Lethem had been 'bored' by this task, 'Now suddenly I did want to write about the trees casting a shadow on the building' (Clarke 2011: 83). He indicates, though, a step change between the two novels. Our discussion of *Fortress* will demonstrate its density of visual description; in *Motherless Brooklyn* we can expect to see a more sparing use of the method.

Geographically, the novels' territories overlap. Both range into Manhattan – a point that will be considered below – and both contain sections outside New York entirely, with *Fortress*'s Vermont somewhat rhyming with *Motherless Brooklyn*'s Maine in taking a native New Yorker into New England. More obviously, both have a home base in Brooklyn: specifically in the far north-west corner of the borough, within a dozen miles from Manhattan. Though both are recognized as major Brooklyn novels, the actual space that they cover within the borough is relatively small: from, say, Brooklyn Heights at the north-west corner, south to Red Hook and east little further than Fort Greene. The vast majority of the borough – from Williamsburg in the north to Brighton Beach in the south, Bay Ridge in the west to Canarsie in the east – remains untouched by both books. Coney Island, one of the borough's most celebrated spots, is visited in a future form in *Girl in Landscape*, but in Lethem's 1990s Brooklyn almost its only trace is in the name of Lionel Essrog's colleague Gil Coney. As Lionel explains as he and Coney arrive in Greenpoint, North Brooklyn, 'Brooklyn is one big place, and this wasn't our end of it' (1999: 20).

Motherless Brooklyn's sense of the borough is primarily centred in the neighbourhoods of Carroll Gardens and, immediately to its north, Cobble Hill, clustered around the north-south thoroughfares of Court Street and Smith Street. *Fortress* makes reference to these, but is primarily set in the area ambiguously known as Gowanus or Boerum Hill (the ambiguity is highlighted, in a novel much interested in naming) to the east of Smith Street. The single road that most strongly links the two novels is Bergen Street, the long road that runs parallel, to the south, to Dean Street, the central street of *Fortress*. At the westernmost end of Bergen Street, on the corner with Smith Street, is the L&L car service which serves as a front for Frank Minna's shady detective agency. Down the block from L&L is the Boerum Hill Inn (239), populated by upwardly mobile young drinkers: in another novel the place could be the focus for a sustained discussion of the ambiguities of gentrification. That glimpse of theme, and the mere presence of the name Boerum Hill, effect a momentary crossover between the two novels. Yet *Motherless Brooklyn* itself never ventures to Dean Street, and rarely touches directly on Dylan Ebdus's immediate neighbourhood. Why this difference?

The first reason is that *Fortress* is a fundamentally *residential* novel, *Motherless Brooklyn* fundamentally one of business. Insofar as it has a spatial centre, this novel needs to be near a thoroughfare densely populated not with anonymous brownstones but with small businesses, public spaces, comings and goings. First Court Street, and then Smith Street, fulfil this role. L&L itself is such a business, open to the public gaze, even if its car service is a facade (93). Much of *Fortress* is spent outside, but in largely aimless or optional activity – sitting on a stoop, throwing a ball, or venturing to spray graffiti on a wall. The contrast reminds us that a detective novel is a novel of work; of the city as a place of action, not reverie – even though, as has been said in Chapter Two above, this novel stretches at the genre it occupies.

Court Street is the initial heart of Frank Minna's fiefdom, and provides the second reason. Lethem is writing a crime novel, and the kind of crime he wants as milieu is Italian American in origin and image. The novel rarely goes as far as to implicate the Mafia as such, but it relies on a sense of organized crime, orchestrated by Americans of Italian descent and moving on an inscrutable yet far-reaching level. (The closest it comes to the pattern of a full-blown Mafia story is the description of Frank Minna's behaviour after crossing his powerful clients: 'He'd refuse to be seated anywhere but in the corners of restaurants, his back to the wall' [167].) This makes Court Street and Carroll Gardens, a historic heartland of Brooklyn's Italian immigrant population, the logical geographical focus. One passage, during Lionel's explanation of his history with Frank, conveys this in a single sustained stroke: 'Minna's Court Street was the old Brooklyn, a placid ageless surface alive underneath with talk, with deals and casual insults, a neighborhood political machine with pizzeria and butcher-shop bosses and unwritten rules everywhere. All was talk except for what mattered most, which were unspoken understandings' (55). The 'political machine' indicates the operation of power through local channels; the bosses are not elected politicians but patrons, perhaps owners, of restaurant and butcher's shop. The notion of a place where 'all was talk' suggests a garrulous Italian-American community of bravado, machismo and vernacular rhetoric, somewhat like those depicted in the films of Martin Scorsese. Frank Minna is himself such a talker: his own language charges the book and offers a partial mirror of, and model for, the Tourettic Lionel. The Court Street community has more such talkers: in the barber's shop 'men passed through constantly to argue sports and wave away offers of haircuts' (55). Yet what Lethem emphasizes is what underlies the talk: 'unspoken understandings' and 'unwritten rules', unfathomable to outsiders. Hence the barbershop which seems not to work as a business but as 'a retirement home, a social club, and front for a backroom poker game', on the basis of a 'conspiracy' that is not to be mentioned. Hence, too, the other example of Court Street behaviour: a curb of Vespas permanently parked and unmolested: 'It didn't need explaining – this was Court Street' (56). That the mopeds are Italian adds to the texture.

This portrait of Court Street is emblematic of the Brooklyn into which Frank inducts Lionel, in a significant way: its combination of something awry, suspicious, perhaps criminal, with the fact that nothing is explicitly, demonstrably wrong. That is also the character of most of the jobs that we see Lionel do for Frank: emptying an electronics showroom into Frank's van (53), hurriedly transporting a rock band's equipment, with the band nowhere to be seen (58–9), and later standing on a street and watching a car until it is towed away (167–9). This last scene is a fine example of the Minna paradox: his Men do nothing illegal, yet are increasingly consumed with unease simply for waiting on an empty sidewalk. At the 'placid dead-end traffic circle' in Brooklyn Heights, with strollers passing by, the very lack of action or information spooks the team. 'The Volvo couldn't have been less conspicuous if it were invisible, but for us it glowed, screamed, ticked like a bomb': the duality well captures the combination of effects in Minna-land, an ostensibly unobjectionable scenario which nonetheless becomes ominous with unstated meaning. Something analogous can be observed in the Clients Matricardi and Rockaforte. Their every word to Frank and his boys is polite, in a formal idiom that bespeaks immigrant roots and perhaps the influence of Damon Runyan's gangsters ('Let us bring a little joy. For orphans to make music is a good thing' [64]; 'Honor us in this time of disappointment and regret' [165]). They seem detached from any actual violence. Yet their secret power over it is what makes Frank flee New York for three years. Their house in Gowanus is suggestive of the doubleness. They greet visitors in the parlour that belonged to Matricardi's mother: 'perfectly elegant, lavishly fitted [...] with gold leaf on the ceiling's plaster scrollwork, antique chairs and desks and a marble-topped side table, a six-foot mirror-lined grandfather clock, and a vase with fresh flowers. [...] It was more like a museum diorama of Old Brooklyn than a contemporary room' (61). Yet the rest of the house is spartan, its historic interior 'stripped and gutted', a functional warehouse. It is not exactly that the 'Old Brooklyn' manner is a public facade over a private reality: after all, the parlour is itself hidden away within the rest of the house, and the Clients themselves can only be seen at their own discretion. To them, the old-world manner is authentic. Yet it subsists on a more brutal world with which its precise connections are never displayed.

The Court Street that Lionel describes is 'the old Brooklyn', and also 'the only Brooklyn, really' (55–6). The sense that this is already an older neighbourhood world chimes with Gerard Minna's description of his brother as 'anachronistic' (231), and Frank's own tendency to adopt a personal image from an earlier time (40). The notion that this is the only real Brooklyn is pure local chauvinism, and may be tacitly racist. Frank's intuition that almost 'everything east of the Gowanus Canal [...] was an unspeakable barbarian tumult' (56) appears to carry an unspoken association of those 'barbarian' lands with African Americans, a group Frank finds uninteresting because 'unfunny' and not part of the 'classic', lighter-skinned New York immigrant communities like Irish or Italian (68). The association of different parts of the borough with racial difference is made more explicit in Tony Vermonte and Lionel's interview with the black homicide detective Lucius Seminole. Seminole '[doesn't] get to work this side of Flatbush Avenue that often', and has had to learn quickly about the Minna Men's neighbourhood. Tony's cheeky query, 'Not so many murders over here, eh, Chief?', is taken by Seminole for the coded racial statement it intends: 'Not so many *niggers* on this side of Flatbush, that what you're trying to say?' (186–7). The conversation points up a difference not just between two areas but between two forms of crime. Seminole concurs that 'you got the lid clamped down pretty tight around here. No murders and no niggers. Nice clean streets, nothing but old guys carrying around racing forms and tiny pencils. Makes me nervous' (187). He has come to the Minna Men, we are to understand, from a professional life dealing with drug deals, muggings, guns and knives in use on the street. Minna's world looks 'clean' and orderly by contrast, but this arouses his suspicion that another kind of crime is going on: a matter of 'unspoken understandings' and acts that cannot be pinpointed as criminal, but that point to a world of power out of plain sight. There is a slight, telling discrepancy with *The Fortress of Solitude* here. Seminole accosts the men on Degraw Street in Gowanus, which in *Fortress* would seem primarily populated by African Americans; yet here he concurs with Tony's insinuation that not many 'niggers' are to be seen. The explanation for the difference is surely, in one word, gentrification: Seminole's visit to Gowanus takes place in the mid to late 1990s, and the area's demographics have changed since Dylan Ebdus's childhood.

How else is Brooklyn depicted and imagined in this novel? To Lionel, Brooklyn instinctively means home. It is that which is close at hand, from which one departs and to which one returns: the norm against which other environments are measured. When Lionel and Gil Coney see the giant's K-car turning off for Queens at 36th Street in Manhattan, they can find 'something comforting about this. The giant and his driver were moving onto our turf, more or less. The boroughs. Not quite Brooklyn, but it would do' (17). Brooklyn is typically spoken of as a rough and ready place, sometimes friendly (as in Zeod's sandwich shop, as consistent a source of warmth as Lionel meets in the novel), often tough, but generally familiar. When Gil Coney tussles with a security guard in Brooklyn Hospital's waiting room ('We stand up we're gonna lay a condition on *your* ass, Albert [...] You unnernstand that?'), 'The whole room was watching, tuned to Channel Brooklyn' (32). The implication is that this kind of scene, with its weary late-night antagonists and vernacular idiom of threat, is characteristic of the borough. Channel Brooklyn might be airing such material twenty-four hours a day.

Far more than any of Lethem's other fiction, the novel returns to urban environments that are workmanlike, dirty, out of the way: 'a gated warehouse yard under the shadow of the Brooklyn-Queens Expressway, in a ruined industrial zone' (48); 'a vacant Red Hook lot' (56); 'the edge of the Brooklyn-Queens Expressway, at the end of Kane Street' (82); most extensively, the industrial zone in North Greenpoint where Frank is killed. Here Lethem's new impulse to write more 'visual information' is exercised early on a peculiarly harsh setting: 'The windowless brick warehouse was laced with fire escapes, wrought-iron cages that ran the length of the second floor and ended in a crumpled, unsafe-looking ladder. On the side street a smallish, graffitied Dumpster was tucked halfway into the shadow of [a] double doorway. The doors behind were strapped with long interior hinges, like a meat locker' (22). Frank is bleeding in the Dumpster – which is presented to the reader almost as a clue in a puzzle to solve: given this description of the setting, can we guess where Frank is before Lionel does, over a page later? The suggestion of a 'meat locker', in this context, adds an extra touch of blood-stained brutality befitting the crime scene. But the broader impression is of the unforgiving character of the whole environment: a place designed for getting business done, loading and unloading heavy goods ('The other entrance was a roll-up gate on a truck-size loading dock' [22]), rather than for pleasant interactions between human beings. Lethem has called *Motherless Brooklyn* 'a very male book' (Clarke 2011: 115); this extends to an exploration of environments that are themselves effectively masculine – battered places of manual work, left abandoned and sometimes commandeered for brutal violence. That this environment is strongly connected to the genre of urban crime is suggested by the fact that it features so heavily here, and so rarely across Lethem's work outside the genre.

Even away from crime as such, the book's embrace of such harsh environments is announced in Lionel's opening description of his own place of origin, St Vincent's Home for Boys. In a flamboyantly long sentence, Lionel situates the home amid a series of uncompromising coordinates: 'on eight lanes of traffic lined with faceless, monolithic civil courts'; 'by Brooklyn's central sorting annex for the post office, a building that hummed and blinked all through the night, its gates groaning open to admit trucks'; 'by the Burton Trade School for Automechanics'; 'by a desolate strip of park benches'; 'by a car lot surrounded by a high fence topped with wide curls of barbed wire and wind-whipped fluorescent flags' (36–7). These reference points share a functional character: they involve ways to pass through, to achieve a necessary, perhaps unwelcome task or at most briefly to pause, with minimal frills. As Lionel summarizes, the whole space at the edge of 'the battered, ancient borough' is 'a place strenuously ignored in passing through to Somewhere Else' (37).

By the same token, the 'battered' borough typically connotes authenticity, an unvarnished, unpretentious reality by contrast with more aspirational or fanciful regions. The most obvious point of contrast is Manhattan. The Brooklyn-Queens Expressway, Lionel tells us early on, has the 'rottenest surface in the boroughs. Like the G train, the BQE suffered from low self-esteem, never going into citadel Manhattan, never tasting the glory' (25). Here a roadway is personified, as Brooklyn's physical infrastructure is imagined bearing its personality. The description here sounds defensive, yet such self-deprecation can easily flip into chauvinism, through a form of inverted snobbery. Lionel is bemused by Kimmery's view of the Manhattan Zen pupil Wallace as a 'hippie': 'In Brooklyn we would have just said *loser*' (144). He is likewise unimpressed by Gerard's disavowal of his own borough in the name of his Zen reinvention ('Gerard Minna's a punk from Brooklyn', he insists to the credulous Kimmery [216]), and in his interview with the beatific Gerard is on the lookout for unwitting fragments of authentic speech: 'Was *crapped* a chink in Gerard's Zen facade, a bit of Brooklyn showing through?' (232). At the very outset of the novel, he makes plain how foreign he and Gil Coney feel on the Upper East Side: in terms of Monopoly pieces, 'we were off our customary map, *Automobile* and *Terrier* in Candyland' (3). To refer to uptown Manhattan as Candyland acknowledges its wealth while also hinting at a defiant resistance to it in the name of a more authentic place. All this corresponds closely to the image of Brooklyn extensively documented by James Peacock: 'a sentimental, lyrical, nostalgic impulse to some extent counterbalanced with a knowing, sometimes cynical toughness' (2015: 18). If Frank Minna has such a romance of Brooklyn, so too, initially, does Julia, who is told stories of it at a distance by him and Gerard: 'In some way Brooklyn, where she'd never been, became a romantic ideal, something truer and finer than the city life she'd glimpsed in Boston' (288).

As Lionel's Monopoly image makes clear, the idea of Brooklyn is often constructed through a contrast with Manhattan. Peacock points out (2015: 16) how far Manhattan is constitutive of the proud self-image sometimes advanced on behalf of Brooklyn, and notices that Lionel sees the affluent clientele of the Boerum Hill Inn as a 'Manhattanized' (239) presence in Brooklyn. Manhattan plays a major part in this Brooklyn novel, but is naturally seen selectively, in particular aspects. Primarily, what we see is the Upper East Side: the Zendo that is Gerard Minna's base is in Yorktown on East 84th Street. This naturally brings associations of socio-economic class: the Zendo is surrounded by 'giant doorman apartment buildings' (3), while there is also a degree of gentility, by Lionel's standards, in the 'Upper East Siders' who by mid-morning have 'retaken their streets, and walked obliviously crinkling doggie-doo bags and the *New York Times* and wax paper around bagels' (144), if only in their fastidious readiness to clean up after their dogs. The Fujisaki Corporation's building at 1030 Park Avenue is in the same area, and more definitively signals wealth: 'The oak doors split the difference between magnificence and military sturdiness', while the building's discreet lack of a name indicates that at this financial level, 'nothing remained to be proved, and anonymity was a value greater than charisma'. In keeping with his more downmarket experiences of industrial zones and abandoned lots, the uptown Lionel is again scanning the environment as a place of work whose features are clues to its precise character: 'The building had a private loading zone and a subtle curb cut, though, which sang of money, payoffs to city officials, and of women's-shoe heels too fragile to tangle with the usual four-inch step' (157). The multiple white-gloved doormen who accost him in the building's lobby are another index of material resources.

Lionel's walk to the building gives us a glimpse of uptown Manhattan. The scene around him punctuates his tense cell-phone call to Tony Vermonte back at L&L in Cobble Hill. Thus 'A well-coiffed man in a blue suit turned off Lexington ahead of me', cell phone to his ear – this in an era when mobile telephone use is still sporadic and typically an index of wealth and purposeful business (152). On Park Avenue itself, 'the monolithic walls of old money stretched out, a furrow of stone' (155). In one of the book's fullest descriptions of an urban scene, Lionel crosses the avenue and stops on a traffic island with its 'thumbnail of garden': 'Park Avenue's giant apartment buildings were ornate with shadow in the midmorning light. I was like a castaway on my island there, in a river of orange cabs' (155). A minute later, 'The light changed and the cabs crossing Park blared their horns, working through gridlock. Another raft of pedestrians passed over my island and back into the river' (156). Though Manhattan is not the novel's home, it gains solidity from being sketched here; the other pole to Brooklyn emerges in its combination of enduring grandeur and daily commotion. Unostentatious metaphors bring it to our attention: the traffic island suggests an actual island in a body of water, making the lonely investigator a 'castaway' and the crowd of pedestrians seem to pass from land to water. It matters that Manhattan is brought to life on the page, as at this point in the novel Lionel experiences a kind of quandary about the relative reality of his immediate, uptown environment and that of Brooklyn, which is more than once on the other end of the telephone.

Finding that he distrusts Tony, Lionel decides not to tell him his true location. He reports that he is in Brooklyn, and a tic further suggests that he is in Greenpoint, where Frank Minna was killed the night before. Tony already sounds sceptical, but becomes more so at the fanfare of yellow cabs' horns: 'Doesn't sound like Greenpoint'. Now Lionel unfurls an unlikely scenario: 'They're filming a movie out here. You should see this. They've got [...] Greenpoint Avenue set up to look like Manhattan. All these fake buildings and cabs and extras dressed up like they're on Park Avenue or something. So that's what you're hearing' (156). Tourette's aside, this is one of Lionel's odder rhetorical ventures. Faced with a question of auditory evidence, Lionel produces a pretence of visual evidence: if

Greenpoint doesn't sound like itself right now, that's because it doesn't look like itself either. His fantasy is surely much less credible than simply saying that the traffic on Greenpoint Avenue is heavier than usual. As such, it seems not a real effort to deceive, more a disguised confession that he is on Park Avenue after all, in the recognition that his initial lie has been penetrated. There is a kind of intimacy in the veiled confession, characteristic of the affection that Lionel repeatedly expresses for Tony while receiving only contempt in return (248). In this context, perhaps the oddest thing about the exchange is that Tony does not necessarily seem to realize that Lionel is lying: after confirming that Mel Gibson is in the film, Tony asks the surprisingly earnest-looking question, 'And they really got fake buildings out there?' (156).

Lionel's fantasy is suggestive as a reflection on New York itself. One subtext is Manhattan's tendency to be filmed. Lionel's notion of a simulated Upper East Side plays upon the idea of these streets – unlike those of homely, overlooked Brooklyn – as already a stage set, but ludicrously redoubles it by suggesting that Hollywood, for unexplained reasons, would rebuild this ready-made environment a few miles away across the East River. In this scenario, Brooklyn is remade to look like Manhattan, its inhabitants pretending to be Upper East Siders. A further subtext, then, is Brooklyn's actual contemporary development: the 'Manhattanization' that Lionel sees in the Boerum Hill Inn, and that James Peacock (2015: 18–19) uses to name Brooklyn's gentrification, is given literal form in Lionel's putative film set.

The fantasy has one more aspect. Lionel has only just started using a cell phone, taken from one of the doormen who has tried to accost him earlier. He feels 'quite Captain Kirk-ish' at the novelty of using it. The ability to talk at long distance while on the move is a new experience for Lionel, and encourages the discrepancy between his actual surroundings and the scenario he weaves for Tony. Sound and vision, or discourse and physical reality, diverge here, as the former fabricates a new version of the latter. The novelty of the phone seems to encourage Lionel to essay a sense that in language, anywhere could be anywhere. If he tells Tony he is in Brooklyn, then he is in Brooklyn – and can fabricate to an absurd length to support the case. We may notice a corollary: if he tells *us* he is in Brooklyn, then he is. Among other things, the exchange plays upon the authority of language, in literature, to make a world – a theme that we have explored in Chapter Three in relation to science fiction, but that here flashes up for a page in a novel ostensibly set in a single and plausible world.

A related experience occurs shortly after this call, when Lionel, still on the Upper East Side, is contacted by the Clients in their Brooklyn house. Once again the condition of remote communication proves a significant issue for exploration. As Rockaforte talks, Lionel looks out of the window:

> Through the window I viewed Eighty-Third Street, midday, November. A couple of women in expensive coats mimed a Manhattan conversation for my benefit, trying to persuade me of their reality. On the line, though, I heard an old man's breathing, and what I saw through the windshield wasn't real at all. (163)

This might look like a case of Manhattan, as such, being dismissed as 'unreal' beside the truth of Brooklyn: a phone call out of Candyland. Yet the expensive coats are not the prime reason for Lionel's reaction. Rockaforte makes the women seem unreal simply because of his own gravity, the sense he brings of menace out of the past: 'Though I'd heard [the Clients] speak just two or three times in fifteen years, I would have known his voice anywhere.' It is in this context that the women appear to be 'trying to persuade [Lionel] of their reality': the everyday world that they occupy suddenly seems less profound than the deep and potentially deadly one of the Clients. In their unwitting 'persuasion' they are a faint reprise of Gwen in *Amnesia Moon*, secreted in a drug and trying to persuade Chaos to make her world the real one, or conversely Philip Engstrand attempting the same with Alice Coombs in *Table*. The poignancy of a character trying to insist on their own solidity and draw another back into solidarity with it is a recurring motif in Lethem, and it is telling that it can appear, for a marginal instant, even in such a seemingly hard-headed setting as *Motherless Brooklyn*. Like those other characters, these sidewalk figures are seen as insubstantial. The voice on the line trumps the view through the windshield. Yet a page later, Lionel tries to reverse this perspective: 'Again I consulted my other senses: I was in the sunshine in Manhattan in an L&L vehicle talking on a doorman's cell phone. I could discard Minna's beeper, forget about the call, go anywhere. The Clients were like players in a dream. They shouldn't have been able to touch me with their ancient, ethereal voices' (164–5). The Clients speak from 'Old Brooklyn'. Yet it is Manhattan, not Brooklyn, that is now quotidian, solid, friendly: an ordinary world that one could return to by hanging up the telephone. Lionel has a related feeling when, back in Gowanus, he is menaced by Tony:

> My home borough had never felt so like a nightmare to me as it did on this bright sunlit day on Matricardi and Rockaforte's block of Degraw: a nightmare of repetition and enclosure. Ordinarily I savored Brooklyn's unchangeability, the bullying, Minna-like embrace of its long memory. At the moment I yearned to see this neighborhood razed, replaced by skyscrapers or multiplexes. I longed to disappear into Manhattan's amnesiac dance of renewal. (179)

The reflection is striking in a novel so rooted in Brooklyn: as strong a case as one can find in Lethem's writing of what *Dissident Gardens* dubs 'boroughphobia' (2013a: 29). Lionel reiterates a traditional sense of Brooklyn as place of tradition; the 'long memory' of local legend is much like that identified by James Peacock as typical of the borough's literary history (2015: 14–19). His momentary desire to replace Brooklyn with Manhattan is partially a desire for amnesia – another of Lethem's major themes, quietly placed here as a geographically specific condition – and akin to J.G. Ballard's more enduring preference for motorways and concrete airports over stifling English tradition.

Yet as we have just seen, Manhattan also stands, at this particular point, for a kind of everyday reality outside the paranoid circuits of the case. The character who seals this connection is Kimmery, who occupies her own uptown world of romantic break-up, Zendo housekeeping and cat-sitting, and who is consistently unable to credit Lionel's detective work as a real activity rather than a displacement from grief at Frank's death: 'Regular people, when someone they know gets killed or something they don't go around trying to *catch the killer*. They go to a *funeral*' (255). Like Julia Minna (300), Kimmery does not even believe in the existence of the giant (212, 254). Lethem himself comments that Kimmery is 'the only other "real" character' beside Lionel himself, and – while within the terms of the novel, the murder investigation is plainly real – he sees her as offering him a way out of this obsession and into a more mundane life, one that Lionel is unable to take (Clarke 2011: 39–40). In this regard, Manhattan, for once, is the more down-to-earth option than Brooklyn.

Brooklyn and Manhattan thus stand as spatial poles in this novel: both keenly sketched, significantly contrasted regions between which Lionel's narrative moves. But how does this movement take place? The answer is, for the most part, very rapidly, with minimum digression. Lethem usually takes the trouble to tell us how Lionel gets somewhere. The return from hospital to L&L is made by car, 'so quickly [...] in a perfect fog of numbness' (90). After Gil is arrested, 'I took an agency car into Manhattan and tried to see Gilbert at the precinct house' (120). The next morning Lionel drives to the Upper East Side in L&L's Pontiac: the journey is marked by the three asterisks that typify the novel's section breaks, then 'By the time I'd parked ...' (132). His return to see the Clients is made by car, though this is not specified till afterwards ('I'd parked in the shade of an elderly, crippled elm' [178]). Returning to the Zendo, he is 'stepping out of another cab' (227). Two notable exceptions to this automotive pattern exist: Lionel's journeys on the subway. The first is dispatched with the statement 'There is nothing Tourettic about the New York City subways' (192): primarily an in-joke in its refusal of Lionel's tendency to link everything to his condition. On his return journey, Lionel withdraws the judgment, noting 'that dance of attention, of stray gazes, in which every rider must engage', and 'the tunnel walls […] layered […] with expulsive and incoherent language' (237). The thought is stimulating, but the main point is to dispel it: 'But I was in a terrible hurry […] I couldn't spare a minute to dwell in myself as a body riding the Lexington train to Nevins Street – I might as well have been teleported, or floated to Brooklyn on a magic carpet, for all that I was distracted by the 4 train's sticky, graffitied immediacy' (237). This statement is very suggestive. This particular subway trip, we can see, is about as detailed as Lionel's journeys get. Mostly, the narrative deposits him outside his destination and he gets to work. Any richness of observation follows from that point. Lionel's image of teleportation can be combined with his earlier notion of the Minna Men's movement around Brooklyn resembling that of a piece in Monopoly (3): this too would be urban travel as sudden leap.

The novel is not, therefore, generally rich in what Lethem dubs 'visual information' about the transition from one part of the city to another. Its vividness is localized to particular venues. Compare *The Fortress of Solitude*:

> One thawing Saturday in March Dylan met Mingus at noon to walk up Court Street, through the scrap-strewn park that stretched beyond Borough Hall […] In the park they bought hot dogs and knishes from a steaming cart […] Just past the war monument the park tilted towards Brooklyn's edge, the crumpled waterfront: parking lots, garbage scows, city scrap yards. The Brooklyn-Queens Expressway was a vibrating shadow, beneath it the streets still showed cobblestone in places, elsewhere old trolley tracks lay half buried in the new tar. (76)

Here a movement through the city, on foot, from one area of Brooklyn to another, culminates in a moment of rich observation of the traces of history in the streets at the borough's edge. It thus differs from the travels that Lionel describes during his investigation. The primary reason for this is a difference of genre. In the crime novel, crosstown travel is purposive, goal-directed and often urgent: what matters is the investigation set to take place at the other end. In the Bildungsroman, on the other hand, the character of place is of central interest. We are seeing both the environment that makes Dylan and the developing process of perception in which he sees it. It is true that, as we noted in Chapter Two, *Motherless Brooklyn* itself has a dimension of the Bildungsroman, and material closer to the passage above can be found in its second, eponymous chapter, where Lionel is recounting his life story and how working for Frank has shown him the borough. But such material is largely excised from Lionel's present-day narrative of detection. Having learned to 'tell his story walking' (69–70), he rarely takes the scenic route.

Frank Minna's phrase reminds us of a simpler difference between the two novels. 'Minna Men drive cars' (90) is given as one of the group's defining characteristics. The novel begins with two of them in a Lincoln, ends with Lionel driving to JFK; its central business is notionally a car service. The adult Dylan Ebdus ends *Fortress* with a relentless drive to Indiana, but for the best part of that novel automobiles are not on the agenda: he walks, takes the subway – or occasionally flies. A novel dominated by these means of movement is readier to find space for urban observation during its journeys. Lionel appreciates his walk around the Upper East Side (153–63), but in his mindset as 'a detective on a case' (132) he is definitively not a *flâneur* ('I couldn't spare a minute to dwell in myself'). He does not walk from one area of the city to another and observe the gradual changes between them.

There is one major exception to all this: the car chase in Chapter One. Here for once we see the space of New York change before us. The named stages of travel include East 84th Street, Second Avenue, 59th Street, 36th Street, the Midtown Tunnel, the Pulaski Bridge, McGuinnness Boulevard. These are all cited, where in Lionel's other, functional journeys to a destination they would be invisible ('By the time I'd parked …'). Whereas those journeys are the means to an end (action, detective work), this journey *is* action and detective work. The chase is not like going from A to B (say, Bergen Street to the Zendo) as usual, because at the outset – and even to the end – the pursuers have no idea where B will be (Greenpoint, as it turns out). Any location along the route could, at the time, be of significance or lead to a different outcome (the giant's K-car might take the 59th Street Bridge to Queens, or go on deeper into Brooklyn): each must thus be registered and considered as it comes. In short, movement across the city must for once be traced in detail in its own right, rather than bracketed as an interlude. As such, it also draws a small stipend of brisk, lively metaphor: 'We all screeched across Fifty-ninth, a madcap rodeo of cabs and cars'; the two bunches of traffic blend 'like video spaceships on some antic screen' (17).

Arriving at the book's start, the chase sequence announces it as a novel of New York, traversing three boroughs. It showcases local knowledge, on the part of characters as well as author, and invites the reader to engage at the same level: 'At Fifty-Ninth Street we hit the end of the cycle of green lights, as well as the usual unpleasantness around the entrance to the Queensborough Bridge' (16); Thirty-sixth Street, Lionel realises, means 'Midtown Tunnel. Queens' (17). The business of the tunnel's toll booth and the K-car's use of an E-Z Pass bring unexpected variation into the sequence, making the specifics of the city's road network into knots of complication in the narrative thread. More broadly, the boroughs are viewed from a specific, situated perspective. If uptown Manhattan, before the chase begins, is 'Candyland' (3), the prospect of Queens means that 'The giant and his driver were moving into our turf, more or less. The boroughs' (17). Yet Queens, as it turns out, is in fact not familiar enough: 'a tangle of indifferent streets' (18). The realization that they are adjacent to Brooklyn – 'we both turned our heads like cartoon mice. The Pulaski Bridge' (20) – is at once a narrative gear-change and a signal of the Minna Men's (and by extension the novel's) sentimental or sheltered attachment to the idea of their own borough: twenty pages in, *Motherless Brooklyn* can finally travel 'into the mouth of Brooklyn'.

The opening chapter makes automobiles central to the novel. As we have seen, this association will largely remain intact. A later chapter is titled 'Auto Body': primarily a pun on the generic sign on automobile repair shops (as in *The Fortress of Solitude*, where Brooklyn's Fourth Avenue is marked by 'oil-stained auto-body shops' [2003: 136]), this is also a reply to the more Zen chapter title 'One Mind', and suggests the way that Lionel blends his subjectivity into the automotive experience during the novel's second car chase, out of the city. Some of Lethem's other works feature automobiles significantly: *Amnesia Moon*, definable as a 'road trip'; 'Access Fantasy', set in a vast traffic jam; the close of *Dissident Gardens* in which Sergius Gogan experiences a memorable drive to the airport. Yet no other work of this scale immerses itself so thoroughly in the realm of the motor car. There is, finally, an intriguing element of incongruity here. Lethem wrote the novel on returning from the West Coast, where constant car use was the norm. As the complainer says in *You Don't Love Me Yet*: 'I don't like to drive anyplace I can walk […] I know that outlook's a rarity in this burg' (Lethem 2007: 69). Indeed, even the comparatively low-income young band members of that novel all drive their own cars (2007: 175). Lethem has talked of bringing back the *noir* techniques of Los Angeles and here applying them to his home city, rather than 'tackling Brooklyn as Brooklyn' as he would do in the next novel (Clarke 2011: 39). In doing so he brings an automotorized world that is comparatively unusual in New York fiction, and certainly in Lethem's own other depictions of the city, in which almost no major character – from Rachel Ebdus to Miriam Zimmer, Perkus Tooth to Lenin Angrush – drives a car. That this is congruent with the city is demonstrated by Lethem's recollection of his own first relocation to California, in which he initially 'imposed my New Yorker's paradigm on the place and took buses, subways and did things within walking distance' (Clarke 2011: 162). Looking down from the Brooklyn Bridge, Dylan

Ebdus and Mingus Rude still occupy that paradigm: they consider that 'People in cars weren't New Yorkers anyway, they'd suffered some basic misunderstanding' (2003: 78). The observation might be a wry reflection on the New Yorkers of their author's previous novel.

The Street's History

We have seen that in *Motherless Brooklyn*, the city is navigated in specific areas, traversed by known routes, and a character like Lionel can be suddenly out of place in his own city. This sense of an urban environment that is known not in total but in pieces, in greatly varying degrees of intensity, is heightened in *The Fortress of Solitude*. For the duration of part one, 'Underberg', the focal point of the book's map is the house on Dean Street where Dylan Ebdus is raised, primarily through the 1970s, by his father Abraham (and his mother Rachel until her departure for Indiana). Geographical limitation is consistent with Lethem's project here. This is a novel centred around one individual's experience, from age five upwards; for the most part it does not presume to range far beyond his sphere of experience, though it does occasionally follow the paths of other characters around the city. Within that range, we shall see, it nonetheless comes to seek panoramic quality.

Beyond the family home itself, the primary unit of experience in the novel is 'the block': a section of Dean Street between Nevins Street and Bond Street which run south-west to north-east across it. These are 'vents into the unknown' (Lethem 2003: 13), leading away from the known block to other parts of the local area which, while geographically close, are unfamiliar to a young child. As the novel progresses, a number of other streets emerge into its lexicon. Bergen Street runs parallel to Dean Street on the grid, one block south; Wycoff Street, one block beyond it, is a name associated with housing estates and trouble; Pacific and Atlantic Avenues are their counterparts to the north, and Fulton Street leads into downtown Brooklyn to the north-west. Both Hoyt Street and Smith Street cross Dean Street further west; the major traffic artery of Flatbush Avenue to the north marks a spatial limit beyond which the protagonist is often reluctant to think himself. The book comes with no map (a scholarly edition would surely contain at least one), and was published before Google made instant access to detailed online maps the norm for many readers. Yet it makes little effort to situate the uninitiated reader amid its spatial coordinates: they are presented not systematically but occasionally, as narrative or the protagonist's thought demands. To reprise once again one of Farah Mendlesohn's terms for fantastic narrative (2008: xx–xxi), *The Fortress of Solitude* is an immersive world, even though its geographical terms are not Lethem's invention. It plunges the reader into an environment that they must accept and piece together from multiple references – spatially as in other ways. Readers here follow a protagonist who is usually, if only slightly, more familiar than us with the immersive world; his learning process, often including his desire to conceal his lack of prior knowledge, is one of the prime trajectories of the narrative.

In this, *The Fortress of Solitude* follows one of its major precursors, Henry Roth's *Call It Sleep* (1934), a semi-autobiographical novel about a Jewish boy growing up in the tenements of Brooklyn and the Lower East Side in the early twentieth century. Roth's novel does not progress beyond childhood: it is a modernist, stream-of-consciousness novel of the city narrated almost entirely from a child's point of view. What Lethem records especially taking from Roth is the sense of two worlds of experience, inside the home and on the street (Clarke 2011: 91). Roth's protagonist David Schearl is emotionally tied to his mother, in a way that Dylan Ebdus initially seems ready to emulate (his mother cracks an egg on his head for cooking: 'He'd rub his head, half hurt, half in love' [11]), but is denied when she abruptly departs the narrative. Outside the home David awkwardly joins the children's street games, with a tentativeness akin to Dylan's – 'He drew near, warily. That was Sidney, Yonk. He knew them. The others? They lived around the corner maybe' (Roth 2006: 86) – and talks to them in a guttersnipe slang that Roth phonetically renders ('"He was standin' dere awreddy"' [86]). The intensity of the contrast between home life and street life is taken up by Lethem, who writes at the outset that 'There were two worlds' (8). A rich account of Dylan's home life follows, until the narrative winds from the attic to the front door and ejects Dylan, 'from the first of his two worlds, the house, into the second. The outside, the block. Dean Street' (13). With the arrival of Mingus Rude, who addresses Dylan in street games with a series of improvised nicknames, the protagonist begins to understand that 'he and Mingus were to be one thing to each other indoors, off the street, and entirely another outside. On the block' (59).

The sidewalk is the centre of what becomes a gradual concentric movement through urban space. Dylan perceives 'an arrangement of zones in slate', the paving stones of which he quickly becomes an expert scholar, through 'long communion' which enables him to choose the best place to chalk a board for the children's game of skully (21). Beyond the slates, the 'peeling painted fronts of the row houses – pink, white, pale green, various tones of red and blue, always giving way to the brick underneath' – appear as 'the flags of undiscovered realms' (13). Lethem's narration is moving at a microscopic level, methodically following the child's curiosity about the composition of his street. Pieces of space are only tentatively put together. A collective focal point in the street, for the local children, is the house inhabited by Henry, a boy three years older than Dylan, with its paved front yard and cement fence (13). Two doors down from this is 'the abandoned house': though described in Gothic terms ('It wore cinderblock bandages over the windows and doorway like a mummy with blanked eyes and stilled howling mouth' [14]), for the children it is primarily known for its practical utility as a target for thrown rubber balls.

A known world is thus produced from the child's point of view and the interests of the group of children who become a kind of collective agent in these opening chapters. 'From Henry's and the abandoned house to his own Dylan knew the slate precisely' (17): the statement signals how small the urban world is at this stage, in a novel which will ultimately open on to much larger distances. Lethem follows the limits imposed by his character's life. The terms of reference also follow those colloquially known to the character, rather than official ones: to any adult in range, the house would not be 'Henry's house', but to Dylan the relevant identifying term is the child who occupies it. When Dylan is sent around the corner for a quart of milk, the limit of his familiarity with the world nearby is emphasized: his side of the street has been 'a surfaced iceberg, one with Dylan's own flag planted on it [...] The rest of the block was under water. Dylan for years had clung to this one face, bent over the slates as though they were sheets of Spirograph paper on the floor of his room, not noticing until too late that they were part of an edifice which curled past Bond and Nevins Street, into the unknown' (36). Lethem's metaphor suggests how foreshortened the range of urban cognition can be: one or two streets away are no distance, yet to venture to them may take the urban voyager out of accustomed patterns and into uncharted water.

'The stoop of the abandoned house', Lethem records, 'was also a proscenium arch for secrets, hidden in plain sight in the middle of the block' (15). The image suggests the urban block's role as a stage set, crossed by the cast of characters in varying combinations for set-piece scenes. Around particular events on the street Lethem also weaves a sense of place as abiding rather than confined to individual scenes. Walking the sidewalk that he has memorized, Dylan 'could say when he was in front of Henry's or the abandoned house without glancing up, just by the shapes at his feet, the long tilted slabs or the one sticking-up moonlike shape or the patch of concrete or the shattered pothole which always filled with water after those summer thunderstorms which came and instantly broke the humid afternoons into dark, electrified pieces' (15). This sentence moves from the deeply specific – a single, unrepeatable, shape of slate, as though vividly encountered in a particular moment – to the more general – 'those summer thunderstorms', a recurrent series of events on multiple days – imperceptibly; the generic time-scale at the end of the sentence emphasizes that these encounters with the ragged pieces of sidewalk are themselves generic, repeated day after day.

These first chapters depict time's passage over a sustained period, even as they also present individual encounters. Some passages clearly describe extended periods of time: 'Winter days were static glimpsed between channel flips. Rotting snow like black diseased gums in the street. The projects were sealed up, the kids didn't come out' (76), or at a wilfully accelerated clip: 'Whole days were mysterious, and then the sun went down' (16). On another occasion we witness time spooling, as if on fast-forward, through a single afternoon as Dylan haplessly waits for his bicycle to return: 'Dylan stood naked in the minutes as they accumulated, as they stacked up indifferently on the distant face of the Williamsburg Savings Bank tower clock. The day was like an unanswered telephone, the mute slate ringing' (43). The recurrent local landmark of the clock brings a combination of fixed place and passing time.

The narrative subtly moves between events which are generic and repeatable, and those that only happen once. The 'stolen time between passing cars and the Dean Street bus', capitalized upon by players of street sports, is generic, though it is limned with the immediacy of a present action: 'The bus stopped the game the longest, the players pressed impatiently against the doors of parked cars to make room, waving the bus on, faster, faster, go' (15). When Robert Woolfolk accosts Dylan on Bergen Street, a bus travelling the same route is visible 'up near Smith Street, where it seemed to rest at a tilt, fatigued' (36): a unique moment. The same is true a few pages later when Robert casually rides away on Dylan's bicycle, leaving him standing helpless before his home: 'The tonguelike latch of Dylan's black ironwork gate rattled with the vibration of the bus going by' (43).

The local bus is an understated, recurrent presence in 'Underberg'. It passes again as Mingus arrives in his first street game, 'taking a lean on a parked car to let the bus go by' (58), and again on an Autumn evening: 'The block an island of time, school a million miles away, mothers calling kids inside, the bus lit inside now, fat ladies coming home from offices at the Board of Education on Livingston Street, their weary shapes like black teeth inside the glowing mouth of the bus' (66). It is the first syntactical subject of the scene in which the Funk Mob visit Brooklyn: 'The Dean Street bus, unable to slip past the white stretch limousine double-parked in front of Barrett Rude's place, nestled at its bumper instead, humming like a refrigerator, traffic behind stacking to Bond Street. The bus carried just two passengers, one intermittently asleep, but the thing still had its dumb round to make, its loop' (154). No named character, let alone Dylan Ebdus, ever takes this bus: it remains not a vehicle for narrative propulsion but a mobile piece of background. Its disuse by actual characters lets it stand apart from them, as a nudging force from outside the block: a piece of civic infrastructure, state-owned like the Public Schools righteously favoured by Dylan's mother, a structural connection to the unseen city beyond Dean Street, and also something that must move to regular schedules ('its dumb round [...] its loop'). It thus suggests a circling, rhythmic passage of time: across a day and by extension, in the more lyrical sentence above, across the seasons. It is a tiny, telling detail that Arthur Lomb's block on Pacific Street – 'the Bermuda Triangle of Boerum Hill, a space arranged [...] to fall under no domain whatsoever' – is 'eerie, kidless, no bus' (125): the absence of the public transport connection heightens the block's strange sense of isolation.

Extended through time, Dylan's block becomes a site of memory – not merely for the Dylan Ebdus imprisoned by its legacy two decades on (319), but during 'Underberg' itself. As early as Chapter Three, 'The block was empty [...] Dylan didn't know where the kids were. It was October, getting colder, everyone was wearing jackets and ranging away from the block' (35). By 1974 Dylan can already suddenly reflect that 'come to think of it you couldn't say when the last time was anyone played wallball, it might be another lost art. Forgotten games stacked up like the grievances of the losers of wars, unrecorded in the street's history' (45). The block, which has been the beginning of Dylan's spatial and social awareness, in 1975 is suddenly declared 'so useless now, no skully, no ball games, any kid you could think of off in some cluster or gang, like survivalist cells' (91). In 1977, around eight years into the book's catalogue of events, Dylan and Mingus find themselves playing ball once more, prompting the narrative reflection: 'The block was like an open-air museum of their former days, the slate cracked and skewed in all the usual places, the abandoned house still theirs any time they wanted to reclaim it' (159). Their contemporaries come out to the street or 'back to the block' to join in, drawn by the sense of a local history being revisited: 'Nobody knew they were nostalgic until they saw Dylan Ebdus and Mingus Rude in the golden leaf-light that covered the middle of the block, a dream of a summer ago, ripened into history while nobody noticed' (160).

Lethem's portrait of a place thus also noticeably occupies the dimension of time, which in the fast-changing consciousness of the child can make 'history' of events a year or two earlier. There is an element of irony in this, as the child's intuitive sense of 'the street's history' is framed by the mature author. From an adult perspective the notion that a year or two's street ball games amount to historical change is an entertaining error of scale – as though a historical novel could be written about, say, 1972 from the perspective of 1975 – yet the narrative is committed to following Dylan's perspective on its own emergent terms. By the early 1980s, as Dylan prepares to leave Brooklyn for Vermont:

> Sometimes when you walked around the neighbourhood now it was like you were already a visitor from the future.
>
> The pavement, the slate's not changed, but though you'd never flown higher than one precocious spaldeen catch you might be drifting now, a released balloon, too far off to discern distinctive cracks formerly memorized, let alone rain-rinsed skully ghosts. (271–2)

Dylan begins the novel distinguished for his scholarship of the sidewalk slates. His relative alienation from the city block that has been his home is demonstrated by his distance from this expertise, while 'skully ghosts' – his own game-board etchings on the sidewalk – are erased by time and weather. To be a 'visitor from the future' picks up the imagery of science fiction that runs through the novel and Dylan's life (for instance in the paperbacks whose covers Abraham Ebdus paints), but also gestures forward to the future of Brooklyn that the characters do not yet know but the author does. This theme of urban transformation will be taken up shortly.

The depiction of the block has one further, subtle aspect. This is its connection to the film being painted, day by day, in the attic by Abraham Ebdus. The frames of the film, it is stated early on, 'made a diary of painter's days' (31). Abraham inserts representational content, like figures, into this abstract work, then removes or sublimates it: 'They'd melted into blobs of light' (31). 'Blobs' hints at the connection between the painting and the street, for it is also quietly recurrent in Lethem's depiction of that 'second world'. Dean Street's trees are 'inclined to cover the abandoned house in dappled shade, blobs of light' (15). On an afternoon in 1977, 'Blobs of yellow-green sun refracted through trees grew elliptical, spanned the white [limousine] hood, moved on' (155). On a hot day Barrett Rude Jr opens his windows: 'The sunlight on the strewn mirror [was] blobby, swimmy' (105). These small touches imply a painterly approach to light, consonant with the presence of the painter who is at work above the street each day. This point is emphasized later in 'Underberg', as, during a sequence narrated from Abraham's point of view, the narration breaks into single sentences, isolated like tentative lines of poetry:

> Bus purring through leaf-blotched shadow.
> Run-on sentence of cracked slate.
> Cornices a horizon, lintels slag in a canyon or quarry wall. (234)

Each of these lines is left to stand unexplained, but each suggests an artistic relation to the street. If the first feels like a fragment of Imagist poetry, it also hints at the painter's eye for light and shade. The second imagines the slates of the sidewalk as a text: an image reminiscent of Dylan's study of this surface, but here perhaps shown as viewed on high by his father. The third line reimagines architecture as a natural environment, as though the painter pictures the street as a mountainous landscape. That these compressed perceptions are connected to Abraham's practice is suggested by what follows: 'Dean Street of course infiltrated the work, it couldn't not. Abraham painted house-row façades, then blacked them over, presences drowned in abstraction' (234). We can extrapolate an analogy between painter and author, painstaking artists of the city block. In Lethem's career, the various lines quoted above are integral to an unprecedentedly dense and sustained attempt to render the texture of place. As such, an implicit surrogate within the text is not only the child with his shifting perceptions, but the abstract painter, obsessively dedicated to texture, who finds himself painting the street almost despite himself.

These readings have shown that the city of *Fortress* is, in the first instance, profoundly local; at its heart is the lore and emotion sunk into a particular stretch of street. Yet as Dylan grows, the book's spatial range also expands. How does Brooklyn emerge? In significant moments, it is revealed as Dylan walks into it, the narrative once again closely tied to the protagonist's movements and boundaries. Thus when his mother takes him to the furniture store Pintchik on Flatbush Avenue, Dylan wonders what he would find 'if he walked across Flatbush, past its shops selling dashikis, and T-shirts which read I'M PROUD OF MY AFRICAN HERITAGE, past Triangle Sports, past Arthur Treacher's Fish and Chips, past Pintchik itself? Who knew. His world found its limit there' (52). We are halted at his limit, 'immersively' confronted with a series of locations that the narrative does not trouble to explain further. In another episode, Dylan is led by Mingus 'toward Brooklyn's edge, the crumpled waterfront' and on to the Brooklyn Bridge: 'over the river, traffic howling in cages at their feet, the gray clotted sky clinging to the bridge's veins, Manhattan's dinosaur spine rotating into view as they mounted the great curve above the river' (78).

The traffic 'howling in cages' might suggest a menagerie of tormented animals, yet the 'cages' are not merely figurative but a reference to the bridge's physical structure. A location that can appear picturesque is here visually impressive, certainly, yet also a cold, uncompromising environment, dominated by automobiles above which the pedestrians are perilously suspended. The last clause conveys the movement of the observers across the river – the skyline is 'rotating into view' as they walk – while also rendering both skyline and bridge in compressed phrases pregnant with suggestion. 'Manhattan's dinosaur spine' suddenly refreshes an image familiar (unlike Triangle Sports or Pintchik) to most readers, while (through the connotations of 'dinosaur') hinting at distance, scale and danger. 'The great curve', lastly, is a buried, semi-conscious trace of a song title from Talking Heads, unreleased at the moment of the scene but long familiar to Lethem and, by virtue of the band's career, implicitly associated with New York. (The phrase is taken up again, more ostentatiously, to describe the New York cityscape early in *Dissident Gardens*, when Miriam Zimmer promises to disclose 'the greatest curve' in the subway network, a phrase that acquires parallel reference to her own body [2013a: 30].)

This is one of the novel's first sightings of Manhattan. As in *Motherless Brooklyn*, the city's central borough figures significantly. Frequently its primary association is with distance. 'Dylan knew Manhattan, knew David Copperfield's London, knew even Narnia better than he'd ever know Brooklyn north of Flatbush Avenue' (52): the primary emphasis here is on the inaccessibility of large parts of Brooklyn itself. But into the bargain Manhattan is also posited as a remote realm, on a par with places far-flung in time and space, or a realm of sheer fantasy. This view recurs. On a wintry night watching the Super Bowl in Dean Street, 'Somewhere ice-laden planes might be crashing, Manhattan might have snapped in two and drifted out to sea' (75). When Barrett Rude Junior contemplates in turn a Ray Charles concert at Radio City Music Hall, recording the demo of a song, and buying an ice cream, he concludes: 'the four-track recorder was impossibly distant, a rumor as farfetched and unlikely as the ice-cream cone, as Manhattan' (109). He and Abraham both realize, on a rare trip to the island, how entrenched they have become on their own block: 'Brooklyn a mind-state peeling further from Manhattan each day, like continental drift' (131). Brooklyn was a city in its own right until 1898; these characters' reclusive consolidation into it seems to promise to reverse the process of its affiliation to New York City, making it feel increasingly an autonomous zone once more. Even after Dylan commences study in Manhattan, his time split between two worlds, his return to Mingus leaves 'Manhattan unlikely as Neptune or Vulcan, restored to its status as an unexplored planet, the future' (223). For a long time it is mainly descried from afar: 'the trace of Manhattan's high teeth visible past downtown Brooklyn' visible through Arthur Lomb's binoculars (127). Visible from Brooklyn's Promenade, the skyline is 'a channel no one watched that played anyway, like an anthem, like famous static' (92): the emphasis here is on its iconic quality, screened many times over in the twentieth century yet unimpressive to the Brooklynite to whom it is an all too familiar background. This only changes when, in the wake of Mingus's arrest as Aeroman, Dylan broods at 'the whole watery mouth of the city' (239), tiring of Brooklyn and ready for 'escape': 'Another option, Manhattan, was so prominent it was nearly sticking in his eye' (241).

Dylan's partial departure to Manhattan offers a perspective on Brooklyn itself by contrast: a realm of crime and danger, so that after Robert Woolfolk's theft of his money in the East Village, 'Brooklyn's chased you to the ground and nobody's going to comprehend except that you're marked, cursed, best avoided' (269). It has a similar role in Vermont, which is innocently 'permeable to Brooklyn ways' like shoplifting (175), and where at Camden Dylan can use his 'inner-city knowledge' to impress (387). Yet Brooklyn is not truly as simple as this. At moments, *Fortress* seeks to register the borough's range by rising to a more synoptic view. In the previous chapter we saw that the superhero motif allows the novel a different approach to the city. The point can be taken further here. A crucial passage is Dylan's first venture onto his own block's roof, in an abortive bid to try flying. What that notion enables is a spectacular vision of the city. Manhattan's towers, viewed from the roof, 'place you, fix you in a firm relation of puniness and awe':

> What's unsettling is to put Manhattan at your back and face the borough. Up from the canyon floor, out of the deep well of streets, gazing out into the Brooklyn Beyond is like standing in a Kansas prairie contemplating distance. Every rooftop for miles in every direction is level with that where you stand. The rooftops form a flotilla of rafts, a potential chessboard for your knight-hops, interrupted only by the promontory of the Wycoff housing projects, the skeletal Eagle Clothing sign, the rise of the F-train platform where it elevates past the Gowanus Canal. Manhattan's topped, but Brooklyn's an open-face sandwich in the light, bare parts picked over by pigeons and gulls. (153)

The first notable idea here is almost explicit in the first sentence: to 'put Manhattan at your back and face the borough' is to reverse the perspective on New York shown by a majority of stories and representations, turning from the city's most obvious iconography to seek a different repertoire of legends. Those would include the specific sights and names here: Wycoff, F-train,

Gowanus Canal, typical of the universe of local particulars in which this novel immerses us. The sentence thus stands as a description of one of the undertakings of *Fortress* (and even, to a degree, *Motherless Brooklyn*). In a novel that has worked for 150 pages to familiarize Dylan and us with Brooklyn, the passage also performs an instant defamiliarization: seen from on high, the borough is different once again. A basic feature like the homogeneous level of the rooftops' heights is hitherto unsuspected, while those landmarks that rise above it take on spatial relations different from those they have at street level. The defamiliarization is a simple enough matter of perspective, but Lethem enriches it with a battery of metaphors. The canyon (the 'well' of the street below the roofs); the prairie (the new flat land of unimpeded long-distance views at rooftop level); the rafts and chessboard (two different ways, in quick succession, to envisage the multiple, delineated surfaces of the grid formed by the roofs); the sandwich (an image for the openness to the sky that has its own Brooklyn provenance, at least in the wake of Lionel Essrog's passion for Zeod's sandwiches): the vista travels through five metaphorical registers in 113 words.

Dylan sees the 'Brooklyn Beyond'. The narrative voice, though, goes higher still, as though in emulation of this view, to describe Brooklyn to us in a different way. One instance here is the narrative's location of Samuel J. Underberg's store itself: 'on the other side of Flatbush, beyond the newsstand on the traffic island, in the region of flattened lots and stilled warehouses in the shadow of the Williamsburg Savings Bank tower. The area is a big zero in most senses, a region of lack. Past the Brooklyn Academy of Music, the Long Island Rail Road terminal, there's nothing doing, nobody home. In fact, though no one seems to know it, this is the site once slated for Ebbets Field's relocation, before the Dodgers defected' (186). The narrative voice here does not coincide with a single character's perception, but rather is a consciousness full of Brooklyn lore. (In fact it is very close to Lethem's vignette 'Breakfast at Brelreck's', published during the composition of *Fortress* and interested in such shared local mythology [2011: 413–7].) If the voice could be part of a *Rough Guide* travelogue, it also connotes the sense of an aerial view, from which the multiple landmarks can all be seen and coordinated. This is still more explicit in a lengthy passage which, before Dylan even knows of the magic ring, draws on the conceit of flight for its vantage: 'Rise up, the way the flying man no longer can. Look' (136). The conceit offers an alibi for what the passage is already doing: scanning the district of Gowanus and Boerum Hill and judging their uncertain borderline, assessing the rate of social change.

The theme of gentrification – the transformation of relatively impoverished or ordinary urban areas into more affluent and fashionable ones, with higher property prices, differently composed populations, and different businesses and services – is often associated with *The Fortress of Solitude* (Godbey 2008; Nadell 2010: 119; Williams 2018), yet remains submerged or implicit for much of its course. It is introduced by the elderly Isabel Vendle, who single-handedly invents Boerum Hill as a more upscale name for Gowanus as she looks out over the slow transformation of Dean Street. From her point of view, the Ebdus family is potentially a harbinger of a more desirable future for the area: white, artistic and middle-class in culture if not financially wealthy. But Isabel dies sixty pages in, and there is scant evidence of her dreams' fulfilment until late in the novel. The passage under consideration is an exception, directly addressing the issue: '[T]his gentrification is strange and slow and not at all as coherent as Isabel Vendle had hoped. There's a cluster of antique shops now on Atlantic between Hoyt and Bond, new families on Pacific and Dean, Bergen too. […] Some eager beaver's opened a French restaurant on Bergen and Hoyt, jumping the gun perhaps but worth a shot' (136). The account is dense with local knowledge, street-by-street detail of the degree of renovation or new business. As the point of view rises above Brooklyn, it draws more distinctions: 'Here Fourth Avenue's a wide trench of light-industrial ruin, oil-stained auto-body shops and forlorn, graffitied warehouses'; in a nod back to Frank Minna, 'Court Street's an old Italian preserve, the side streets south of Carroll hushed in the grip of Mafia whispers, old ways enforced with baseball bats and slashed tires'. The lengthy passage suggests that even this small tranche of one borough must be understood on very local terms, each street differentiated from the next with precise cultural connotations. In making these judgments, the general notion of gentrification becomes premature at best: the renovators are 'a set of ghosts from the future haunting this ghetto present' (136). In this they resemble what Dylan feels like, another 130 pages on: 'a visitor from the future'.

The novel's unusual structure allows it both to visit from the future and to visit that future (1999, the setting of Part Three, 'Prisonaires') as a kind of exotic destination itself, owing to the density with which the 1970s have been reassembled. Almost the first sighting of Brooklyn in this section of the book is the restaurant Berlin, with its 'fresh, expensive renovation, one hip to the virtues of a century-old shopfront': 'impoverished Smith Street had been converted to an upscale playground' (426). Euclid Barnes, Dylan's former Camden classmate, complains that the neighbourhood is 'too trendy. In just like six months everybody came and spoiled it' (428–9). Given the novel's deep investment in reconstructing the earlier historical moment, it would be easy enough to assume that it endorses Euclid's judgement, considering the 1970s Brooklyn as the authentic model and disdaining the social changes that Berlin represents. But again things are more complicated. In a key passage, the thirty-five-year-old Dylan reflects:

> My possessive feelings were silly. I saw the changes here in terms of Rachel's war on the notion of gentrification [...] I walked an invisible map of incidents, shakedowns, hurled eggs, pizza muggings, my own stations of the cross. But imagining that those terms should be relevant to the hipsters who'd colonized the place was like imagining that 'Play That Funky Music' heard on a taxicab's radio was a message of guilt and shame intended for my ears. No, Isabel Vendle was dead and forgotten, and Rachel was gone. Euclid's Boerum Hill was the real one. The fact that I could see Gowanus glinting under the veneer wasn't important, wasn't anything more than interesting. (429)

The reflection is perceptively generous. Though provoked to feel 'weirdly bitter' at the transformation of his old home, Dylan has enough perspective to see that he has no special claim on a place that he has visited 'three or four times in nearly two decades' (427). His own history with the place is certainly 'interesting', but not 'important' in the sense of giving him the right to define the experience of one who lives there now. That 'Euclid's Boerum Hill was the real one' is in one way a statement of the obvious, in another a bold declaration that the present is as authentic as the past.

The Fortress of Solitude is Lethem's richest portrait of New York, though it is also one carefully limited in scope: limning a neighbourhood and following particular trajectories across the city, its urban excavation achieves depth rather than seeking excessive breadth. We have seen that it is rooted in a *pointilliste* reconstruction of the individual block on Dean Street, as dedicated as Dylan's scrutiny of the sidewalk tiles, but that it gradually builds outward from this to produce striking redescriptions of the city. It also aspires, figuratively, upward, to make a synoptic scan of the territory and issue a more sociological account. Meanwhile this is also a novel profoundly immersed in the passage of time: if its painting of Dean Street takes on this dimension, so on a larger scale its overall structure allows it to take a wider view of the ambiguities of urban renewal. With this novel behind him, Lethem had made as major a statement about Brooklyn as anyone in his generation of novelists could do. In his next major novel of New York, Lethem would reverse the motion of Dylan on the roof: putting Brooklyn at his back and facing the borough of Manhattan.

Tiger Island

'Everybody lives on some island', says the mayoral aide Richard Abneg in *Chronic City* (2010: 157). The assertion obliquely suggests the island where the conversation is taking place, and where everyone in it lives. The action of *Chronic City* never ventures off Manhattan. Even the dialogue and imagination of the novel rarely go further. In a taxicab late in the novel, the cultural critic Perkus Tooth rhetorically wonders: 'I wonder what would happen if we asked this cab to take the [...] Lincoln Tunnel? What sort of world [...] is left out there?' (407). The implication is that beyond Manhattan lies 'fallout-strewn [...] wasteland' or 'Chinese slave dictatorship' (417), if not simply a void. Richard's response – 'There never was much of one' – is primarily sardonic, a version of the Manhattanite's blinkered notion that the rest of the world is not worth bothering with, though in this context it looks like an endorsement of Perkus's increasing disbelief in that world's existence. Perkus's own reflection, 'Probably we wouldn't [...] be allowed to try', is unsupported by any evidence in the novel: no 'Manhattan Border Patrol' (407) is seen preventing people from leaving the island. It is not needed, as outside this conversation no character in the novel ever thinks of leaving. When the protagonist, retired actor Chase Insteadman, later considers that he could demonstrate his free will by taking a cab off the island 'to call Perkus's bluff' (441), he nonetheless proceeds to the Metropolitan Museum on Fifth Avenue. His own name plainly echoes his location: metrically, it suggests the bank Chase Manhattan (as it was known until a merger in 2000), with 'Insteadman' appearing instead of the borough, just as the fictional novel *Obstinate Dust* recalls David Foster Wallace's *Infinite Jest* (100). His sometime partner, the ghostwriter Oona Laszlo, is also, in her way, emblematic of the borough: 'a rib of Manhattan torn out to make a woman' (242).

The novel contains much large talk of 'the city', but in practice these references are to its central island. Staten Island is mentioned as a place where police officers live (417); a senior doctor has a 'deep Bronx' voice (423); a radio station is located 'at the mouth of the Brooklyn Bridge' (233). In a throwback to earlier cityscapes, a hospital nurse is housed 'behind sliding Plexiglas, like Chinese food in Brooklyn' (408) – a reference native to Lethem that seems improbable from Chase. Otherwise the other boroughs are almost unmentioned in over 450 pages. The only other states to figure even distantly are Chase's home of Indiana, recalled in the penultimate chapter (454–9), and Connecticut, mentioned as the home of Perkus's sister and as evidence that Perkus's theory of Manhattan's isolation 'wasn't concretely true' (461). To a remarkable degree, Lethem's novel makes Manhattan a self-sufficient world. When Perkus Tooth calls Manhattan a 'pocket universe', in which nobody believes in news from beyond its boundaries (386), he is on a late paranoid streak, yet it is a fair description of the borough as it appears in this novel. Brooklyn in the earlier novels and Queens in *Dissident Gardens* prove to be intricately connected with the rest of the city, above all with Manhattan itself. *Chronic City* suggests that the view might not need to be mutual; that while these boroughs cannot ignore Manhattan, it can more readily forget them.

Even within Manhattan itself, movement is somewhat circumscribed, as the novel recapitulates its predecessors' focus on particular sites and routes. A long journey uptown takes Chase and Oona to 191st street to view a public artwork: almost as far as one can go and remain in Manhattan, 'the island's own provinces and badlands, its margins' (106). Chase and Perkus each make one trip downtown (233, 74) as far as the Lower East Side or Chelsea. Chase's life consists heavily of invitations to high-society gatherings, so he will travel to the Metropolitan, to a funeral on the Upper West Side (55) or to a party at the Mayor's townhouse on Park Avenue and 64th Street (260). Perkus ends up occupying a set of 'canine apartments', intended for dogs, on 65th Street (313). Elsewhere on the Upper East Side, Perkus lives on East 84th Street, Chase six blocks away (8), Oona on 94th street, Richard Abneg on 78th Street, and his partner Georgina Hawkmanaji in a penthouse on Park Avenue (33). When Perkus Tooth travels downtown he realizes that he has not left his 'quarantine', 'east of Lexington, north of Grand Central Station', for perhaps over a year; even in midtown he has come to feel like a foreigner in need of a guidebook (74–5). The eccentric Perkus is an extreme case, but he dramatizes the way that an urban world can become circumscribed to a familiar radius.

The most elementary fact about these locations is that they are affluent, at least by comparison with the Brooklyn of Dylan Ebdus's and Lionel Essrog's childhoods. A relevant circumstantial detail is the amount of travel undertaken by cab: Chase, unlike Mingus Rude or Miriam Zimmer, can disdain the subway and insist 'I always take taxicabs' (102). The fact that he can take a cab a hundred streets downtown, while leaving African American residents of the far north of the island waiting for a bus, is pointed out as a class distinction that shapes his sense of mobility around town (115). *Chronic City* is Lethem's lengthy foray into a New York of wealth and class status, a place that knows itself as 'capital's capital' (65). Richard Abneg considers that 'Dollars resided intrinsically here in Manhattan. Their transfer elsewhere was only a mystical wish' (130). In a reprise of Marx's thought in the Paris Manuscripts, capital can make space malleable: 'Money had its solvent powers, could dissolve the rear walls of a nineteenth-century town house to throw a dining room into what must have been the backyard' (269). Big money is immensely powerful, yet can also be discreet. Richard Abneg reflects that the benefit gala circuit discloses the true ownership of the city, as seemingly public spaces like museums and galleries are retaken at night by their rightful owners (127–8). Set pieces to this effect include the Woodrows' party, with its etiquette of cocktail small talk and Cuban cigars (28–42); the vast funeral gathering at the Society for Ethical Culture where Chase spots Salman Rushdie and Lou Reed (56); the annual fundraiser for the Manhattan Reification Society, held in the Museum of Natural History, where Richard Abneg eats 'two-thousand-dollar pork medallion and scalloped potatoes' (130); the elaborate evening brunch at Le Parker Meridien in midtown, where the wealthy Danzigs take the prize of an evening in Chase's company (188–95), won at a charity raffle featuring Bono and Damien Hirst (176); and most significantly, the Mayor's Christmas party, 'a scene of glowing golds and browns against monumental windows [...] guests [Lou Reed again included] busy emptying flutes of Prosecco and vodka shots and trays of tiny sushi and blini shopped among us by the catering staff', beneath 'a thirty-foot-high plaster scrollwork ceiling painted and lit to resemble buttercream icing on an inverted wedding cake' (260). We have come a long way from Lionel's delight in sandwiches from Zeod's, let alone Chaos's struggles for food in Hatfork. *Chronic City* takes on a social milieu almost unprecedented in Lethem – perhaps its closest precursor is the exclusive virtual reality party of his early story 'Forever, Said the Duck' – and as such seems to remove its characters from the claims of dissidence or counterculture. In Lethem's favoured binary, Chase Insteadman moves in a 'white elephant' world.

Yet there is, initially, still space for the termite. Even within the spatially limited zone of the Upper East Side, Lethem insists on divergence. Perkus Tooth inhabits 'one of those anonymous warrens tucked behind innocuous storefronts, buildings without lobbies, let alone doormen' (8): quite different from, for instance, the extraordinary townhouse of Maud and Thatcher Woodrow (28) with its double layer of doormen, yet not geographically distant from it. Inside Perkus's hallway, the dowdiness is plain: 'the corridor floor's lumpy checkerboard mosaic, the cloying citrus of the superintendent's disinfectant oil, the bank of dented brass mailboxes, and the keening of a dog from behind an upstairs door'. This is a long-standing, scuffed residential environment, minimally maintained and seemingly without fundamental renovation in decades. Chase expands: 'To live in Manhattan is to be persistently amazed at the worlds squirreled inside one another, the chaotic intricacy with which realms interleave'; 'We only pretend to live on something as orderly as a grid' (8). The Upper East Side turns out to contain multitudes, social niches adjacent yet often not acknowledging each other. Lethem has made this explicit when asked about the novel's location:

> There's this quarter of power, Park Avenue and Madison Avenue, and Fifth, along the edge of the park, that is rightly resented and envied and treated as a kind of palace of fantasy [...] And yet the trick to the Upper East Side is you go a bit further east, past Lexington Avenue and onto Third and Second Avenue and beyond that, and you're in a kind of Podunk zone of Manhattan, very drab and unfashionable and sometimes quite affordable; there are a lot of rent-controlled apartments there and the shops never change. [...] And so these two things are side-by-side. (Clarke 2011: 170)

Lethem had given a preview of this residential, less glamorous facet of the Lower East Side in his story 'Lucky Alan', in the *New Yorker* in 2007, whose main characters inhabit 78th Street. That these two elements of the Upper East Side 'never resolve, they just interpenetrate, endlessly' is what Lethem describes as 'useful' for his purposes. Chase confirms that the 'secret' of the area is 'its quarantine from the boom-and-bust of Manhattan's trends and fashions. [...] what's here is entrenched and immutable' (65). The binary of Manhattan vs. Brooklyn has thus been replaced by a more local one, Manhattan vs. Manhattan, and not even uptown vs. downtown. Chase realizes that he is a crux between two irreconcilable versions of Upper East Side society: 'Maud [Woodrow] at her regular table at Daniel, vibrantly awake to an invisible yet omnipotent web of social power, and Perkus, in his Eighty-fourth Street burrow, testing his daily reality on a grid of cultural marginalia, simultaneous views of mutually impossible worlds' (122).

Given Lethem's past tendency sometimes to romanticize and metaphorize his own borough – 'Science fiction was a literary Brooklyn for me', and the like (2011: 46) – it is curious to realize that Perkus Tooth, dissident celebrant of subversive cultural marginalia, has no connection with the place at all: the native of Connecticut is disoriented below 42nd Street. During the novel a sense grows (especially in Perkus himself) of Perkus as an 'enemy' of the city, hunted by its authorities (447). Yet this phrasing takes 'the city' only as its present administration. In another sense Perkus Tooth is part of the city, a long-standing facet of Manhattan as integral as the cultural figures Chase sees at his galas. Richard Abneg recalls Perkus as a 'broadsider', plastering messages to Manhattan walls 'when the city had still been open to Beat or punk self-invention, that city

Perkus had always chided me for failing to know' (429–30). A major underlying dynamic of *Chronic City* is that one aspect of Manhattan is seeking, literally or figuratively, to bulldoze another out of existence. The Manhattan of wealth and power is gradually cleansing the streets of the Manhattan of dissidence. Memory thus becomes an important stake. If Perkus is one of those who hold certain memories of the city and its traditions, the powers that be prefer to spread amnesia.

This brings us to the fantastic elements of the novel, because the subtle operations of power suggested in *Chronic City* are closely bound to what Chase experiences as 'a wrongness everywhere' (66) that he cannot easily name, and one way that Lethem brings this 'wrongness' to the reader's consciousness is through the estrangement effects of a 'reality-shifted' New York. A mundane example is Perkus Tooth's claim that Mayor Arnheim's 'quality-of-life police' (221) travel the city in black vans looking for petty crime, though this suggestion – a transposition of Mayor Giuliani's 'zero tolerance' policy on crime – is not fully substantiated. More striking is the existence of the War Free Edition of the *New York Times*, which Perkus realizes he is reading after wondering 'where were all those pieces nobody ever read, but everybody relied upon to be there?' (74). 'You could opt out now', Perkus remembers: out, presumably, of news of America's wars, which in the real world of the time were taking place in Afghanistan and Iraq. A War Free Edition sounds loosely reminiscent of Orwell's *Nineteen Eighty-Four* (1949), where misinformation about war is fed to the population daily. But it is subtly different from that more fully dystopian model: first because the *withholding* of such news is an opposite strategy from the relentless dissemination of it to stir fear and jingoism, seeming instead to promote oblivious serenity; second because the reader 'opts out', choosing whether or not to engage with the world's more onerous news. If obliviousness is being cultivated, *Times* readers are doing this willingly rather than simply being lied to. The War Free Edition is thus a model of complicity rather than oppression. If it resembles anything in reality it is the argument, much more frequent since the novel's publication, that media consumers are constructing 'bubbles' of their own preferences and thus entering feedback loops that shield them from the world's real complexity. Perkus eventually opts out entirely, declaring that 'The *Times* isn't the commissar of the real, not anymore, not as far as I'm concerned. It's the cover story' (367).

In the real world, America's Middle Eastern wars were launched in the wake of the terrorist attacks of 11 September 2001, which destroyed the World Trade Centre and made lower Manhattan a site of mourning and memorialization. Numerous writers have responded to these events, producing what came to be categorized as the 9/11 novel (Araújo 2017). *Chronic City* is among other things Lethem's post-9/11 novel: most specifically because of one of its most mysterious features, the 'gray fog' that has settled over lower Manhattan. When first introduced, this sounds like a metaphor: a rich wife remarks that her husband Reggie Spencer is 'stuck at work' in the financial district – 'It's all dreadful down there now' – and Chase pictures 'The money men, effortful and exhausted, slumping through the gray fog' (31). It is only on Reggie's return that the reader unambiguously understands that the fog is not a figure for an emotional condition, but a physical reality: 'I thought I could see shreds of the gray fog still clinging to his creased pinstripe three-piece, to his scuffed chestnut wingtips' (35). It is implied that working life amid this atmospheric condition is a struggle: 'There was something tragical about the men who worked downtown' (36), and Chase notes the public imperative that 'we're all in something together, especially after the gray fog spread out to cover the lower reaches of the island. I ought to feel sympathy with the moneymen, ashen and dim in aspect, forgetful, sleepy, never quite themselves anymore' (65). The ominous character of the fog is made clear on Chase's own trip downtown, when he realizes he is afraid of it: 'It swallowed daylight right up to the [Brooklyn] bridge's on-ramp, hazy tendrils nestling into the greens around city hall' (234). He is doubly troubled to hear sirens.

The transposition of 9/11 is subtle. The fog recalls that event first simply in its location; second, in its close resemblance to the clouds of dust that did cover lower Manhattan in the wake of the twin towers' destruction; third, in the sense of an official narrative of civic solidarity. The 'moneymen' might stand for those real workers of the financial district who returned to Wall Street after 9/11, their fortitude in the face of trauma an example to the rest. As victims of the conditions ('never quite themselves anymore'), they also sound like first responders from the emergency services, more obviously heroic figures who could claim to have experienced post-traumatic stress disorder. In their grim, ghostly aspect, they may even suggest the dead of 9/11, including the 'moneymen' who were forced to leap from the towers. Although in *Chronic City* the World Trade Centre still stands, the fog is also tied to 9/11 in generating memorialization: the architect Laird Noteless, whose works all involve large holes in the ground, is constructing a *Memorial to Daylight* downtown (110). The sirens that Chase hears downtown turn out to signal that a financial worker has thrown himself into the pit, briefcase and all (234). The memorial is generating death. Perkus Tooth finally asserts that the grey fog 'or some other disaster' has caused a rupture in Manhattan's sense of reality (389). The suggestion is at once wildly science-fictional and congruent with actual history. A major difference from 9/11, though, is the lack of clarity over the phenomenon's origins. The clearest account we get is 'the gray fog that had descended or some said been unleashed on the lower part of the island, two or three years ago' (173). The sheer vagueness about the date of the fog's arrival is in stark contrast to the punctual, calendrical marking of 9/11; the same can be said about its causes. War may be going on somewhere, but it does not seem to be against the fog's perpetrators. Fog suggests forgetting, and thus blends intuitively with the novel's pervading atmosphere of amnesia. Doubling this effect, the origins of the fog are also shrouded in forgetful uncertainty.

The fog is itself echoed, more mildly, in 'the weird pervasive chocolate smell that floated like a cloud over Manhattan' (173). The smell seems initially a local contingency, then turns out to be an island-wide phenomenon, prompting mayoral comment and casual conversation in the street: 'Lexington Avenue sidewalks, normally muffled in regular hostility, broke out suddenly in Willy Wonka comparisons' (173). Rivka Galchen (2009) points out that this development recalls an actual 'Maple Syrup Event' whose scent affected New York City in 2005. In Lethem's rendition the smell is suggestive in two ways. First it is an instance of collective urban experience, illustrating the way that the vast numbers of citizens crowded onto an island can share and reinflect such a phenomenon. Chase describes it in collective terms, using the first person plural: 'We'd already woken one November morning to the first snow'; 'It was a news item the exact size of our childish wishes' (174). The declaration that 'a chocolate mystery reminded us that we all dwelled in Candyland, after all' (174) registers this collectivity, while emphasizing the way that the smell is like an obverse to the fog: a mysterious experience of softness and sweetness, more analogous if anything to the seductions of media than to traumatic destruction. ('Candyland' also reprises Lionel Essrog's term for the Upper East Side.) Second, on the other hand, the experience also proves highly, unexpectedly subjective: some individuals, including Perkus, experience no smell at all, but a high-pitched ringing (177). The novel does not belabour this question, but it is plainly strange that a sensory phenomenon could be experienced in such alternate ways. Against the emphasis on a shared urban experience, the hint is that reality might be radically relative.

The chocolate scent is also intuitively tied to weather, another disconcerting element in *Chronic City*. The blizzard that falls in December is hardly incongruous (259). The snowstorms that arrive in spring are more so: 'now it was March and you felt something was wrong, or anyway different. Winter had stayed' (360). 'Amazing about this weather, don't you think?', asks journalist

Anne Sprillthmar at the next snowstorm (401). Perkus Tooth concurs: he shows Chase an old episode of *The Twilight Zone*, in which a vision of the world overheating as it nears the sun is shown to be a dream from an Earth which is actually hurtling away from the sun and 'Manhattan is locked in a fatal deepening freeze' (366). Perkus, typically relying on popular cultural history as allegory of reality, finds the episode uncannily parallel to the state of real life, including 'the state of the weather' (366). This fictional vision may have little direct purchase on the real, but it discloses a version of climate change, which is plainly at work by the end of the novel, when Chase breezily notes that 'We've only had two snows in August so far. The newspapers are calling it summer, and mostly I find people are content to do the same' (463). Part of the point here is the extreme weather itself; another is its normalization in media talk and public understanding.

To talk of weather in the city is to unite nature and artifice. Such a combination is peculiarly characteristic of *Chronic City*, whose Manhattan is also marked by the appearance of animals. As Susan Kollin observes, the novel explores how ecological change brings human and non-human beings into unfamiliar proximity, as animals tenaciously establish niches within urban environments (2015: 264–6). A comparatively mundane example is the flock of birds that Chase repeatedly watches from his apartment window circling a church tower (67, 126, 200), and eventually finds at close range, having been dragged to the site by the dog he inherits from Perkus (467). More unusual are the coyotes that enter Manhattan and by the novel's end are 'terrorizing joggers at the Central Park Reservoir' (164, 464), and the minke whale, 'perhaps deranged by ocean fungus', that wanders up the East River to die (73). Richard Abneg battles a family of eagles nesting on his apartment building (49–55). All these animals circle around the most insistent one, 'the gargantuan escaped tiger that was ravaging sections of the East Side' (22). Regularly making the front page of the *New York Times* (74), to the point where a journalist can suggest producing a Tiger Free Edition (464), the tiger has become a piece of city folklore, adduced to explain disruptions: 'Traffic was a nightmare. The cabbie was saying something about that escaped tiger getting loose again on Lexington Avenue' (36). Characters talk of the tiger as an animal that might be handled by a hunter (36–7), and Chase wonders where it goes in the rain or why it does not favour Central Park (61) – as, in fact, the quasi-feline Sufferer does in Lethem's much earlier story (1996: 155). Yet all this squares poorly with the repeated reports of the tiger's destruction of urban infrastructure, razing 'a twenty-four-hour Korean market on 103rd street' (74) or tearing up subway track in North Manhattan (113).

The tiger hovers incoherently between these notions, whose incompatibility is remarked upon but never really pressed through to a logical conclusion.

A degree of plausibility arrives with Richard's worldly, insider's explanation that the tiger is really a mechanical device, a giant boring machine that is building the Second Avenue subway but has gone haywire: 'At night sometimes it comes up from underneath and sort of, you know, ravages around' (163). The authorities do not stop it, he says, as it is 'mostly doing a good job with the tunnel': the damage is judged a price worth paying (164). While this is presented as the truth behind the rumours, its own lack of coherence is barely remarked: the claim that the machine is lonely for the lack of a partner (163); the question of why, like a nocturnal animal, such a machine would only come out at night; the puzzle of why citizens eager for sightings of it fail to notice that it does not resemble a tiger. It is as though the supposed machine is still conceived in animal terms. Sociologically, Richard explains the confusion as a case of 'the power of popular delusions and the madness of crowds' (162). In that sense it joins a major theme of the book: the maintenance, through media and rumour, of perhaps deluded collective consciousness across the city. The establishment of a Tiger Watch website (200) with colour-coded danger levels (227) adds to the tiger's presence as what Claire Carter calls 'a distraction' (447), and the drug dealer Foster Watt responds to the zeitgeist by naming his products after it, explaining that 'People do love them some fear' (307). Aesthetically, the confusion leaves the reader subtly disoriented, piecing together an account that we may sometimes forget does not quite cohere. This lack of resolution brings us closer to Chase Insteadman's befuddled state, in which clear explanation can usually be deferred till after the next cocktail or hamburger.

A sidenote in Richard's explanation is that the machine's destructive actions are not necessarily unwelcome to the authorities: 'Anyway, a certain amount of the buildings it's taken out were pretty much dead wood in the first place', to which Perkus adds that this is 'how urban renewal works. [...] You find an excuse to bulldoze stuff so that the developers can come in' (164). Apart from this first moment, Richard is never pressed on this point, but it comes to seem as though the supposedly randomly destructive 'tiger' is in fact wreaking a more systematic pattern of destruction on the part of the city's authorities. This is consistent with Chase's final observation that the phenomenon 'goes on wrecking only things it seems to me the city can spare' (464). The abrupt destruction of Perkus Tooth's favourite hamburger joint, Jackson Hole (237), leads to Perkus's own block being declared unsafe and Perkus's departure into eventual oblivion. Perkus asks Richard 'Did this happen because of us?' (239), implying careful agency behind the destruction. Perkus, growing more paranoid than ever, later thinks: 'The creature, which Richard Abneg had claimed was a machine operated by the city, might have been on a Perkus-eradication course to begin with' (321). This 'legend of the tiger, his own personal destroyer' (386) is surely incorrect, though Chase continues with it in later demanding whether the tiger is being used against the city's enemies (447). But there is reason to believe that the destruction is a deliberate piece of urban clearance: Richard has earlier considered that Perkus will be safe unless 'the planners of the Second Avenue subway issued an eminent domain seizure of Jackson Hole, and tore the restaurant down' (133). The supposed tiger gives them a rapid way to accomplish this. On this plausible view, it is a machine being covertly used by the state to reshape the urban landscape: a vehicle for what the economist Joseph Schumpeter called creative destruction, under cover of mere animal chaos. With Perkus and his neighbours evacuated from their rent-stabilized apartments, we can hypothesize that this 'Podunk' region of the Upper East Side will be redeveloped into something no longer, in Lethem's words, so 'drab and unfashionable and sometimes quite affordable'. Outside Perkus's abandoned block, Chase reflects: 'these were merely uninhabitable buildings, destined to come down and be replaced with something newer, and soon they'd be hard to remember. The city had moved on' (294–5). In this respect, *Chronic City* is as much a novel of gentrification as *The Fortress of Solitude*, suggesting it with the quasi-fantastic image of the rampaging tiger rather than the gradual arrival of the bohemians in the brownstones.

Yet the entire mechanical explanation of the tiger is itself undercut when Chase and Richard encounter the animal late in the novel, in the middle of the night after Perkus's death (433–4). After so much anticipation and uncertainty around the phenomenon, the moment – 'At the corner of Eighty-fourth we came upon the giant escaped tiger' – is extraordinarily understated, presented as though the characters were merely catching sight of an acquaintance. Lethem lingers over its physique: 'the great burgeoning white-and-yellow fur of its ears and ruff'; 'striped, smooth-ridged fur'; 'leather-black nostrils steaming above a grizzly muzzle'; 'the psychedelically deep-flat headlamps of its pale gaze'. Chase's emphasis is that 'The tiger had no remotely mechanical aspect to it […] [It] seemed instead to be wholly of flesh and fur'. We are curiously back where we began: the giant animal was real after all. This animal – which Chase thinks has no subterranean aspect – has surely not destroyed the urban fabric. It has perhaps become conflated, in the city's fevered collective imagination, with the machine that does. Chase supposes that there are two tigers: one animal and one machine. That the tiger appears at Perkus's old home on the night of his death also suggests a symbolic value, as though it is here to observe a dissident spirit at its extinguishing, even if it cannot, as Chase imagines, put back together what has been destroyed. That the tiger remains so mysterious and multivalent ultimately enhances its power as the novel's most memorable icon.

Social control in *Chronic City* takes less obviously material forms than destroying unwanted infrastructure. It also involves distraction, urban myth – like the notion of the tiger itself – and sheer falsehood. The ultimate example of this is Janice Trumbull, Chase's supposed fiancée, an astronaut stranded on a space station and posting missives back to him that are printed in the *New York Times*. As a result, most people Chase meets congratulate him for his role as diligent fiancé to the lost heroine. The Mayor himself earnestly tells Chase: 'You keep the faith [...] You bring honor to this city [...] We learn from your example' (280-1), and at the end is still commiserating with Chase on Janice's death. But by that point we know that her entire engagement with Chase has been a fabrication, her letters to him concocted by Oona. A piece of New York's reality falls away – not altogether without warning, as the lie has been gradually hinted, especially by Perkus (334). Indeed we earlier glimpse Chase's meeting with two 'producers' who offer him 'the role of a lifetime' and never send him a script (64-5; 262). The implication is that the role is Chase's whole life since, 'enlisted in this city's reigning fictions' as Perkus sees it (74), and perhaps that the script comprises specifically Janice's letters, to which Chase publicly plays out his response. The broader sense is also that all this benefits the authorities, as another sentimental distraction for the masses. Chase is seen as an emblem of the city, admired simply for carrying on; by the same token, Perkus finally calls him 'the perfect avatar of the city's unreality' (407). In this episode of bread and circuses, Chase the actor is a sad clown.

Memory and its failure are also involved. Chase fails to remember that he has no sustained history with Janice; he can only perceive, when he admits it, that he does not clearly remember her (166). The roots of his amnesia are never clarified, only elided with the general vagueness of this man without responsibilities. This plot line revives one of Lethem's great themes, from the Forgettol that triggers the story of *Gun* to the green fog in which Chaos forgets his name – and which is echoed in *Chronic City*'s own grey cloud. 'What I couldn't remember could fill a book' (441), Chase realizes, a line that artfully suggests Lethem's making of books from the failure of memory. This context makes a little more sense of Perkus Tooth's obsession with cultural touchstones and byways. Amid his clutter of old films and records, his relentless connection of names and artefacts from

Norman Mailer to Marlon Brando and back again is an attempt to remember in a society bent on forgetfulness or false memory, albeit one that comes unstuck in its recursiveness and inability to affect the wider world.

As the book progresses, Perkus talks increasingly of Manhattan as a place of illusion. 'Your city's a fake, *a bad dream*', he tells Richard (152). Lionel Essrog's brief fantasy of Park Avenue being recreated in Greenpoint is reprised in this novel's larger vision of a Manhattan so swathed in simulation that reality can no longer be readily discerned. An even stronger version of the case is that Manhattan itself is literally a simulation, constructed from elsewhere: shortly before his death, Perkus explains 'his simulacra theory of Manhattan', in which the strangest features (like the fog and the tiger) are 'typical of the slippage at the edges of our reality by its handlers, who were for all their contrivances and capital unequal to the task they'd set themselves' (412). This view arises from the discovery of the virtual reality site Yet Another World, which prompts Perkus and Oona to speculate that the world as they know it could be a simulation set up an unknown programmer, and further to debate whether the creation of virtual reality would be likely to lead to the simulated world being switched off for draining too much computing power (228–9, 266–7).

Such extreme ontological scepticism was characteristic of Philip K. Dick, who influenced *Chronic City* by virtue of Lethem's work on his Library of America edition while writing the novel (Clarke 2011: 175–6). Yet *Chronic City* does not declare its fictional world a wholesale fake, rather abiding in mixture and ambiguity. It is suspicious, in a black-comic final touch, that the view from Chase's window seems to have altered (467). But Chase also cleaves to the sense that 'everything around me, every tangy specific in the simulation in which I found myself embedded, militated against the suggestion that it was a simulation: the furls of stale smoke and gritty phosphenes drifting between my eyes and the kitchen's overhead light', and so on (228–9). Chase's reflection is also a sidelong aesthetic comment, as a celebration of an aspect of Lethem's fiction at this point: the relish of 'tangy specifics' that the novel lingers over marks a shift from the starker narration of *Amnesia Moon*, the novel which is otherwise closest to *Chronic City*'s themes of simulation. The same is true of Chase's later citation of such particulars: the scar on Perkus's dog, the skin of the pregnant Georgina, the taste of sugar dust on a croissant (449). In *You Don't Love Me Yet*, likewise, the awakening Lucinda experiences what she feels is a dream but we know is reality, with the sensory 'whirling racket of coffee beans in a miniature grinder, the tap-tap of the grind being emptied into the espresso machine's strainer', followed by the 'richly olfactory […] fumes of sizzling bacon grease and butter' (2007: 210,

212). The textures of particularity at once offer some ground for believing in one's own reality, while also being a property available to the kind of immersive simulation that we call the novel.

Chronic City leaves the extent of simulation, like the true character of its tiger, undecided. The closest it comes to a statement is not Perkus's suspicion that he is living in a construction (340) but Chase's more nuanced reflection: 'Our sphere of the real (call it Manhattan) was riddled with simulations, yet was the world at hand. Or the simulation was riddled through with the real. […] The world was ersatz and actual, forged and faked, by ourselves and unseen others. Daring to attempt to absolutely sort *fake* from *real* was a folly' (448–9). The book's ambience is then not one of absolute deception and revelation, but of 'real characters in an unreal world' (Clarke 2011: 176), muddling through a zone of uncertainty. It is plainly relevant that Manhattan is the place of forgetting and falsehood. For it is not only recently that it has become 'a kind of virtual reality': as Lethem recognizes, 'It's always been susceptible to so much projection, so much transference that the real lives that are being lived there are always under the shadow of an enormous cloud of these projections of money and power and fantasy' (Clarke 2011: 176). In his next novel, the borough of Queens would figure in an opposite way, mundane streets ('Somewhere at the intersection where Forty-Seventh Road crossed Sixty-Fourth Terrace on its way to Seventy-Eighth Place' [2013a: 267]) dominated by an ageing woman consumed by memory and grudges.

Still more consistently, as we have seen, Brooklyn has figured for Lethem as a place of memory, even to excess. Thus Dylan Ebdus looks back to childhood as 'the only part of my life that wasn't […] overwhelmed by my childhood' (2003: 319), and Lionel Essrog tires of its 'long memory' and longs 'to disappear into Manhattan's amnesiac dance of renewal' (1999: 179): in effect, longing to be a character in *Chronic City* instead. A lesser-known figure, and in part an outer-borough precursor of Perkus Tooth, is Lethem's 'Mad Brooklynite', who appeared in vignettes published before *Fortress*: a small man wearing 'a blue cap with a B on it, a typography I associated with the departed Brooklyn Dodgers' (2011: 418). He delights in reciting local history to strangers, above all the ghostly history of the Brooklyn Dodgers' never-built baseball stadium, abandoned when they departed for Los Angeles (2011: 417). His author would eventually do the same, but not before rendering his home city in these 'walls of language' that have made it legible in new ways.

Conclusion

'It was there when I woke up, I swear. The feeling' (1994: 3): with that reflection from Conrad Metcalf, Jonathan Lethem's career as a novelist began. Two decades later, his tenth novel commenced: 'It was there when he woke up. Presumably also when he slept. The blot' (2016a: 3). The echo is unmistakable, suggesting the author's awareness of his own trajectory and a readiness to string textual connections across the decades. In fact, though this is unusually blatant, the underlying impulse is characteristic. To read across Lethem's work is to realize how densely its words are woven together.

This book has argued for Lethem's status as a writer of New York City, so it cannot be too surprising that different works visit the same urban places: for instance that Richard Abneg, in the Museum of Natural History, takes a private telephone call 'near a long display full of penguins bunched on floes of ice' (2010: 132), the same display that the child Lionel Essrog enters, Touretically touching every penguin to the amusement of Gil Coney (1999: 41). It is more pointed that, having in *Motherless Brooklyn* turned the actual hot dog restaurant Papaya King into Papaya Czar, Lethem repeats the fictional location in *Chronic City*. The garish signs that for Lionel make it 'my kind of place', 'layered with language' (160), put Chase Insteadman off (97). One scene clearly calls back to the other, though the reader need not know both; the relation is trivial. It feels less trivial that Perkus Tooth's apartment is located a block or two east on the same street as the Yorkville Zendo, a place that the giant tiger has thus just passed when Chase and Richard encounter it. Perkus's apartment and the Zendo are in their differing ways the mysterious hearts of each novel's quest; that they are so close is plainly evident to the author, but any frisson from this goes unspoken.

Does the tiger actually pad past a building hitherto occupied by Gerard Minna? Are the worlds of these novels really the same world? That they are is suggested by the continuity of character names across them. Dylan Ebdus takes Lucinda Hoekke to a Jonathan Richman concert in Oakland in the mid-1980s; they never meet again (2003: 410). In restitution to Lucinda for her bit-part status, Lethem makes her the protagonist of his next novel, set in Los Angeles a few years later. Among the audience for Lucinda's band is the Rain Injuries' drummer Richard Abneg (2007: 92): the same unusual name as Perkus Tooth's high school friend and later municipal official (2010: 429). Tommy Gogan in *Dissident Gardens*, releasing the LP inspired by Miriam Zimmer, encounters the scorn of seventeen-year-old 'P.K. Tooth' in the *East Village Other* (2013a: 187). On the face of it, these four successive novels are all thus related, if only by sharing a single character apiece. Glancingly implicated too is *The Feral Detective*, which remembers *Chronic City*'s installation artist Laird Noteless not only by reusing the name 'Laird' for an unrelated character but with specific reference to Noteless's work (Lethem 2018b: 44, 321). Also apparently linked are *As She Climbed across the Table* and *A Gambler's Anatomy*, by the brief reappearance in the latter of the therapist Cynthia Jalter. The later novel's Cynthia is 'peroxided' (2016a: 74–6) while the earlier incarnation was 'the least blond woman I had ever met' (2001: 103). That detail at once posits the two versions as opposites, while leaving the logical possibility that they could be the same person.

The apparent implication is that Lethem has discreetly constructed his novels to overlap, to the point where they form a single fictional universe. The immediate parallel is with his contemporary, the English novelist David Mitchell, who has openly done this with his entire fictional oeuvre, gradually showing it as a world traversed by occult powers. Yet to reach the same conclusion about Lethem is ultimately misguided. Simple details do not add up across the texts. Richard Abneg in *Chronic City* has a New York past, not a Los Angeles musical one. Perkus Tooth in the mid-2000s is 'in his early forties' (2010: 3), much too young to have reviewed Tommy Gogan in 1964. And New York is not the same place in *Chronic City* and *Dissident Gardens*: most simply, in the former 9/11 never happened, while in the latter it is affecting airport security (2013a: 366). It is better to say that these characters inhabit parallel worlds, similar to each other yet subtly different: in their contents (9/11 does or does not happen), but also more pervasively in their tones. The different modes of writing that Lethem adopts – romantic comedy, family saga, and so on – shape their fictional worlds accordingly. A theme of this book has been Lethem's fascination with the construction and multiplicity of worlds. We can add that the novels themselves represent such multiple worlds, coexisting as alternatives as do the worlds inside Lack, the differing zones within Yet Another World, or even the multiple simulations that Perkus comes to fear include his own universe.

Dispensing with the notion that the novels literally overlap, we can perceive other kinds of textual recurrence. The repetition of the kangaroo, from its evolved, gangland state in *Gun* to its more naturalistic form in *You Don't Love Me Yet*, is an example so blatant that Lethem has been asked about it: at this point, he replied, 'I can fool around with my own cache of images and jokes a little bit. It's like that way you begin to see your own material up for grabs, too' (Clarke 2011: 137). The implication here is that the artist's 'own material' is on a par with the archive of pre-existing imagery to be spun into second use, on the 'Ecstasy of Influence' model. Sometimes we can see Lethem deliberately doing this. It was incongruous enough for his second detective novel to centre on a Buddhist Zendo; it is beyond coincidence that his third, published almost two decades later and set at the other end of the continent, does the same (2018b: 73). The radio show on which Lucinda plays, 'The Dreaming Jaw', lends its name to the supposed blog in a story published two years later (2007: 116; 2015: 135). Whether the Archbuilders' entertaining predilection for backgammon (1998: 238) is deliberately taken up by the game's centrality to *A Gambler's Anatomy* is harder to judge. But Carl the Complainer's recommendation not to disturb Bedwin from his delusory world – 'Not unless you've got a better one to offer in its place' (2007: 156) – is plainly taken up at greater length in Perkus Tooth's identical ethic (2010: 341).

Narrative motifs echo each other. In the midst of dealing with a *femme fatale*, Conrad Metcalf orders a pizza – 'I had to wheedle a bit to get them to put mushrooms on a small, but they finally came around' (1994: 125) – which he then cannot bring himself to finish. The scene is replayed for greater comic effect in *Table*, written around the same time, where Philip does the same, seeking first 'a small pizza without cheese', then choosing mushrooms as his only special topping, with 'no cheese' and 'no pineapple' as the other required specials, and finally realizing 'I don't want a pizza. No cheese was the giveaway' (2001: 116–7). This is a play on the novel's theme of absence and depletion – in a world where Lack is adored, 'no pineapple' might be considered a delicacy. It also stretches a gustatory trail between the two novels, which is more often taken up by the motif of sandwiches so beloved of Lionel Essrog – and of Lethem, who muses that 'books are sandwiches' (2017: 299), collapsing his whole output into this culinary format. Lack closes up at the end of his novel, but proves curiously insistent. Philip's experience inside Lack is reactivated in Lionel's experience of being knocked out – 'distinguished only by nothingness, by blankness, by lack and my resentment of it. Except for grains. It was a grainy nothing. A desert of grains' (1999: 205) – while the process of offering items to Lack's maw is replayed by the ritual grant of an item to Laird Noteless's vast hole in the ground (2010: 111). *Chronic City*'s holes in the ground, in turn, have a haunting precursor in *Girl in Landscape*, where Caitlin's death 'would forever be linked for Pella to the collapse of the subway. The tunneling devices that had hollowed out too much of the city's bedrock, the failed surgical incursion that had destroyed Caitlin' (1998a: 37). Here two images are already linked, in a primal condition of mourning and resentment; they offer a more emotionally loaded response to the havoc caused by the mechanical tiger than is actually conveyed by *Chronic City* itself. At this level – and perhaps with the grey Manhattan fog that resembles the amnesiac green fog of the west in *Amnesia Moon* – we are moving from the playful manipulation of incidental details to something more like an authorial imaginary, a battery of ideas that suggest continuity of purpose across a writing career.

That also applies to a still smaller unit of repetition, at the level of words and phrases. It may not signify much that Alexander Bruno's final incarnation is as 'The Mummy' (2016a: 282), while the empty house in Dean Street is 'like a mummy with blanked eyes and stilled howling mouth' (2003: 14); or that Gil Coney's coat makes him resemble Lewis Carroll's Red Queen (1999: 58), an identity taken on much more extensively by Rose Zimmer. These repetitions suggest an author bouncing off familiar reference points in the practical search for means of description. Some verbal echoes are stronger. Rockaforte's banal reassurance that 'Frank Minna is a good man' (1999: 62) is close to Hiding Kneel's increasingly obsessive insistence that the same applies to all his persecutors, in a novel published a year earlier (1998a: 246–52). It is suggestive of a verbal pattern that the Complainer's itchy phrase, 'monster eyes', echoes not only *Motherless Brooklyn*'s 'interrogation eyes', belonging to Lucius Seminole (1999: 106), but also the 'paradigm eyes' that Philip yearns for in *Alice* (2001: 1). Each phrase contains the hint of an excessive, confected verb: 'monsterize', 'paradigmize'. Lionel's increasing fascination with finding 'edge', of the road or the continent, in New England recalls the first character and word that we encounter in *Amnesia Moon* (1999: 257, 264; 1995: 1). Lionel is of course a ready outlet for any verbal fancies, and as if to confirm Lethem's pattern of cross-textual echoes he outrageously hears 'Alfred Hitchcock' as 'Ilford Hotchkiss', the ultimate villain from *Amnesia Moon* (1999: 46; 1995: 138).

At this level of highly deliberate repetitions, Shelf the kangaroo recalls Kimmery's borrowed cat Shelf – a name that she and Lionel agree is 'completely stupid' (1999: 213). If we wonder why the word would have any valence for Lethem, the best available answer is Lethem's fondness for Terry Carr's story 'Stanley Toothbrush' (1962), in which a character repeats the word 'shelf' until his actual shelves disappear (Clarke 2011: 16–17). Lethem takes up the title in *Table* itself, where Philip compares Lack to 'Stanley Toothbrush', the name of a fabricated romantic rival in Carr's story (Lethem 2001: 41). The name was already an obscure private joke here; what is stranger is its reappearance in

Chronic City, where Oona tells Chase that it is the name of her neighbour and assistant (2010: 251). In this context, though, the name primarily recalls their mutual friend Perkus Tooth. This in turn connects Perkus's name to Lethem's unfolding verbal process, for *Table* also contains the deconstructionist Georges De Tooth, and Lucinda's band considers the name Idiot Tooth ('The opposite of a wisdom tooth') – not without confounding it with the alternatives Mystery Tooth and Spooky Tooth (2007: 58). In fact *Idiot Tooth* was the name of a fanzine that Lethem and his first wife Shelley Jackson produced in Berkeley in the early 1990s (2017: 270), so the broadsider Perkus's surname appears a belated tribute to this venture. 'Tooth' is plainly a recurrent element; the same might be said, less prominently, of 'phone', from Danny Phoneblum in *Gun*, through Lionel's fascination with Phil Fonebone – 'lastingly traceable in my tendency to append *phone* or *bone* to the end of a phrase' (1999: 223) – and thence with an actual carphone (260), to the 'Oonaphone' given to Chase (2010: 296). Outside fiction, Lethem has confirmed his interest in telephony (2011: 236–9): the phone's place in his writing merits study, but it also seems, like 'tooth', to function more elementally, as a sound to return to and recombine.

The Roland Barthes who talked of a text as a galaxy of signifiers liked to entertain the sense that literature was autonomous, referring only to itself. The examples listed above indicate how far Lethem's oeuvre can be experienced this way, an array of signals back and forth across its continually expanding space. More expansively, Barthes also saw literature as intertextual, one text opening on to another. This too is plainly true of Lethem. Chapter One above demonstrated his commitment to a conception of culture as a common resource to be borrowed, sampled and returned; Chapter Two showed how far genre has been such a resource for him. The names of other writers can find their way in. That Fancher Autumnbreast is a disc jockey for KPKD (2007: 116) is a merry reference to Philip K. Dick, but is redoubled by his unusual forename, as Hampton Fancher was the screenwriter of *Blade Runner*, who in turn asked Lethem if he could adapt *Gun, with Occasional Music*: given that novel's debt to *Blade Runner*, the two writers were in 'a circular influential mirror' (2011: 63). (Rivka Galchen [2009] also considers the real Hampton Fancher to be both the source of Lethem's story 'Lucky Alan' and a close analogue to Perkus Tooth.) Intertextuality can also occur at the micro level, as shown in *Chronic City*'s brief list of borrowings, or by other unacknowledged fragments. In the story 'The Spray', a spray used by police 'settled like a small rain through the house' (2004: 48): the image here derives from Thomas Pynchon's story 'The Small Rain' (1959), a phrase counter-intuitive (as against, say, 'light rain') at first encounter, but rendered more evidently cogent in Lethem's usage. Lionel Essrog recounts that Frank Minna sent his boys to driving school thanks to 'an arrangement with a certain Lucas' (1999: 86). The insertion of the title of a 1979 collection by Julio Cortázar is gratuitous, but quietly buries another literary work in the texture of this one. In a last example, the opening of *Dissident Gardens* is a shock tactic:

> *Quit fucking black cops or get booted from the Communist Party.* There stood the ultimatum, the absurd sum total of the message conveyed to Rose Zimmer by the cabal gathered in her Sunnyside Gardens kitchen that evening. Late fall, 1955. (2013a: 3)

Yet this too, for all its immediacy, is a reference: now to Philip Roth's *Sabbath's Theater* (1995), which commences:

> Either forswear fucking others or the affair is over.
> This was the ultimatum, the maddeningly improbable, wholly unforeseen ultimatum, that the mistress of fifty-two delivered in tears to her lover of sixty-four on the anniversary of an attachment that had persisted with an amazing licentiousness – and that, no less amazingly, had stayed their secret – for thirteen years. (Roth 1995: 3)

The two texts are too different for one to be called a plagiarism, even by those less keen on the Commons than Lethem. At the same time they are close enough that we can perceive that he opens his novel by playing a variation on someone else's score, and leaves it to us to recognize this, or not. The text can work either way: demonstrating Lethem's audacity in opening on this uncompromisingly obscene note, or suggesting a different kind of audacity in modelling his own text on a predecessor. What all these examples have shown is that while Lethem's work is profoundly involuted, it is also extroverted in its dealings with the rest of literature.

Yet, for all literature's scope, this still sounds insular. There is, after all, also a world beyond literature. But it is not merely beyond, for it is also what is refracted and transformed, through diverse means, into the matter of literature itself. Better then to say that the world outside literature can be continuous with, certainly profoundly influential upon, the world within it. Having established how far Lethem's galaxy of writing is about writing, it should finally be affirmed how far it is also about what *Chronic City*'s closing note calls 'everywhere else'. Abraham Ebdus paints a film in which he attempts to banish figuration – though the street outside 'couldn't not' infiltrate the work at times (2003: 234). Lethem works in a medium considerably more predisposed to referentiality than Abraham's. The critic Michael Wood cites Borges' story 'The Lottery in

Babylon' (1941) for its provocative suggestion that even someone who thought they were dissimulating might be telling the truth: 'Who can boast of being a mere impostor?' (Wood 2005: 64). To write a fiction of, say, New York might offer a way to nod to Cortázar or Roth, or indeed oneself. But it might also, more emphatically, tell us something about New York that we would not have perceived any other way. In weaving, like Spider-Man, these intricate webs of words, Lethem also necessarily depicts versions of things that pre-exist them. The Brooklyn Bridge that Chase mentions (2010: 233) presumably resembles the one that Miriam Zimmer walks halfway across from Manhattan (2013a: 25) and the one that Dylan and Mingus mount from the other side (2003: 78) – and that Lethem and many of his readers, too, have walked across.

Of course, in Lethem's case it is insufficient to say that the content of the work mirrors the real world, for so much of it makes a point of not doing so. The Planet of the Archbuilders, Aaron X. Doily's ring, the giant tiger, testify to a commitment to writing not as humble replication of the real but its transmutation. But these figments, though often rich in their own right, are not mere evasions: they stay implicitly on terms with the world in which they were written, and offer another way of seeing or saying something about it – to stay with these particular cases, respectively, about grief and colonialism; race and adolescence; the transformation of the city by power and the displacement of nature. Borges also liked to imagine tigers, and we could recast his question to ask: Who can be sure that their tiger is merely imaginary? 'If you find this world bad', cautioned Philip K. Dick, 'you should see some of the others'. Lethem has shown us many of the others, and our own.

Works Cited

Alford, Robert. (2012) 'Celebrating the Possibilities of Fiction: A Conversation with Jennifer Egan'. *Popmatters*, 20 February 2012. https://www.popmatters.com/154523-celebrating-the-possibilities-of-fiction-a-conversation-with-jennife-2495885422.html?rebelltitem=1#rebelltitem1

Allen, Graham. (2000) *Intertextuality*. London: Routledge.

Araújo, Susana. (2017) *Transatlantic Fictions of 9/11 and the War on Terror: Images of Insecurity, Narratives of Captivity*. London: Bloomsbury.

Arnaudo, Marco. (2013) *The Myth of the Superhero*, trans. by Jamie Richards. Baltimore, MD: Johns Hopkins University Press.

Barthes, Roland. (1974) *S/Z*, trans. by Richard Miller. New York: Farrar, Straus & Giroux.

Beckett, Samuel. (1970) *Proust and Three Dialogues with Georges Duthuit*. London: Calder & Boyars.

Benjamin, Walter. (2008) *The Work of Art in the Age of Its Technological Reproducibility, and Other Writings on Media*, ed. Michael W. Jennings, Brigid Doherty and Thomas Y. Levin. Cambridge, MA: Belknap.

Blackbeard, Bill. (1982) 'Pulps'. In *Concise Histories of American Popular Culture*, ed. M. Thomas Inge (Westport, CT: Greenwood Press), pp.289–307.

Bloom, Harold. (1973) *The Anxiety of Influence: A Theory of Poetry*. Oxford: Oxford University Press.

Brooker, Joseph. (2016) 'Involutions of the Word: Lorrie Moore and Jonathan Lethem'. In *The Contemporaneity of Modernism: Literature, Media, Culture*, ed. Michael D'Arcy and Mathias Nilges (New York and London: Routledge), pp.105–118.

Campbell, Andy. (2010) 'Jonathan Lethem Resigns as "Bard of Boerum Hill"'. *Brooklyn Paper*, 27 September 2010. https://www.brooklynpaper.com/stories/33/40/dtg_lethemleaves_2010_10_01_bk.html

Cancalon, Elaine F., and Antoine Spacagna (eds). (1994) *Intertextuality in Literature and Film*. Gainesville: University Press of Florida.

Cawelti, John G. (1976) *Adventure, Mystery, and Romance*. Chicago, IL: University of Chicago Press.

Chabon, Michael. (2000) *The Amazing Adventures of Kavalier & Clay*. New York: Picador.

Chandler, Raymond. (2010) [1940] *Farewell, My Lovely*. London: Penguin.

Chandler, Raymond. (1952) [1944] *The Lady in the Lake*. Harmondsworth: Penguin.

Clarke, Jaime (ed). (2011) *Conversations with Jonathan Lethem*. Jackson: University Press of Mississippi.

Clute, John. (1997) 'Polder'. *The Encyclopedia of Fantasy*. http://sf-encyclopedia.uk/fe.php?nm=polder
Coughlan, David. (2011) 'Jonathan Lethem's *The Fortress of Solitude* and *Omega: The Unknown*, a Comic Book Series'. *College Literature* 38: 3 (Summer 2011), 194–218.
Davis, Ray. (2009) 'High, Low, and Lethem'. *Genre* 42: 3–4 (Fall/Winter 2009), 61–78.
Davis, Ray, and Jonathan Lethem. (1998) 'Mistakes Were Made: An Exchange'. *New York Review of Science Fiction* 11: 4 (December 1998). http://www.pseudopodium.org/repress/shorts/Davis_and_Lethem-Mistakes_Were_Made.html
DeLillo, Don. (1985) *White Noise*. London: Picador.
Derrida, Jacques. (1980) 'The Law of Genre', trans. by Avital Ronell. *Critical Inquiry* 7: 1 (Autumn), 55–81.
Dick, Philip K. (1978) 'How to Build a Universe that Doesn't Fall Apart Two Days Later'. http://deoxy.org/pkd_how2build.htm
Dinnen, Zara. (2012) 'In the Mix: The Potential Convergence of Literature and New Media in Jonathan Lethem's "The Ecstasy of Influence"'. *Journal of Narrative Theory* 42: 2 (Summer 2012), 212–230.
Eaglestone, Robert. (2013) 'Contemporary Fiction in the Academy: Towards a Manifesto'. *Textual Practice* 27: 7, 1089–1101.
Eagleton, Terry. (2003) *Figures of Dissent*. London: Verso.
Ellis, Bret Easton. (1987) *The Rules of Attraction*. New York: Simon & Schuster.
Eve, Martin Paul. (2014) *Open Access and the Humanities: Contexts, Controversies and the Future*. Cambridge: Cambridge University Press.
Eve, Martin Paul. (2016) *Literature against Criticism*. Cambridge: Open Book Publishers.
Fiedler, Leslie A. (1972) *Cross the Border – Close the Gap*. New York: Stein & Day.
Franzen, Jonathan. (2002) *How to Be Alone*. London: HarperPerennial.
Franzen, Jonathan. (2012) *Farther Away*. New York: Farrar, Straus and Giroux.
Frow, John. (2006) *Genre*. London and New York: Routledge.
Gaiman, Neil, with Kazuo Ishiguro. (2015) 'Let's Talk about Genre'. *New Statesman*, 4 June. https://www.newstatesman.com/2015/05/neil-gaiman-kazuo-ishiguro-interview-literature-genre-machines-can-toil-they-can-t-imagine
Galchen, Rivka. (2009) 'In between the Dream and the Doorknob: On Jonathan Lethem's Fictions'. *Ecotone* 5: 1 (Fall 2009), 162–180. https://ecotonemagazine.org/nonfiction/in-between-the-dream-and-the-doorknob-on-jonathan-lethems-fictions/
Godbey, Matt. (2008) 'Gentrification, Authenticity and White Middle-Class Identity in Jonathan Lethem's *The Fortress of Solitude*'. *Arizona Quarterly* 64: 1 (Spring 2008), 131–151.
Gourevitch, Philip (ed). (2006) *The Paris Review Interviews, I*. New York: Picador.
Hammett, Dashiell. (2005) [1930] *The Maltese Falcon*. London: Orion.
Hess, Charlotte, and Elinor Ostrom (eds). (2011) *Understanding Knowledge as a Commons: From Theory to Practice*. Cambridge, MA: MIT Press.

Hyde, Lewis. (2011) *Common as Air: Revolution, Art, and Ownership*. New York: Farrar, Straus and Giroux.
Jameson, Fredric. (1991) *Postmodernism, or, the Cultural Logic of Late Capitalism*. London: Verso.
Jameson, Fredric. (2015) *The Antinomies of Realism*. London: Verso.
Jameson, Fredric. (2016) *Raymond Chandler: The Detections of Totality*. London: Verso.
Joyce, James. (1993) [1922] *Ulysses*. London: The Bodley Head.
Kafka, Franz. (1960) *Description of a Struggle and The Great Wall of China*, trans. by Willa and Edwin Muir and Tania and James Stern. London: Secker & Warburg.
Kafka, Franz. (1991) *The Great Wall of China and Other Short Works*, trans. by Malcolm Pasley. Harmondsworth: Penguin.
Kelley, Rich. (2007) 'Jonathan Lethem on Philip K. Dick: "I Call Him Science Fiction's Lenny Bruce"'. https://www.loa.org/news-and-views/486-jonathan-lethem-on-philip-k-dick-i-call-him-science-fictions-lenny-bruce
Kollin, Susan. (2015) 'Not Yet Another World: Ecopolitics and Urban Natures in Jonathan Lethem's *Chronic City*'. *Lit: Literature Interpretation Theory* 26 (2015), 255–275.
Kress, Nancy. (2007) 'The King of Sentences'. 14 December 2007. http://nancykress.blogspot.com/2007/12/king-of-sentences.html
Latham, Rob. (2015) 'American Slipstream: Science Fiction and Literary Respectability'. In *The Cambridge Companion to American Science Fiction*, ed. E.C. Link and G. Canavan (Cambridge: Cambridge University Press), pp.99–110.
Lessig, Lawrence. (2002) *The Future of Ideas: The Fate of the Commons in a Connected World*. New York: Vintage.
Lessig, Lawrence. (2008) *Remix: Making Art and Commerce Thrive in the Hybrid Economy*. London: Bloomsbury.
Lethem, Jonathan. (1994) *Gun, with Occasional Music*. San Diego, CA: Harcourt Brace & Company.
Lethem, Jonathan. (1995) *Amnesia Moon*. San Diego, CA: Harcourt Brace & Company.
Lethem, Jonathan. (1996) *The Wall of the Sky, the Wall of the Eye*. San Diego, CA: Harcourt Brace & Company.
Lethem, Jonathan. (1998a) *Girl in Landscape*. New York: Doubleday.
Lethem, Jonathan. (1998b) 'The Squandered Promise of Science Fiction'. *Village Voice*, June 1998. http://hipsterbookclub.livejournal.com/1147850.html
Lethem, Jonathan. (1999) *Motherless Brooklyn*. New York: Doubleday.
Lethem, Jonathan. (2001) [1997] *As She Climbed across the Table*. London: Faber.
Lethem, Jonathan. (2003) *The Fortress of Solitude*. London: Faber.
Lethem, Jonathan. (2004) *Men and Cartoons*. New York: Doubleday.
Lethem, Jonathan. (2005) *The Disappointment Artist*. London: Faber.
Lethem, Jonathan. (2006a) *How We Got Insipid*. Burton, MI: Subterranean Press.

Lethem, Jonathan. (2006b) 'My First Novels'. *Bookforum*. http://jonathanlethem.com/my-first-novels/
Lethem, Jonathan. (2007) *You Don't Love Me Yet*. London: Faber.
Lethem, Jonathan. (2008) *Omega: The Unknown*. New York: Marvel Comics.
Lethem, Jonathan. (2010) [2009] *Chronic City*. London: Faber.
Lethem, Jonathan. (2011) *The Ecstasy of Influence*. New York: Doubleday.
Lethem, Jonathan. (2012) *Fear of Music*. New York: Bloomsbury.
Lethem, Jonathan. (2013a) *Dissident Gardens*. New York: Doubleday.
Lethem, Jonathan. (2013b) 'Cyberpunk'. In *Exercises in Style*, ed. Raymond Queneau and Barbara Wright (New York: New Directions), pp.247–248.
Lethem, Jonathan. (2015) '*Lucky Alan*' *and Other Stories*. New York: Doubleday.
Lethem, Jonathan. (2016a) *A Gambler's Anatomy*. New York: Doubleday.
Lethem, Jonathan. (2016b) 'Stealing Is Much Harder than People Think'. Interview with Chris Woolfrey, *Right to Copy*, November 2016, pp.34–45.
Lethem, Jonathan. (2017) *More Alive and Less Lonely: On Books and Writers*. New York and London: Melville House.
Lethem, Jonathan. (2018a) 'Nancy, All Too Nancy'. *McSweeney's* 50, 15 May 2018. https://www.mcsweeneys.net/articles/mcsweeneys-issue-50-nancy-all-too-nancy
Lethem, Jonathan. (2018b) *The Feral Detective*. New York: Ecco.
Lethem, Jonathan, and Carter Scholz. (1999) *Kafka Americana*. New York: W.W. Norton.
Levitz, Paul. (2015) 'Man, Myth and Cultural Icon'. In *Many More Lives of the Batman*, ed. Roberta Pearson, William Uricchio and Will Brooker (London: British Film Institute), pp.13–20.
Luckhurst, Roger. (2005) *Science Fiction: A Cultural History*. Cambridge: Polity.
Luter, Matthew. (2015) *Understanding Jonathan Lethem*. Columbia: University of South Carolina Press.
Mason, Paul. (2018) 'Neoliberalism Is a Real Economic Model – Here's How the Left Can Overturn It'. *New Statesman*, 16 May 2018. https://www.newstatesman.com/politics/economy/2018/05/neoliberalism-real-economic-model-here-s-how-left-can-overturn-it
McHale, Brian. (1987) *Postmodernist Fiction*. London: Methuen.
McHale, Brian. (2009) 'Genre as History: Genre-Poaching in *Against the Day*', *Genre*, 42 (2009), 5–20.
McIlvain, Ryan. (2016) 'Provisionally Speaking: An Interview with Jonathan Lethem'. *Los Angeles Review of Books*, 16 October 2016. https://lareviewofbooks.org/article/provisionally-speaking-interview-jonathan-lethem/
McLintock, Scott, and John Miller (ed). (2014) *Pynchon's California*. Iowa City: University of Iowa Press.
Mendlesohn, Farah. (2008) *Rhetorics of Fantasy*. Middletown, CT: Wesleyan University Press.
Mosley, Walter. (2009) 'Poisonville'. In *A New Literary History of America* ed. Greil Marcus and Werner Sollors (Cambridge, MA: Belknap), pp.598–602.

Nadell, Martha. (2010) 'Writing Brooklyn'. In *The Cambridge Companion to the Literature of New York*, ed. Cyrus R.K. Patell and Bryan Waterman (Cambridge: Cambridge University Press), pp.109–120.
O'Hara, Frank. (1994) *Selected Poems*, ed. Donald Allen. Harmondsworth: Penguin.
Orr, Mary. (2003) *Intertextuality: Debates and Contexts*. Cambridge: Polity.
Ostrom, Elinor. (1990) *Governing the Commons: The Evolution of Institutions for Collective Action*. Cambridge: Cambridge University Press.
Pak, Chris. (2016) *Terraforming: Ecopolitical Transformations and Environmentalism in Science Fiction*. Liverpool: Liverpool University Press.
Peacock, James. (2012) *Jonathan Lethem*. Manchester: Manchester University Press.
Peacock, James. (2015) *Brooklyn Fictions: The Contemporary Urban Community in a Global Age*. London: Bloomsbury.
Porter, Dennis. (2003) 'The Private Eye'. In *The Cambridge Companion to Crime Fiction*, ed. Martin Priestman (Cambridge: Cambridge University Press), pp.95–113.
Rieder, John. (2015) 'American Frontiers'. In *The Cambridge Companion to American Science Fiction*, ed. E.C. Link and G. Canavan (Cambridge: Cambridge University Press), pp.167–178.
Roberts, Adam. (2006) *The History of Science Fiction*. Basingstoke: Palgrave Macmillan.
Roth, Henry. (2006) [1934] *Call It Sleep*. London: Penguin.
Roth, Marco. (2009) 'The Rise of the Neuronovel'. *n+1* 8 (Fall 2009). https://nplusonemag.com/issue-8/essays/the-rise-of-the-neuronovel/
Roth, Marco. (2010) 'Throwback Throwdown'. *n+1*, 18 May 2010. https://nplusonemag.com/online-only/book-review/throwback-throwdown/
Roth, Philip. (1995) *Sabbath's Theater*. New York: Houghton Mifflin.
Rzepka, Charles J. (2005) *Detective Fiction*. Cambridge: Polity.
Still, Judith, and Michael Worton. (1990) 'Introduction'. In *Intertextuality: Theories and Practices*, ed. Michael Worton and Judith Still (Manchester: Manchester University Press), pp.1–44.
Suvin, Darko. (1979) *Metamorphoses of Science Fiction: On the Poetics and History of a Literary Genre*. New Haven: Yale University Press.
Tartt, Donna. (2007) [1992] *The Secret History*. London: Penguin.
Westfahl, Gary. (2015) 'The Mightiest Machine: The Development of American Science Fiction from the 1920s to the 1960s'. In *The Cambridge Companion to American Science Fiction*, ed. E.C. Link and G. Canavan (Cambridge: Cambridge University Press), pp.17–30.
Williams, Stacie. (2018) *Bizarro Worlds: Jonathan Lethem's 'The Fortress of Solitude'*. New York, San Francisco, Providence: Fiction Advocate.
Wittgenstein, Ludwig. (1974) [1921] *Tractatus Logico-Philosophicus*, trans. by D.F. Pears and B.F. McGuinness. London: Routledge & Kegan Paul.
Wolfe, Gary K. (2011) *Evaporating Genres: Essays on Fantastic Literature*. Middletown, CT: Wesleyan University Press.

Wood, James. (2004) *The Irresponsible Self: On Laughter and the Novel*. London: Jonathan Cape.
Wood, Michael. (2003) 'On Edward Said'. *London Review of Books* 25: 20 (23 October 2003), 3–6.
Wood, Michael. (2005) *Literature and the Taste of Knowledge*. Cambridge: Cambridge University Press.
Wright, Bradford W. (2001) *Comic Book Nation: The Transformation of Youth Culture in America*. Baltimore, MD: Johns Hopkins University Press.

Index

2000AD (comic) 114
9/11 7, 187–9, 197

Action Comics 120
Adams, Neal 126, 150
Adorno, Theodor 31
Alden, Scott 128
Allen, Graham 11
Altman, Robert 22
Amazing Stories 47, 48
Argosy, The 47
Asimov, Isaac 95
Astounding Science Fiction 7
Astounding Stories 48
Auster, Paul
   The New York Trilogy 49

Bachelard, Gaston 88
Ballard, J.G. 34, 50, 60, 167
   The Atrocity Exhibition 94
Barth, John 49, 87
   The End of the Road 26
   Giles Goat Boy 41
Barthelme, Donald 22, 78, 86, 87
Barthes, Roland 15, 200
   S/Z 2
Beatles, The 125
   John Lennon 22
   Paul McCartney 22
   Yellow Submarine (film) 109
Beattie, Ann 27, 75
Beckett, Samuel 84
Bedtime Stories 47
Bellow, Saul
   Humboldt's Gift 39
Benjamin, Walter
   The Arcades Project 13
   'The Work of Art in the Age of Mechanical Reproduction' 15
Bennington College 4, 21, 40–2
Berry, Chuck 23
Black Mask 48

Blade Runner 200
Bloom, Harold 24, 26, 29, 30–2
   The Anxiety of Influence 12, 16
Bogart, Humphrey 48, 68, 70
Bollier, David
   Silent Theft 17
Borges, Jorge Luis 50, 86, 98, 201–2
   'Pierre Menard, Author of the *Quixote*' 36
   'The Lottery in Babylon' 201–2
Boucher, Christopher 79
Bowie, David 23, 34
Bradbury, Malcolm 26
   The History Man 26
Brando, Marlon 194
Breton, André 35
Brooklyn 2–3, 5, 11, 22, 30, 34, 58, 64–72, 74–5, 81, 88, 91–5, 128, 139–44, 155–82, 183–4, 186, 195, 202
Brooklyn Paper, The 155
Bugs Bunny 16, 58
Burke, James Lee
   Purple Cane Road 72
Burroughs, Edgar Rice 120
Burroughs, William S.
   Red Night trilogy 49
Burton, Tim 151
Bushmiller, Ernie 39
   Nancy 39–40
Byrne, David 32

Calvino, Italo 86
   If on a Winter's Night a Traveller … 86
Campbell, John W. 7
Carpenter, John
   They Live 4
Carr, Terry 26
   'Stanley Toothbrush' 199–200
Carroll, Lewis 26, 109
   The Hunting of the Snark 109
Carter Angela 50
   The Passion of New Eve 49

Cassavetes, John 22–3
Catcher in the Rye, The (J.D. Salinger) 65
Cawelti, John G. 55–6, 94
Chabon, Michael 52
  The Amazing Adventures of Kavalier & Klay 122
  The Escapist 122
Chandler, Raymond 1, 4, 55–63, 66, 67–72, 121
  Farewell, My Lovely 70
  The Lady in the Lake 57
  'The Simple Art of Murder' 69
Christie, Agatha 55
Clowes, Daniel
  Ghost World 120
Clute, John
  Encyclopedia of Fantasy 112
College Stories 47
Collins, Wilkie 48
Comics. *See* Superheroes
Commons, The 16, 17–19, 39, 42, 201
Coover, Robert 49
  A Night at the Movies 49
Cortázar, Julio 22, 202
  A Certain Lucas 201
Coughlan, David 152
Crime fiction. *See* Detective fiction
Crumb, Charles 23
Crumb, Robert 23

Dalrymple, Farel 147, 149
Dark Knight, The 123
Davis, Miles 22
Davis, Ray 47, 51
DC (Detective Comics) 121, 124, 126, 129, 137–8
Delany, Samuel R. 4, 50
DeLillo, Don 26, 29, 31, 49, 50, 113
  Ratner's Star 26
  White Noise 26, 103, 104
Derrida, Jacques 60
Detective fiction 4, 35, 45–9, 55–73, 119, 121, 156–71, 198
Dettmar, Kevin J.H. 7
  Cambridge Companion to Bob Dylan, The 14
Diaz, Juno
  The Brief Wondrous Life of Oscar Wao 122

Dick, Philip K. 2, 3–4, 7, 21, 22, 25–8, 32, 42, 50, 59, 103, 109–10, 113, 116, 117, 194, 200, 202
  'The Defenders' 116
  'Foster, You're Dead!' 116
  The Man in the High Castle 138
  Do Androids Dream of Electric Sheep? 116
  Ubik 107, 109, 116
  'How To Construct a Universe That Doesn't Fall Apart Two Days Later' 109
  The Exegesis of Philip K. Dick 4
Dickens, Charles 48
  Great Expectations 28
Diddley, Bo 23
Dienst, Richard 12
Dime Detective 47
Dinnen, Zara 15
Disch, Thomas 50
Disney 16, 36
Dixon, Willie 24
Downs, Cathy 97
Doyle, Sir Arthur Conan
  Sherlock Holmes 48, 62, 121
Dylan, Bob 14, 22–3
  'Song to Woody' 78
  'Love and Theft' 14

Eagleton, Terry 12
Earp, Wyatt 97–9
Egan, Jennifer 29–30, 32
  A Visit from the Goon Squad 29–30
Einstein, Albert 18
Eisenstadt, Jill 4, 40–1
  From Rockaway 40
Eliot, T.S.
  'Gerontion' 12
  'The Waste Land' 12
Ellin, Stanley 4
Ellis, Bret Easton 1, 4, 40–2
  Less Than Zero 40
  The Rules of Attraction 40
Éluard, Paul 35
Erickson, Steve 50
Ernst, Max 35–7
Eve, Martin Paul
  Taxonomographic metafiction 49–50, 56

Fancher, Hampton 200
Farber, Manny
    White Elephant vs Termite Art 73, 81, 185
Faulkner, William 50
Fiedler, Leslie 48–9
    Love and Death in the American Novel 14
Finger, Bill 129
Fonda, Henry 97
Forbidden Planet 48
Ford, John 23, 27, 90, 97–8
    My Darling Clementine 97–8
    The Searchers 21, 27, 89–91, 97
    The Man Who Shot Liberty Valance 97–8
Ford, Richard 76
    The Sportswriter 86
Forster, E.M. 30
    A Passage to India 27–8
Foucault, Michel 15, 42
Fox, Paula 32
Frankenstein (Mary Shelley) 47
Franzen, Jonathan 1, 30–2
    'Why Bother?' 13
    The Corrections 32, 146
    Freedom 32
    'On Autobiographical Fiction' 30–2
Freud, Sigmund 12, 63
Frow, John 55

Gaddis, William 31
Gaiman, Neil 52
Galaxy (magazine) 2, 25
Galchen, Rivka 49, 189, 200
Gas (magazine) 129
Gates, David 27
Gerber, Steve 150, 153
Gernsback, Hugo 48
Goetz, Bernhard 144
Gold, Horace 2
Gold Dagger award 72
Graffiti 142–3, 153
Greene, Graham 22
Grossman, David
    See Under: Love 78
Gun Molls 47

Hammett, Dashiell 4, 48, 68
    The Maltese Falcon 68

Harper's 13
Harriet the Spy 36
Heinlein, Robert
    'The Unpleasant Profession of Jonathan Hoag' 35–6
Hernandez, Jaime
    Love & Rockets 120
Hess, Charlotte 18
Highsmith, Patricia 50
Hitchcock, Alfred 22
    The Birds 36
Hoban, Russell 50
Horkheimer, Max 31
Hornschemeier, Paul 147, 149
Horror Stories 47
Hosler, Mark 16
Hyde, Lewis 14–15, 17–18

Ingarden, Roman 85
Interzone 4
Isaac Asimov's Science Fiction Magazine 4, 77
Ishiguro, Kazuo 52
    Never Let Me Go 52

Jackson, Pamela 4
Jackson, Shelley 9, 78, 80, 200
Jackson, Shirley 27
Jaeger, Lukas 34
Jameson, Fredric 49, 61, 80
Jefferson, Thomas 16
Joyce, James 8, 156
    Ulysses 54
    Finnegans Wake 71

Kafka, Franz 1, 33–6, 50, 79, 129–33
    The Trial 34
    'A Crossbreed' 129–32
    'The Vulture' 129
    'The Burrow' 129–32
Kane, Bob 129, 132
Karloff, Boris 48
Kelleghan, Fiona 25, 52
Kelly, James Patrick 34
Kessel, John 34
Kirby, Jack 22–4, 123, 124, 135, 137
Kollin, Susan 190
Kornbluth, C.M. 25
Kress, Nancy 73
Kubrick, Stanley 50

Lariat (magazine) 47
Latham, Rob 51–2
Le Guin, Ursula K. 85
　Earthsea 86
Led Zeppelin 24
Lee, Stan 22, 124–5
Lefebvre, Henri 88
Lem, Stanisław 26, 50
Leon, Donna
　Friends in High Places 72
Lessig, Lawrence 16, 18, 19, 36
Lessing, Doris 50
Lethem (film) 7
Lethem, Jonathan
　Books:
　Gun, with Occasional Music 4–6, 31, 51, 55–63, 64, 69, 71, 73, 76, 111, 132, 145, 156, 193, 196, 197, 198, 200
　Amnesia Moon 4–5, 25, 46, 60, 74–5, 76, 81, 83, 86, 89, 110–17, 124, 153–4, 166, 170, 193, 194, 199
　The Wall of the Sky, The Wall of the Eye 5, 77
　As She Climbed across the Table 4–6, 26–7, 29, 76, 83, 86, 102–10, 117, 119, 166, 197, 198, 199, 200
　Girl in Landscape 5–6, 27–8, 30, 34, 73, 75, 80, 83, 87–102, 116–17, 145, 157, 198–9, 202
　Motherless Brooklyn 5–6, 7, 8, 9, 49, 64–73, 78, 85, 119, 124, 146, 153, 155–71, 178, 180, 196, 198, 199, 200, 201
　This Shape We're In 6, 85
　The Fortress of Solitude 6, 7, 8–9, 11, 27–8, 41, 46, 75, 76, 78, 80, 121–3, 125, 126, 127, 131, 133–47, 153, 156–8, 161, 168–9, 170, 171–82, 192, 195, 196, 199, 201, 202
　Men and Cartoons 6, 77, 121–2
　The Disappointment Artist 6, 20–5
　How We Got Insipid 77
　You Don't Love Me Yet 6, 31, 37–9, 170, 194–5, 196–7, 198, 199, 200
　Omega the Unknown 6, 122, 147–54
　Chronic City 2, 7, 28, 39, 76, 83, 84, 107, 117, 156, 183–95, 196–7, 198–200, 201, 202
　They Live 4, 6

　The Ecstasy of Influence 6, 8, 12, 30, 32–3, 78–9, 122, 123
　Fear of Music 6, 31
　Dissident Gardens 7, 18, 24, 73–5, 76–7, 79–81, 86, 167, 170, 178, 184, 197, 199, 201, 202
　Lucky Alan 7, 77–8
　A Gambler's Anatomy 7, 11, 76, 77, 196, 197, 198, 199
　More Alive and Less Lonely 6, 123
　The Feral Detective 7, 11, 77, 81, 156, 197
　Edited books:
　The Vintage Book of Amnesia 7
　Shake It Up 7
　Stories:
　'Using It and Losing It' 5
　'The Happy Man' 83
　'Vanilla Dunk' 73, 81
　'Forever, Said the Duck' 25, 73, 77, 83, 185
　'The Notebooks of Bob K.' 121, 129–33
　'The Insipid Profession of Jonathan Hornebom' 35–7
　'Light and the Sufferer' 7, 52–4, 190
　'The One about the Green Detective' 5
　'How We Got In Town and Out Again' 25, 77, 83
　'Access Fantasy' 170
　'The Spray' 200
　'K for Fake' 33–7
　'Breakfast at Brelreck's' 180
　'The Dystopianist, Thinking of His Rival, Is Interrupted by a Knock on the Door' 86–7
　'The Vision' 121–2, 128
　'Super Goat Man' 41–2, 121–2, 127–8
　'Their Back Pages' 77–8
　'Lucky Alan' 77, 186, 200
　'The King of Sentences' 76
　'The Dreaming Jaw, The Salivating Ear' 78, 83, 198
　'The Epiphany' 123, 128–9
　'Nancy, All Too Nancy' 39–40
　Essays:
　'The Squandered Promise of Science Fiction' 51
　'Defending *The Searchers*' 21, 91
　'Izations' ('My Spidey') 122–3, 125–6, 139

'Top Five Depressed Superheroes' 123, 126–8
'Identifying with Your Parents, or The Return of the King' ('My Marvel Years') 22–4, 122–3, 125
'Speak, Hoyt-Schermerhorn' 21, 140
'The Beards' 21, 39
'The Ecstasy of Influence' 12–20, 23–4, 33, 36, 38–9, 102, 133, 148, 152, 198
'*Supermen!*: An Introduction' 123–5
'Somatics of Influence' ('The Afterlife of "Ecstasy"') 20
'My Disappointment Critic' 33
'The Only Human Superhero' 123
Co-written works:
Idiot Tooth (with Shelley Jackson) 200
'The Elvis National Theatre of Okinawa' (with Lukas Jaeger) 34
Kafka Americana (with Carter Scholz) 33–7, 129–33
'Receding Horizon' (with Carter Scholz) 33
'Ninety Per Cent of Everything' (with John Kessel and James Patrick Kelly) 34
'Always Crashing in the Same Car' (with David Bowie et al) 34
Conversations with Jonathan Lethem (with Jaime Clarke et al) 8
The Blot: A Supplement (with Laurence A. Rickels) 7
Lethem, Judith 3, 11
Lethem, Richard Brown 3, 11
Lewis, C.S. 146
 The Lion, the Witch and the Wardrobe 85
Liddell, Alice 103
Life (magazine) 47
Los Angeles Review of Books 1
Lott, Eric 14
Love Story Magazine 47
Luckhurst, Roger 51, 62
Luter, Matthew 8, 24

Mad (magazine) 71
Magritte, René 22
Mailer, Norman 3, 194
Malamud, Bernard 3
Marlowe, Philip. *See* Chandler, Raymond

Marvel Comics 6, 20, 22–4, 121–7, 129, 133–41, 147–54
Marx, Karl 184
Mason, Paul 17
McCarthy, Cormac 22
McCullers, Carson 27
McGruff (crime dog) 68
McHale, Brian 49, 112, 116–17
 Postmodernist Fiction 84–7
McSweeney's 39
Means, David 76
Mendlesohn, Farah 53, 80, 85, 95, 108, 145–6, 172
 Rhetorics of Fantasy 60–1
Mickey Mouse 18
Miller, Frank 120, 151
Millhauser, Steven
 Portrait of a Romantic 28
Mitchell, David 197
Moody Blues, The 31
Mooney, Jim 149
Moore, Alan 151
 Miracleman 127
 Swamp Thing 127
 Watchmen 127, 137, 141
Mosley, Walter 55, 60
Muir, Edwin 34
Muir, Willa 34
Munro, Alice 32
Murakami, Haruki 50

n+1, 19
Nabokov, Vladimir
 Lolita 14
New Maps of Hell (Kingsley Amis) 25
New York City 2–3, 35, 52, 60, 76, 79–80, 85, 91–2, 95, 122, 125, 146–7, 151, 153, 155–95, 196–7, 202
New York Times 1, 140, 187, 190, 193
New Yorker, The 7, 41, 47, 73, 76, 77, 186
Newley, Anthony 23
Nixon, Richard 73
Nolan, Christopher 151

O'Brien, Flann
 At Swim-Two-Birds 86
O'Hara, Frank 155
O'Neill, Dennis 126
Orwell, George 60

Nineteen Eighty-Four 187
Ostrom, Elinor 17–18
Oulipo 51
Over the Top 47

Pak, Chris 101
Panter, Gary 147
Paolozzi, Eduardo 13
Paris Review, The 8, 27, 28–9
Parker, Charlie 22
Peacock, James 8, 163, 165, 167
Pessoa, Fernando 156
Picasso, Pablo 22–3
Playboy 123
Poe, Edgar Allan 47, 48
Pohl, Frederik 2, 25
Pollock, Jackson 22
Pomona College 7, 11
Porter, Dennis 55
Portis, Charles
   True Grit 27
Postmodernism 49, 84–5
Price, Richard 28–9, 32
   The Breaks 29
Prince (musician) 71
Proust, Marcel 29–30
Pulp fiction 2, 4, 47–8, 73, 120
Puzo, Mario 68
Pynchon, Thomas 4, 8, 31, 49, 50, 77, 113, 156
   'The Small Rain' 200
   Gravity's Rainbow 49, 51
   Inherent Vice 77
   Bleeding Edge 77

Ramones, The 6
'Rapper's Delight' (The Sugar Hill Gang) 138
R.E.M.
   'Little America' 113
Rhys, Jean
   Wide Sargasso Sea 27
Rickels, Lawrence A. 7
Rieder, John 89, 99
Right to Copy 13
Roberts, Adam 87, 120
Robinson, Edward G. 16, 58
Robinson, Kim Stanley 80, 101
Rolling Stone 123

Roth, Henry 146
   Call It Sleep 28, 172
Roth, Marco 19–20
   Neuronovel 71–2
Roth, Philip 3, 27, 202
   Sabbath's Theater 201
Rothko, Mark 89
Runyan, Damon 160
Rusnak, Karl 22, 123, 125, 137, 147–54
Rzepka, Charles J. 55, 62, 64

Sacks, Oliver 71–2
Said, Edward 85
Saturday Evening Post 47
Sayers, Dorothy L. 55
Scholz, Carter 33
Schumpeter, Joseph 192
Science fiction 2, 3–5, 7, 25, 27, 45–54, 59–63, 64, 71, 73, 77, 80, 87–102, 104, 110–17, 119–21, 122, 146, 165, 176, 186, 188
   Planetary romance 95–6, 116
   Cyberpunk 51
   Slipstream 51–2
   Geoengineering 101
Science Fiction Studies 25
Scorsese, Martin 159
Scott, Sir Walter 80
Serling, Rod 4, 34–5, 36
   The Twilight Zone 4, 34–5, 190
Shakespeare, William 11, 19, 22
Sheckley, Robert 2
Shields, David
   Reality Hunger 13, 19
Shuster, Joe 120
Siegel, Don 14
Siegel, Jerry 120
Silverblatt, Michael 28
Sky Birds 47
Sophie's Choice (William Styron) 29
Sopranos, The (TV series) 29–30
Stapledon, Olaf 4, 101
Star Trek 87, 94, 165
Star Wars 20–1, 120
Stein, Lorin 9
Sterling, Bruce 51
Stewart, James 97
Still, Judith 14–15
Strand (magazine) 48
Sun Ra 23

Superheroes 1, 2, 22–4, 119–54
   Superman 23, 119–22, 124–6, 129, 138, 142, 145
   Batman 48, 119, 121, 123, 124, 126–7, 129–33, 134, 135, 138, 139, 150, 151
   Blue Beetle 137
   Captain Marvel 136, 149
   Captain America 122, 137
   Wonder Woman 124
   Flash 121, 124, 129
   Fantastic Four 22–3, 121, 124, 138, 149
   Thing 137, 147
   Incredible Hulk 121, 124, 147, 148
   Spider-Man 6, 121, 123, 125–6, 136, 137, 139, 202
   Scarlet Witch 128
   Black Bolt 125–7
   Silver Surfer 121, 137
   Deadman 125–7
   Vision 125, 126, 128
   Luke Cage 125, 137
   Omega the Unknown 125–6, 138, 141, 147–54
   Ragman 125–7
   Rorschach 127
   Nite Owl 127
Suvin, Darko 46, 62, 96, 147

Talking Heads 6, 31, 178
Tartt, Donna 1, 4, 40–2
   The Secret History 40–2
Tiptree Jr., James 50
Tolkien, J.R.R. 22, 85–6, 95, 122
Tomine, Adrian 149
Tourette's Syndrome 5, 65–6, 67–8, 70, 71–2, 119, 155, 159, 164, 167–8, 196
Trashmen, The
   'Surfin' Bird' 36
Trump, Donald J. 113
Tzara, Tristan 35

Unknown Worlds 35

Verne, Jules 48
Village Voice 51

Wallace, David Foster 8
   'E Unibus Pluram: Television and U.S. Fiction' 13, 15
   Infinite Jest 183
Warhol, Andy 36
Waugh, Evelyn 40
Wayne, John 34, 89, 91, 97–8, 101
Welles, Orson 34, 36
   The Trial 34
   F for Fake 34
Wells, H.G. 48, 101
West, Adam 123
Western (genre) 5–6, 27, 46–9, 88–102, 119–20
Wild Cherry
   'Play That Funky Music' 144, 182
Willeford, Charles 50
Wittgenstein, Ludwig 84
Wolfe, Gary K. 27, 47, 52
Wolfli, Adolf 23
Wood, James 33, 146
Wood, Michael 201–2
Wood, Natalie 89
Woolf, Virginia 156
   Orlando 78
Woolrich, Cornell 25
Worton, Michael 14–15
Wright, Steven 39

Yates, Richard 27, 75
Year's Best Science Fiction, The (series) 77

www.ingramcontent.com/pod-product-compliance
Lightning Source LLC
Chambersburg PA
CBHW050327020526
44117CB00031B/1906